W9-BZM-791

The Social History of Poverty:
The Urban Experience

Francesco Cordasco
EDITOR

POVERTY

BY

Robert Hunter

With a New Foreword by

LOIS AND SAMUEL PRATT

GARRETT PRESS, INC.
New York, 1970

SBN 512-00761-6
Library of Congress Catalog Card
Number 72-106742

The text of this book is a photographic reprint of the first edition,
published in New York by The Macmillan Company in 1904.
Reproduced from a copy in the Garrett Press Collection.

First Garrett Press Edition Published 1970

Manufactured in the United States of America

GARRETT PRESS, INC.
Publishers

250 West 54th Street, New York, N.Y. 10019

FOREWORD

Poverty (1904) by Robert Hunter is an account of the poor in large American cities at the turn of the century. It is a personal document by a man with a strong moral indignation about the treatment of the working poor in that day and an ambivalence about the non-working poor. Hunter says his work should be treated as a personal narrative based on direct observation, and the book is valuable to read solely as a statement of an impassioned reformer; but there are other values in it as well.

There are descriptive materials on the condition of the working poor and the non-working poor (*circa* 1900) that will deepen one's understanding of the conditions of life at the poverty line and below it. In the final chapter, Hunter has this sentence: "On cold, rainy mornings at the dusk of dawn, I have been awakened two hours before my rising time, by the monotonous clatter of hobnail boots on the plank sidewalks, as a procession to the factory passed under my window. Heavy, brooding men, tired, anxious women, thinly dressed, unkempt little girls, and frail, joyless little lads passed along, half-awake, not one uttering a word as they hurry to the great factory." Such imagery makes us feel the meanness of life of the working poor. Hunter develops as clear and concise a statement of the grinding down of men who live in the conditions of poverty as any we have read. No one can read his account and, comprehending that in the present day there are people who still face equally devastating conditions, will not reaffirm the goal of creating conditions of life truly conducive to human development. The book makes insistent the demand: time enough has passed.

Poverty is also instructive in that it clearly reveals the moral attitudes at the turn of the century and thus provides a background for understanding some of today's moralizing about the poor. Hunter's view of paupers as parasites with "a lust for gratuitous maintenance" persists today in widely-held sentiments about welfare freeloaders. He was concerned for the dilution of the quality of American stock by immigrants, stating that "the most vicious, confirmed, and incorrigible child criminal is the child of foreign parents." He also classified cigarette smokers as part of the degenerate and vicious segment of society. These and similar attitudes are valuable to read so that we may reflect on some of the equally unquestioned nonsense spoken about the supposed characteristics of the urban poor today. When an observer as skilled as Hunter projects some of the attitudes we now find so appalling, it helps each of us to pause and consider which of our contemporary attitudes will in a few decades seem equally outrageous to future generations.

Hunter's *Poverty* is historically significant in that it was one of the very earliest statements utilizing the then developing statistical materials and unemployment data. In this respect it is a benchmark book. It helps us recall that quantitative studies of the poor date from late in the 19th century, a circumstance that today's great avalanche of statistical studies obscures for us. High on Hunter's list of recommendations was that there be periodic research on the poverty classes and that collection of statistical data be expanded.

It is now clear that the collection of statistical data is not sufficient for the elimination of many major social problems. Statistics about the poor, unemployment, housing, levels of education and health have stimulated some improvements in conditions. By hindsight we can see that the type of study of the culture of poverty that is exempli-

fied by the work of Oscar Lewis has been equally needed
to create the social comprehension which is so necessary an
ingredient in fundamental reform.

While clearly limited by the attitudes of his society,
Hunter did reveal a surprisingly contemporary grasp of the
complex social forces involved in creating and maintaining
poverty. He described the interrelations between poverty,
unemployment, sickness, occupational injury, insufficient
wages to create savings, limited education, technological
change, and family needs, the demeaning circumstances of
the poor neighborhood, and so on. In his last chapter he
says, "The first difficulty [in removing poverty] lies in the
complex nature of the problem itself. It is inextricably
woven in with all other social and economic problems. . . .
But complex as the problem is, and varied as the remedies
must be, we may be sure that poverty is, to a considerable
extent, due to social causes which are clearly to be seen
and which are possible of remedy." The solutions he proposed are modern in at least two respects. He stressed
prevention of individuals being recruited into poverty,
rather than amelioration of the condition of those who
find themselves in impoverished circumstances. He further
proposed that the solution lies in broad social action rather
than in individual therapy. For example, he insisted that
industrial accidents, unemployment, maldistribution of
wealth, inadequate housing and the spread of communi-
cable diseases are caused by malfunction of the society and
must be corrected by legislation and social programs.

Hunter's specific solutions to the problems of poverty
are, of course, more out of date than his basic approach to
the problems. Many of the things he recommended in his
book have now been instituted. These include his recommendations for improved quantitative analysis, improved
industrial safety, workmen's compensation, urban sanitation, public responsibility for employment and fair wages,

prohibition of child labor, retirement programs, medical benefits, and control of immigration. All of these were meant to make life less arduous, and, as expressed in one of his metaphors, "In other words, the process of Justice is to lift stony barriers, against which the noblest beat their brains out, and from which the ignoble (but who shall say not more sensible?) turn away in despair." Many of his recommendations have been fulfilled, and rereading his impassioned plea made some 70 years ago gives us encouragement that we can move further ahead.

Perhaps the greatest value of Hunter's book lies in the perspective it gives to the rediscovery of poverty in America that occured in the 1960's. It makes one wonder why that rediscovery had to take place. It also brings to fuller public attention the fact that the urban poor have been with us for as long as we have had industrial cities and that they are not solely the result of recent internal migration, new welfare laws, individual laziness or moral depravity. The groups of impoverished that Hunter spoke about, such as the Jews and the Irish, are gone in large measure from the poverty class of today. Different groups have replaced them. As Hunter forecast, there must be a consciously directed effort involving resources and determination if the causes of poverty are to be eliminated.

Lois Pratt
Jersey City State College
Samuel Pratt
Montclair State College

POVERTY

·The· Co·

POVERTY

BY

ROBERT HUNTER

New York

THE MACMILLAN COMPANY

LONDON: MACMILLAN & CO., Ltd.

1904

Norwood Press
J. S. Cushing & Co. — Berwick & Smith Co.
Norwood, Mass., U.S.A.

PREFACE

THE main objects of this volume are: To define poverty and to estimate its extent at the present time in the United States; to describe some of its evils, not only among the dependent and vicious classes, which constitute the social wreckage in the abysses of our cities, but also among the unskilled, underpaid, underfed, and poorly housed workers; furthermore, to point out certain remedial actions which society may wisely undertake; and, finally, to show that the evils of poverty are not barren, but procreative, and that the workers in poverty are, in spite of themselves, giving to the world a litter of miserables, whose degeneracy is so stubborn and fixed that reclamation is almost impossible, especially when the only process of reclamation must consist in trying to force the pauper, vagrant, and weakling back into that struggle with poverty which is all of the time defeating stronger and better natures than theirs. In order to fulfil these purposes, the first chapter deals with poverty in general, with our ignorance of its extent, with our lack of information, and with the several reasons for believing that, in fairly prosperous times, no less than ten million persons in the United States are underfed, underclothed, and poorly housed. The Pauper and Vagrant are dealt with in other chapters as types of those who are beaten and who are sunk into a satisfied dependence from which they can only rarely be reclaimed. But especial attention is directed to the larger mass from which the dependent classes are mainly recruited. Although it comprises several million wage-workers, it is, strange to say, almost a forgotten class, confused on the one side with the vicious and dependent and on the other with the more highly paid workers. The chapters on The Sick, The Child, and The Immigrant deal with certain phases of this larger problem of poverty and with some of the reasons for its continuance amongst us.

It should be said that the book is not a scientific or exhaustive study, endeavoring to deal with all of the conditions, causes, and problems of poverty. Mr. Charles Booth in his study of London has approached most nearly to such a work, and it required several large volumes to print the results. It is unnecessary to say that this book is a much more modest undertaking. It is first of all a personal narrative, telling of things seen while living among the poorest of the working people and among the most degraded elements in several cities of this country and abroad. It makes public certain notes concerning the misery, the wretchedness, the sorrow, and the hopelessness of old neighbors, many of whom are friends and acquaintances. It is not,

however, the result of any definite investigation or
of inquiries and notes made for the purpose of
writing a book. Whatever knowledge of the question is manifested herein comes largely from my
work in a variety of movements intended either to
diminish the number of dependents or to ameliorate
the conditions of poverty. The facts drawn from
books and official publications are such as seemed
to me necessary to a rounded statement of that
portion of the problem of poverty with which I am
most familiar, or to support the generalizations which
are here and there made in the various chapters
concerning tendencies, causes, and remedies. It is
perhaps unnecessary to remark that mere observation cannot take the place of careful inquiry; and
therefore wherever I could make use of material
gained by the latter method, I have freely availed
myself of it. Those who are looking to find in this
book a thoroughgoing treatise on poverty will, for
these several reasons, be disappointed. It has all
the limitations of a book which, if not altogether
personal, is at any rate based entirely upon facts
gained by personal observation.

The limitations are many. I shall mention but
two of those which exist in my description of conditions. The poor of the rural districts have hardly
been mentioned, and the working woman and the
mother are left almost entirely out of consideration.
I have been content to pass over these important
problems because I have been less observant of

these phases of poverty than of other phases, and I
have kept to my original determination not to write
of conditions with which I am not personally familiar.   Similar limitations may be observed in my
dealing with causes and remedies.   I have purposely
ignored individual causes, and I have mentioned
among remedial measures only those for which I
have worked or those which have been in certain
places and at certain times tried and found of value.
The more far-reaching and radical reforms proposed
by the socialist, single taxer, and individualist have
not been examined here, and therefore not con-
demned or endorsed.   In so far as possible conditions are described as seen; causes which have been
watched and studied are mentioned, and remedies
which have appealed to me as of immediate importance have been urged.   The book as a whole has
one aim; namely, to show the grievous need of certain social measures calculated to prevent the ruin
and degradation of those working people who are
on the verge of poverty.   I am at a loss to understand why well-known and generally recognized
poverty-breeding conditions, which are both unjust
and unnecessary, are tolerated for an instant among
a humane, not to say a professedly Christian people.

I am happy to take advantage of this opportunity
to express my sincere thanks to Professor Richard
T. Ely, to Professor John R. Commons, and to my
brother-in-law, Mr. J. G. Phelps Stokes, for many
criticisms and suggestions.   They were interested

enough in the purpose of the book to take time from their many duties to read the entire manuscript. I am also indebted to Dr. William H. Maxwell, Superintendent of Schools in New York City, to Dr. Herman Biggs, General Medical Officer of the Board of Health of New York City, to Mr. Frank P. Sargent, Commissioner General of Immigration, to Dr. Edward T. Devine, General Secretary of the Charity Organization Society of New York City, to Mrs. Florence Kelley, Secretary of the National Consumers' League, to Mr. James Forbes, the agent of the Mendicity Committee of the N. Y. C. O. S., and to Mr. English Walling for reading those chapters of the book which deal with problems in which they are practically interested specialists. Each of these friends has made criticisms and suggestions which have been most helpful. Most of all I am indebted to my wife, who has patiently and painstakingly toiled through every page of the manuscript and proofs.

HIGHLAND FARM,
NOROTON, CONN.,
September 15, 1904.

CONTENTS

POVERTY

CHAPTER I

POVERTY

WILLIAM DEAN HOWELLS said to me recently, after
I had told him of a visit to Tolstoy : " It is wonderful
what Tolstoy has done.   He could do no more.   For
a nobleman, with the most aristocratic ancestry, to
refuse to be supported in idleness, to insist upon
working with his own hands, and to share as much
as possible the hardship and toil of a peasant class,
which, but recently, was a slave class, is the greatest
thing he could do.   But it is impossible for him to
share their poverty, for poverty is not the lack of
things; it is the fear and the dread of want.   That
fear Tolstoy could not know."   These remarks of
Mr. Howells brought to mind the wonderful words
of Thomas Carlyle : " It is not to die, or even to die
of hunger, that makes a man wretched; many men
have died; all men must die. . . .   But it is to live
miserable we know not why; to work sore and yet
gain nothing; to be heart-worn, weary, yet isolated,

unrelated, girt in with a cold, universal Laissez-faire." *
To live miserable we know not why, to have the
dread of hunger, to work sore and yet gain nothing, — this is the essence of poverty.

There are many people in the world who believe
that the provisions of charity are in the present day
so generous and varied that no one need suffer; but,
even if this were true, it would not materially lessen
the sorrow of the poor.   To thousands and thousands
of working-men the dread of public pauperism is the
agony of their lives.   The mass of working-men on
the brink of poverty hate charity.   Not only their
words convey a knowledge of this fact, but their
actions, when in distress, make it absolutely undeniable.   When the poor face the necessity of becoming paupers, when they must apply for charity if
they are to live at all, many desert their families and
enter the ranks of vagrancy; others drink themselves
insensible; some go insane; and still others commit
suicide.   Recently a man who had been unable to
find work and in despair committed suicide, left a
note to his wife, saying: " I have gone forever; there
is one less in the world to feed.   Good-by.   God help
you to care for Tony; don't put her away."   This is
the fear and dread of pauperism; "don't put Tony
away" is the last thought of the man whose misery
caused him to take his own life.

* Refer by page and number to the appendix on Authorities.

These are the terrible alternatives which the working people in poverty accept in preference to pauperism, and yet it is a curious fact, which psychology alone explains, that the very men who will suffer almost anything rather than become paupers are often the very ones who never care to be anything else when once they have become dependent upon alms. When a family once become dependent, the mental agony which they formerly had disappears. Paupers are not, as a rule, unhappy. They are not ashamed; they are not keen to become independent; they are not bitter or discontented. They have passed over the line which separates poverty from pauperism.

This distinction between the poor and paupers may be seen everywhere. There are in all large cities in America and abroad, streets and courts and alleys where a class of people live who have lost all self-respect and ambition, who rarely, if ever, work, who are aimless and drifting, who like drink, who have no thought for their children, and who live more or less contentedly on rubbish and alms. Such districts are certain portions of Whitechapel and Spitalsfield, etc., in London, Kitrof Rynock in Moscow, parts of Armour Avenue in Chicago, Rat Hollow in Cincinnati, and parts of Cherry Hill and the Minettas in New York City, and so on in all cities everywhere. The lowest level of humanity is reached in these districts. In our American cities Negroes, Whites, Chinese,

Mexicans, Half-breeds, Americans, Irish, and others are indiscriminately housed together in the same tenements and even in the same rooms. The blind, the crippled, the consumptive, the aged, — the ragged ends of life; the babies, the children, the half-starved, underclad beginnings in life, all huddled together, waiting, drifting. This is pauperism. There is no mental agony here; they do not work sore; there is no dread; they live miserably, but they do not care.

In the same cities and, indeed, everywhere, there are great districts of people who are up before dawn, who wash, dress, and eat breakfast, kiss wives and children, and hurry away to work or to seek work. The world rests upon their shoulders; it moves by their muscle; everything would stop if, for any reason, they should decide not to go into the fields and factories and mines. But the world is so organized that they gain enough to live upon only when they work; should they cease, they are in destitution and hunger. The more fortunate of the laborers are but a few weeks from actual distress when the machines are stopped. Upon the unskilled masses want is constantly pressing. As soon as employment ceases, suffering stares them in the face. They are the actual producers of wealth, who have no home nor any bit of soil which they may call their own. They are the millions who possess no tools and can work only by permission of another. In the main, they live miserably, they know not why. They work sore, yet gain nothing. They know the meaning of hunger and the dread of want. They love their wives and children. They try to retain their self-respect. They have some ambition. They give to neighbors in need, yet they are themselves the actual children of poverty.

It is with this latter class that this chapter deals. For the purpose of making the distinction perfectly clear between these two social classes, — for it is an important distinction to make, — definitions are necessary. A pauper is one who depends upon public or private charity for sustenance. A man may be in utter destitution and may even die of starvation, but he may not be called a pauper unless he applies for and receives charitable relief. Paupers must be included among those in poverty, but poverty is a much broader term than pauperism. Many, many thousand families, who are in no sense paupers, are in poverty. Those who are in poverty may be able to get a bare sustenance, but they are not able to obtain *those necessaries which will permit them to maintain a state of physical efficiency.*[1] They are the large class in any industrial nation who are on the verge of distress. Only the most miserable of them are starving or dependent upon charity, but all of them are receiving too little of the common necessities to keep them-

selves at their best, physically. It would be difficult
to over-estimate the importance of sufficient food, adequate clothing, and a sanitary home to those men,
women, and children who must depend at all times
upon their labor power and their physical efficiency,
to produce an income sufficient to maintain themselves in working order. There is a fundamental
here. If they must work to live, they must have
those necessities which will enable them to work.
The necessities for maintaining physical efficiency
are very different from those essential to mere living.
A Hottentot, a Lazzarone, or a vagrant may live well
enough on little or nothing, because he does not spend
himself. The modern workman demands a far higher
standard of living in order to keep pace with intense
industrial life. Physical efficiency, not mere existence,
is to him *vital*. His necessities are necessities! It is
a terrible word, for " Necessity's sharp pinch " is like
that of a steel vise. There is no give to it. Necessity is like flint or granite. It is irresistible. It cannot be shuffled with nor altered. If physical efficiency
is an absolute and vital necessity to the workman, so
to him are certain necessities for maintaining that
physical efficiency. The fundamental thing in all
this is that every workman who is expected by society to remain independent of public relief and capable of self-support must be guaranteed, in so far as
that is possible, an opportunity for obtaining those

necessaries essential to physical efficiency. Such a standard is the basis of almost everything; for, unless men can retain their physical efficiency, they must degenerate. To continue in poverty for any long period means in the end the loss of the power of doing work, and to be unable to work means in the end pauperism. A standard of physical efficiency is, of course, purely a materialistic standard; it does not include mental efficiency except as that is involved in physical well-being. It does not mean the maintenance of national efficiency. To live up to the standard, or, in other words, to be above the poverty line, means no more than to have a sanitary dwelling and sufficient food and clothing to keep the body in working order. It is precisely the same standard that a man would demand for his horses or slaves. Treating man merely as the "repository of a certain sort of labor power,"[1] it makes possible the utilization of that power to the fullest extent. No one will fail to realize how low such a standard is. It does not necessarily include any of the intellectual, æsthetic, moral, or social necessities; it is a purely physical standard, dividing those in poverty from those who may be said to be out of it.

The necessaries for maintaining physical efficiency are not difficult to determine. Professor Alfred Marshall says: "The necessaries for the efficiency of an ordinary agricultural or of an unskilled town laborer

and his family, in England, in this generation, may
be said to consist of a well-drained dwelling with
several rooms, warm clothing, with some changes of
underclothing, pure water, a plentiful supply of cereal
food, with a moderate allowance of meat and milk,
and a little tea, etc., some education, and some recreation, and lastly, sufficient freedom for his wife
from other work to enable her to perform properly
her maternal and her household duties. If in any
district unskilled labor is deprived of any of these
things, its efficiency will suffer in the same way as
that of a horse that is not properly tended, or
a steam engine that has an inadequate supply of
coals." [1] This standard is a reasonable one. A sanitary dwelling, a sufficient supply of food and clothing, all having to do with physical well-being, is the
very minimum which the laboring classes can demand.
Anything less means the ruin of that very physical
power which alone suffices to keep them from dependence upon public relief. It resolves itself into the
necessity for "fair wages" and regular employment.
Such a standard has been established naturally by
every one in his treatment of animals; no one would
think of supplying less to any man or beast for whom
he was personally responsible. Serfs and slaves were
always given at least enough to keep them physically
well. But present-day society has ignored the wisdom of this fair provision. Carlyle, even in his day,

protested against this modern injustice of not making
proper provision for the physical well-being of the
working-classes. " Why, the four-footed worker," he
exclaims, " has already got all that this two-handed
one is clamoring for! How often must I remind
you? There is not a horse in England able and willing to work, but has due food and lodging; and goes
about sleek-coated, satisfied in heart. And you say,
it is impossible. Brothers, I answer, if for you it be
impossible, what is to become of you? It is impossible for us to believe it to be impossible. The human
brain, looking at these sleek English horses, refuses
to believe in such impossibility for English men."[1] To
repeat again, poverty means the lack of "due food
and lodging " and clothing.

In England the economists and students of poverty
have determined that in ordinary times from fifteen
to eighteen shillings a week would enable an agricultural laborer to obtain for himself and family the
necessaries of life, and about thirty shillings a week
would enable a city workman to obtain the same
necessaries.[2] Mr. B. S. Rountree, in his study of the
poverty of York, England, fixed a standard of twenty-
one shillings eight pence a week as a necessary one
for a family of ordinary size. Anything less than this
amount would not enable a family to live without
certain deprivations which would in time impair their
physical efficiency. With this sum, as a weekly

income, the family could with care keep themselves
above the poverty line.   But Mr. Rountree says:
" A family, living upon the scale allowed for in this
estimate, must never spend a penny on railway fare
or omnibus.   They must never go into the country
unless they walk.   They must never purchase a half-
penny newspaper or spend a penny to buy a ticket
for a popular concert.   They must write no letters to
absent children, for they cannot afford to pay the
postage.   They must never contribute anything to
their church or chapel, or give any help to a neigh-
bour which costs them money.   They cannot save,
nor can they join sick club or Trade Union, because
they cannot pay the necessary subscription.   The
children must have no pocket money for dolls,
marbles, or sweets.   The father must smoke no
tobacco and must drink no beer.   The mother must
never buy any pretty clothes for herself or for her
children, the character of the family wardrobe as
for the family diet being governed by the regulation,
' Nothing must be bought but that which is absolutely
necessary for the maintenance of physical health,
and what is bought must be of the plainest and most
economical description.'   Should a child fall ill, it
must be attended by the parish doctor; should it
die, it must be buried by the parish.   Finally, the
wage-earner must never be absent from his work
for a single day." [1]

It would seem imperative that every nation should know the number of people in its dominions who, although using their best efforts, are failing to obtain sufficient necessaries for maintaining physical efficiency. How many people in this country are in poverty? Is the number yearly growing larger? Are there each year more and more of the unskilled classes, pursuing hopelessly the elusive phantom of self-support and independence? Are they, as in a dream, working faster only the more swiftly to move backward? Are there each year more and more hungry children, and more and more fathers whose utmost effort may not bring into the home as much energy in food as it takes out in industry? These are not fanciful questions, nor are they sentimental ones. I have not the slightest doubt that there are in the United States ten million persons in precisely these conditions of poverty, but I am largely guessing and there may be as many as fifteen or twenty million! But ought we not to know? If poverty were due to purely individual causes, it would perhaps be fair to deny the moral necessity of national inquiries at periodic intervals into the condition of all the people and especially of the poor. But no one knowing the many active social causes of individual poverty and misery could deny this necessity in a democracy of professedly Christian people. To neglect even to inquire into our national distress is to be guilty of the grossest moral insensitiveness. There are many who would demand not only inquiries, but remedies. A few men, such as Morris, Ruskin, and Emerson, hold up constantly the ideal of the great nation as the one wherein there may be no rich, but wherein there must be "as many as possible full-breathed, bright-eyed, and happy-hearted human creatures." [1] And all great men have universally deplored that nation wherein "wealth accumulates and men decay." They are, of course, right; but until society manifests some desire to know the extent of the misery in which men decay—not until then may we hope for anything more than a petty individual dealing with a question mainly social.

During the entire last century many of the best minds were engaged in the study of social and economic questions. At the beginning of this new century we are still asking "riddles about the starving." After many years of most elaborate investigations, printed in thousands of volumes issued by federal and state governments, we are almost as far from any definite knowledge concerning the extent of poverty as we have ever been. The United States spends more money than any other nation in the world upon statistical investigations, and yet we know less about the poverty of the people than almost any other great nation of the Western world. An immense sum is expended yearly in taking the census and in maintaining the many bureaus in Washington to investigate the conditions of commerce, of labor, of agriculture, of railways, etc. Almost every state has local bureaus existing for the same purpose. After the existence of these bureaus for a period of from twenty to thirty years, no one can tell, or give anything like a fair estimate of, the number of people existing in the community unable to obtain a living wage or its equivalent; or, in other words, unable to obtain the necessaries for maintaining physical efficiency. We cannot now, in any very satisfactory way, tell the number of unemployed, the number of unskilled workers or their wages; we do not know the number of underfed children, or even, and this seems most absurd of all, the number of persons dependent upon the public for support. We do not know the number of men killed by accidents in industry, or injured by dangerous trades. There are immense volumes of wage statistics containing averages so general, and confusing so skilfully all the different classes of labor, that it is next to impossible to make anything specific out of the material. Almost each new publication warns any one from trusting or basing any arguments upon material previously gathered and published. The extent of poverty in the United States is absolutely unknown. Mr. Carroll D. Wright, who of all persons should be able to throw some light on this subject, is unable to quote any statistics whatever when writing

on the subject of poverty in his book. His chapter
on poverty is in itself a restatement of well-known
generalizations of questionable usefulness, and based
largely upon the investigations and statements of
Professor Amos G. Warner, who, largely as a result
of private inquiry, produced an invaluable book upon
" American Charities."[1] With no figures whatever to
bear out his statement, Mr. Wright takes occasion to
speak of the assertion that the "rich are growing richer
and the poor poorer" as "false in its premises and
misleading in its influence."[2] It is unnecessary to say
that we might choose to take Mr. Wright's statement
or choose to take his opponent's statement.   It is
largely a matter of temperament which side one takes
in the matter, for in either case we have no facts to
support our position.

It is difficult without certain fundamental facts, if
it is not indeed impossible, to make any worth-while
estimate of poverty.   This is proved most clearly
by two examples — one in England and the other in
Germany.   A few years ago England did not know
the extent of her own poverty.   Economists and
writers gave opinions of all kinds.   Some said conditions were "bad," others said such statements were
misleading; and here they were, tilting at each other,
backward and forward, in the most ponderous and
serious way until Mr. Booth, a business man, undertook to get at the facts.   No one, not even the most

radical economist, would have dared to have estimated the poverty of London as extending to 30
per cent of the people. The extent of poverty —
the number underfed, underclothed, and in insanitary houses — was greater than could reasonably
have been estimated. Another illustration may be
taken from Germany. A few years ago no one in
that country knew the number of accidents which
occurred yearly in industry. There were various
estimates. It was generally thought that there
might be thirty or forty thousand injuries per year
due to machinery. Mr. John Graham Brooks says:
"The first investigation showed three times this
number; when the investigation became more complete, six times the number." [1] This shows how
impossible it is, without carefully collected data, to
make anything like a correct estimate of existing
social conditions. In both of these cases the facts
proved the actual conditions to be far worse than
any one had dared to estimate them. We are at
present in precisely this state of ignorance, in the
United States, as to accidents, unemployment, pauperism, wages, the number of unskilled, the number
of underfed school children, etc., and, therefore,
ignorant of the extent of poverty. We do not know
whether poverty is gaining or losing ground. We
are uncertain whether or not the causes of poverty
are more active now than they were in the past.

We cannot be sure that we have less poverty than any other country. In the two above-mentioned instances, the conditions abroad proved to be far worse than the highest estimates. Whether this will be true of the United States also must, of course, remain unknown until careful inquiries are made.

Although there are no facts treating of the extent of poverty, there are a great many books filled with descriptions and discussions and riddles. Charles B. Spahr, Walter A. Wyckoff, Mrs. John Van Vorst and Miss Marie Van Vorst, I. K. Friedman, and A. M. Simons have given us some idea of the conditions among the poorest class of laborers in various industrial centres over the country.[1] Jacob A. Riis, Ernest Poole, and Mrs. Lillian Betts have given us most sympathetic descriptions of poverty among the people of the tenements.[2] Flynt and others have given us impressionistic stories of tramps, vagrants, and mendicants.[3] They bring before our very eyes, through books and magazines, stories of needless deaths from insanitary conditions, of long hours of work, of low pay, of overcrowded sweatshops, of child labor, of street waifs, of vile tenements, of the hungry and the wretched.

All these books and articles are extremely valuable and useful, but if anything is to be done about the matter, we should begin as soon as possible to know the extent of these conditions and the causes which bring such terribly serious misery and wretchedness into the world. Some few attempts of real importance have been made to ascertain more detailed facts concerning the living and working conditions of the people, but they also are insufficient. The "Hull House Maps and Papers," Robert A. Wood's "The City Wilderness" and "The Americans in Process," and Dr. Peter Robert's "The Anthracite Coal Communities" are the most important contributions. The investigations of the Bureau of Labor into the conditions of the Italian laborers in Chicago and of the negroes in various cities are all efforts in the right direction, but that is about all that can be said of them. While men in Germany and England have been making exhaustive studies of the poverty and social misery in those countries, and have aroused the people to the grave necessity of social reform, the United States has made almost no progress in obtaining exact knowledge of the condition of the working-classes.

As has been said, it was not until Mr. Charles Booth published in 1891 the results of his exhaustive inquiries that the actual conditions of poverty in London became known. About 1,300,000 people, or about 30 per cent of the entire population of London, were found to be unable to obtain the necessaries for a sound livelihood.[1] They were in a state of poverty, living in conditions, if not of actual misery, at any rate bordering upon it. In many districts considerably more than half of the population were either in distress or on the verge of distress. When these results were made public, the more conservative economists gave it as their opinion that the conditions in London were, of course, exceptional and that it would be unsafe to make any generalizations for the whole of England on the basis of Mr. Booth's figures for London. About ten years later, Mr. B. S. Rountree, incited by the work of Mr. Booth, undertook a similar inquiry in his native town, York, a small provincial city in most ways typical of the smaller towns of England. In a large volume in which the results are published, it is shown that the poverty in York was only slightly less extensive than that of London. In the summary Mr. Rountree compares the conditions in London with those in York. His comments are as follows: "The proportions arrived at for the total population living in poverty in London and York respectively were as under:—

London . . . . . . 30.7 per cent
York . . . . 27.84 per cent

"The proportion of the population living in poverty in York may be regarded as practically the same as in London, especially when we remember that Mr. Booth's information was gathered in 1887–1892, a period of only *average* trade prosperity, whilst the York figures were collected in 1899, when trade was unusually prosperous."

He continues : "We have been accustomed to look upon the poverty in London as exceptional, but when the result of careful investigation shows that the proportion of poverty in London is practically equalled in what may be regarded as a typical provincial town, we are faced by the startling probability that from 25 to 30 per cent of the town populations of the United Kingdom are living in poverty."[1] The invaluable work of these two men, done at their own expense, has had the effect of making the poverty of England understood, and that is the beginning of any reform.

It is, of course, deplorable that we have not made even a beginning in finding out the extent of poverty in America. As has been said, we have no facts which will enable us to make an exact comparison of our conditions with those abroad. There are, however, certain fragments of information which may make us question the prevalent notion that all is well, and that "comparatively speaking," as an economist said to me recently, "we have no poverty." There is a general spirit of optimism, which is not unlike that which existed in England previous to the work of Mr. Booth and Mr. Rountree. It is an optimism which results from ignorance or from the

lack of any real concern.   Such facts as we have are
not sufficient to enable us to make any conclusive
estimate, and they are used only for the purpose of
serving as indications of the extent of poverty in this
country.

These fragments of information, indicative of a
widespread poverty, fall under the following heads :
Pauperism, the general distress, the number of evictions, the pauper burials; the overcrowding and
insanitation due to improper housing; the death rate
from tuberculosis; the amount of unemployment;
and the number of accidents in certain trades.   By
means of such data as we have concerning these
conditions, a partial, but of course a most imperfect,
comparison can be made between the poverty of
England and that of the United States.

In the face of widespread poverty there have not
been for over half a century in England so few
paupers, either actually or proportionately, as there
are now.   The population of England has increased
from about 18,000,000 persons in 1851 to 29,000,000
in 1889.[1]   During this period the number of paupers
actually fell off.   It is said that London "has lost in
pauper population fifteen times as fast as she has
gained in general population."[2]   The total number of
paupers in the United States in the year 1891 was
about 3,000,000 according to the estimates of Professor Richard T. Ely and of Mr. Charles D. Kellogg,

then secretary of the Charity Organization Society of
New York City.[1] The census figures are too incomplete to be relied upon, but the returns from the
almshouses show that the number of paupers
increased almost as fast as population during the
decade from 1880 to 1890.[2] In Hartford, Connecticut,
the number of paupers increased about 50 per cent
during the same decade.[3] An increase not less great
took place in many other cities of the country. It is
questionable whether the same increase occurred in
the last decade. In two or three states a more
economical administration of the poor-law funds,
during the last decade, has diminished the number of
persons dependent upon outdoor relief, although in
several states the number of paupers has increased.
But the figures of most of the states are too incomplete to permit of an exact statement concerning the
increase or decrease of pauperism. Only by means
of an estimate, such as Professor Ely made in 1891,
can we gain any idea of the number of dependent
persons. Taking a similar basis to the one used by
him, there is every indication that not less than
4,000,000 persons are now dependent upon the public
for relief. What relation, if any, pauperism bears to
the poverty of this country has not been determined.
The amount of pauperism in any community depends
so much upon the way in which the poor law is
administered that any comparison of the pauperism

in various cities, states, or countries would yield
no trustworthy data concerning the extent of
poverty.

The general distress, as shown by the demands
made upon *both* public and private charities, is a
better test of the extent of poverty than that furnished by the numbers dependent upon the poor
funds of the state alone.   Mr. Jacob A. Riis, a few
years ago, used some figures which showed that
about one-third of the people of New York City were
dependent upon charity at some time during the eight
years previous to 1890.[1]   The report of the United
Hebrew Charities for 1901 shows very similar conditions existing among the Jewish population of New
York.[2]   But even more astonishing than all other
facts we have are those furnished by the State Board
of Charities.   In 1897 the Board endeavored to
collect figures of the number of persons assisted by
both public and private charities.   It was of course
impossible to prevent duplications or to get returns
from hundreds of the more personal sources of relief-
giving, but it was a creditable and most useful piece
of public work.   Three years later the work was
curtailed by decision of the Court of Appeals, and
consequently the more complete figures are only
available for the three years 1897, 1898, and 1899.   I
quote the following figures from a letter by Robert
W. Hebberd, secretary of the State Board:[3] —

| Year | State Insti- tutions | Hospi- tals | Dispen- saries | Outdoor Relief | | Total |
				In Homes	Homeless	
1897	7720	98,960	1,451,713	266,431	288,380	2,113,204
1898	8272	106,835	1,052,177	364,814	368,101	1,900,199
1899	8161	114,199	932,072	395,632	338,863	1,788,927

These figures unquestionably contain many duplications. How many, it is impossible to say. It would not be reasonable to believe that 29 per cent of the people of New York found it necessary in the year 1897, or 24 per cent in 1899, to apply for relief. And yet it should be said that these figures of the State Board do not include the relief given by the many small clubs, circles, committees, and Trade Unions; nor is the relief given by many benevolent individuals recorded. There must, of course, be many thousand cases of distress receiving relief regularly and solely from these personal or private sources. But even though the figures do not include all persons in distress, it is reasonable to suppose that there are a large number of duplications and that they make the totals considerably larger than they should be.

Excluding half the number of persons relieved by the dispensaries (in order to make some arbitrary allowance for duplications), even then the number of persons relieved would indicate that the poverty of New York State is enormous. In actual figures as reduced, the persons in distress in 1897 number

1,387,348, or about 19 per cent of the people of New
York, and in 1899 they number 1,322,891, or about
18 per cent.

It is possible to compare with these figures those
for Boston just published by the city's official statis-
tician. During the year 1903 over 136,000 persons
were aided by the *public* authorities alone, or, estimating the present population at 606,600, more than 20
per cent of the entire population.[1] It is estimated
that 336,000 persons were aided in *private* hospitals,
dispensaries, asylums, etc.; and these are, of course,
not included, except by duplications, in the above
figures, and the mere fact that such an estimate is
made would indicate that the official figures do not
measure the full extent of the distress. If the figures
are correct as published, the persons in New York
State in distress in 1897, and in Boston in 1903,
would equal proportionately the number of those in
poverty in London.

The amount of actual distress in the community
may be measured also by two additional sets of data.
The number of evictions in any community is a fairly
good measure of the minimum distress. In the year
1903, 60,463 families in the borough of Manhattan
were evicted from their homes.[2] This is about 14
per cent of the total number of families in the
borough. As another indication, the number of
pauper burials should be cited. Every one familiar

with the poor knows how desperately they struggle
to give a decent burial to their dead. A poor
person will resort to almost any means in order to
prevent a member of his or her family having a
pauper burial, or, as they say, " lying in a pauper's
grave." Even the poorest people have friends, politicians or others, who save them, if possible, from
this last disgrace. And yet one in every ten persons
who die in New York is buried at public expense in
Potter's Field.[1] This is, without question, the lowest
limit of misery. If observation counts for anything,
I should say that the number of pauper burials certainly does not represent half of the actual distress in
any community.

The results stated concisely are as follows : —

1903	20 per cent of the people of Boston in distress.
1897	19 per cent of the people of New York State in distress.
1899	18 per cent of the people of New York State in distress.
1903	14 per cent of the families of Manhattan evicted.
Every year.	10 per cent (about) of those who die in Manhattan have pauper burials.

On the basis of these figures it would seem fair to
estimate that certainly not less than 14 per cent of
the people, in prosperous times (1903), and probably
not less than 20 per cent in bad times (1897), are in
distress. The estimate is a conservative one, for
despite all the imperfections which may be found in
the data, and there are many, any allowance for the

persons who are given aid by sources not reporting to the State Board, or for those persons not aided by the authorities of Boston, or for those persons who, although in great distress, are not evicted, must counterbalance the duplications or errors which may exist in the figures either of distress or evictions.

These figures, furthermore, represent only the distress which manifests itself. There is no question but that only a part of those in poverty, in any community, apply for charity. I think any one living in a Settlement will support me in saying that many families who are obviously poor — that is, underfed, underclothed, or badly housed — never ask for aid or suffer the social disgrace of eviction. Of course, no one could estimate the proportion of those who are evicted or of those who ask assistance to the total number in poverty; for whatever opinion one may have formed is based, not on actual knowledge, gained by inquiry, but on impressions, gained through friendly intercourse. My own opinion is that probably not over half of those in poverty ever apply for charity, and certainly not more than that proportion are evicted from their homes. However, I should not wish an opinion of this sort to be used in estimating, from the figures of distress, etc., the number of those in poverty. And yet from the facts of distress, as given, and from opinions formed, both as a charity agent and as a Settlement worker,

I should not be at all surprised if the number of
those in poverty in New York, as well as in other
large cities and industrial centres, rarely fell below
25 per cent of all the people.

Without now making any further efforts to estimate
the extent, we will continue with the various indications of poverty. The amount of unemployment is
an excellent test. Here again our figures are too
imperfect to enable us to compare them satisfactorily
with those of England. The causes of unemployment, however, appear to be more active here than in
that country. Of course, the most serious interrup-
tions to regular employment are industrial depressions, at which times great masses of men are thrown
out of employment for long periods. Depressions,
however, occur periodically in all industrial countries
with much the same regularity. The other industrial
causes of unemployment vary considerably in the
different nations. The reorganization of industry
into trusts, causing many thousands of men to lose
temporarily their employment; the introduction of
new machinery, having the same effect; the speeding
up of the machines, which exhausts and displaces
workmen at an early age; excessive hours in many
trades and a too plentiful supply of labor in many
industrial centres, obtained by artificially stimulated
immigration, are all causes of unemployment which
seem more active in this country than abroad. Even

the contract and sweating systems are more developed
in this country. Englishmen visiting our industrial
centres are amazed at the rapidity of the changes in
industrial methods, from the changing of machines
to the entire reorganization of an industry.[1] Thousands of men are thrown out of employment whenever these changes occur. However beneficial to
society these revolutions in industrial methods are,
they are unquestionably active causes of widespread
unemployment or of irregular employment. Mr. Jack
London, writing in the *Atlantic Monthly* on " The
Scab," refers to the United States as a scab nation,
and to the working-men of this country as scab workmen, because the workers in this country work more
intensely, longer hours, and more cheaply than those
of other great industrial nations.[2] In other words,
we are underbidding the other nations by a lower
standard of work, and underselling them as a result,
not of fair, but of scab methods. Without question,
the causes, which produce on the one hand long
hours and overemployment, result on the other hand
in short periods of work, underemployment, or unemployment.

The figures of unemployment, although very imperfect, show that the evil is widespread, even in
times of prosperity. The census of 1890 shows that
3,523,730, or 15.1 per cent of all of the workers over
ten years of age, engaged in gainful occupations,

were unemployed a part of the time during that
year.[1] These figures are, however, criticised by the
census of 1900 as incomplete. In the last census
the number found to be unemployed at some time
during the year was 6,468,964, or 22.3 per cent of
all the workers over ten years of age, engaged in
gainful occupations.[2] Thirty-nine per cent of the male
workers unemployed, or 2,069,546 persons, were idle
from four to six months of the year.[3] These figures
are for the country as a whole, and for all industries,
including agriculture. In manufacturing alone the unemployment rose to 27.2 per cent of all of the workers.
In the industrial states of the East and North the percentage of unemployment is larger than for the country as a whole. The Massachusetts census for 1895
showed that 8339 workmen were unemployed continuously during that year, and that 252,456 persons
were irregularly employed.[4] This means that over 27
per cent of all persons covered by the inquiry were
idle some portion of the year. That this is not exceptional is shown by the Massachusetts census for 1885.
At that time over 29 per cent of the workmen were
irregularly employed. In other words, the annual
wages of more than one workman in every four
suffered considerable decrease by reason of a period
of enforced idleness, extending in some cases over
several months. In the industrial towns, such as
Haverhill, New Bedford, and Fall River, the irregu-

larity of employment was even greater. In these towns from 39 to 62 per cent of the workmen were idle during some part of the year.[1] Still another investigation, made in 1897 in Massachusetts, showed that there were 100,000 workers in certain factories in that state who found employment when the factories were most active, but who were unemployed when the factories were least active.[2] This fluctuation of the number of employed means that about 30 per cent of the maximum number employed in the busiest season are rendered idle during the slack seasons. This uncertainty of employment is not peculiar to Massachusetts. In every industrial community, the same insecurity of livelihood, due to irregular employment, exists. It has been said that during the anthracite coal strike of 1902 the entire supply of mined coal was exhausted, but the excess of laborers in that district is so great that within a short time after the strike was settled a report was sent out on reliable authority that "intermittent labor is again the lot of anthracite employees. The collieries do not average more than two-thirds time."[3]

Men employed in navigation on the Great Lakes are particularly subject to seasonal demands for their labor. During the three months, January, February, and March, one-third of all the workmen are unemployed.[4] In the clothing trades of New York City it is very much the same. During the first seven

months of the year 1903 there were never less than
one-fifth of the men unemployed, and at times between
one-third and one-fourth of all the workmen were
without employment.[1] In other words, during this
time, from 20 to 30 per cent of the working people
were in enforced idleness. The workers in these
seasonal trades are compelled to have regularly
recurring periods of poverty. The long seasons of
idleness mean in many cases serious distress to large
numbers of workmen and their families.

With the exception of 1885 and 1895 none of the
years for which figures have been quoted are to be
considered as years of industrial depression. In these
times of industrial crises, the number of unemployed
men, who with their families are in poverty, reaches
a point where the whole nation is moved to pity. In
these times the lodging-houses of our cities are overcrowded with idle men. The vagrant class increases
to large proportions, and the despair and wretchedness
of the workless people cause the ruin of thousands.
There is a very large increase in the number im-
prisoned for vagrancy, petty crimes, and drunkenness.
"Modern life," Mr. John Hobson has said, "has no
more tragical figure than the gaunt, hungry laborer
wandering about the crowded centres of industry and
wealth, begging in vain for permission to share in 'hat
industry, and to contribute to that wealth ; asking in
return, not the comforts and luxuries of civilized life,

but the rough food and shelter for himself and
family, which would be practically secured to him in
the rudest form of savage society." [1]

One is apt to forget the tragedies which result
from unemployment. Not only are the better classes
of labor pulled down to the very verge of poverty by
irregular employment, but the poorer classes of
unskilled labor are carried during a season of unemployment into conditions of actual poverty. The
great mass of laborers must in all cases exercise
economy, frugality, and good common sense in order
to obtain for themselves those things necessary to
maintain a standard of living which we proudly boast
is American. For the lower classes of labor, the
maintenance of an American standard, even under
the most favorable conditions, is hardly possible, and
by a period of unemployment, extending from one to
three months in the year, their annual wage is invariably changed from a living one to a poverty one. That
this happens, not only during industrial depressions,
but at certain seasons every year, is, I think, without
question. There is a fierce competition going on,
especially in our cities, among various classes of immigrants for work requiring no special skill. At best,
this labor market is always oversupplied, unemployment is greatest and wages are always at the lowest
level. In consequence, there is a sort of devastation,
due to constantly recurring poverty, which sadly afflicts
this class of common laborers and their families.

There are very few figures regarding the unemployment among unskilled workers; but an investigation into the condition of the Italians in Chicago makes one realize that it is far more extensive among the unskilled than among the skilled workers. The figures given above concern the unemployment of all classes of labor. The federal reports of this inquiry show that " of the 2663 employed in remunerative occupations, 1517, or 56.97 per cent, were unemployed some part of the year . . . . and the average time unemployed for these 1517 persons was therefore over seven months." Two hundred and thirty-two persons were idle eight months of the year; 310 persons nine months; 161 ten months; 68 eleven months during the year.[1] When it is realized that the average earnings, for all classes of work engaged in by the Italians, amounted to less than $6 a week, it is easy to realize the poverty and suffering which result from unemployment.[2] The Italians, for a time, try to do the heavy and intense work required of them here on the same poor diet which supplied their needs in Italy, and superstitiously hang small salt bags about their children's necks to drive away the devil of malnutrition and starvation. Nothing could show the misery resulting from unemployment and underfeeding more clearly than the physical condition of the Italians in this country.

It is doubtful if one is warranted in considering

D

the above conditions to be the same among the unskilled laborers of other foreign colonies. It may,
however, be nearer the average for similar classes of
laboring men than we imagine. The figures of the
last federal census indicate this to be true. It
states that 44.3 per cent of the unskilled workers
were unemployed some part of the year.[1] Common
observation also lends its support to this conclusion.
Everywhere — in the anthracite coal district, in
South Chicago, and in many other industrial communities of Illinois, Pennsylvania, New York, and
Massachusetts — there are among unskilled laborers
indications of extreme poverty. The Irish of "Archy
Road," the Poles and Hungarians of the Stock Yards
district, the Italians of New York and Chicago, and
the Jews of the east side of New York, differ considerably in ability; but from all appearances it seems
that very nearly the same amount of poverty exists
among all those workers, of whatever nationality,
whose labor is unskilled and irregular. The temper-
ance and intelligence of the Jews save them from the
worst miseries. The unskilled and unorganized Irish
laborers, who have been unable to obtain city jobs by
political influence, are, I dare say, as wretchedly
poor as any other class of immigrants. It would, of
course, be unwise to carry this comparison of the
conditions among the unskilled workers of various
nationalities too far. It is necessarily based largely

upon observation, and that is always more or less
limited and imperfect. But it is safe to conclude
that employment is much more irregular among all
classes of unskilled workers than among the workers
in the skilled and organized trades. As the wages
of unskilled workmen, as will be shown later, are in
general only sufficient to keep them above the
poverty line while they are at work, unemployment
means for these classes underfeeding, insufficient
clothing, and uncertain tenure of home. It is hardly
too much to assume that in the larger industrial
states, in ordinary times, 30 per cent of the unskilled
workers are in poverty some part of the year as a
result of unemployment. This, of course, is only one
of many causes of poverty. Sickness and injuries
are perhaps not less important, either as indications
of poverty or as causes.

The indications of poverty which lie in the figures
of accidents, diseases, and casualties, resulting from
industrial employments, are very significant, although the figures are most incomplete. It has
been determined that nine out of every ten working-
class families in Europe require charitable aid after
injuries due to some industrial accident.[1] Probably
not so large a proportion in this country would,
under the same circumstances, find it necessary to
apply for charitable relief; but in nearly all cases
where the breadwinner suffers permanent injury, or

is suddenly killed, the family must receive assistance of some sort, until other members of the family are able to assume the responsibility of its support. Mr. John Graham Brooks, in his recent book, "The Social Unrest," has called attention to "that frightful list of stricken laborers that are now thrown back upon themselves or their families with recompense so uncertain and niggardly as to shock the most primitive sense of social justice." [1]

Unfortunately the facts regarding these industrial causes of poverty are so incomplete as to make it impossible to estimate the amount of distress resulting from them. Such facts as we have apply only to the industries of mining and railroading. The following table, taken from the reports of the Interstate Commerce Commission, will fully illustrate how terribly dangerous is the work of a railway employee:

RAILROAD ACCIDENTS IN THE UNITED STATES [2]

YEAR	EMPLOYEES		PASSENGERS		OTHER PERSONS		TOTAL	
	Killed	Injured	Killed	Injured	Killed	Injured	Killed	Injured
1897	1,693	27,667	222	2,795	4,522	6,269	6,437	36,731
1898	1,958	31,761	221	2,945	4,680	6,176	6,859	40,882
1899	2,210	34,923	239	3,442	4,674	6,255	7,123	44,620
1900	2,550	39,643	249	4,128	5,066	6,549	7,865	50,320
1901	2,675	41,142	282	4,988	5,498	7,209	8,455	53,339
1902	2,969	50,524	345	6,683	5,274	7,455	8,588	64,662

These figures are frightful. In 1901 one out of every 399 employees was killed and one out of every 26

was injured. The trainmen, such as engineers, fire-
men, conductors, etc., are the greatest sufferers. One
was killed for every 137 employed, and one was
injured for every 11 employed. It is difficult to believe that such slaughter is permitted to go on year
after year. It would seem as if the owners of the
railroads would make the safety of their workmen
their first obligation; but, strange as it is, they
resist powerfully every attempt made to have them
adopt safety appliances. The energetic efforts
of the Interstate Commerce Commission have been
but partially successful in compelling the railroads to
put on such appliances as are necessary in order to
diminish the number of accidents and fatalities. Up
to the present the Commission has not been successful in compelling the railroads to introduce the Block
System, which would greatly diminish the number
killed and injured. The railroads consider this
system an "unwarranted luxury," just as a few
years ago they considered the automatic coupler an
"unwarranted luxury." Such increased expenses for
the safety of the employees reduce profits, and
with that only in view the railroads either forget,
or have no concern for, the families whose bread-
winners are lost or injured by this criminal policy
of preferring murder to decreased dividends. The
following are chosen merely as examples of the
injuries : [1] —

Back wrenched	.	.	.	.	workman,	age 24
Leg cut off	.	.	.	.	workman,	age 19
Foot crushed	.	.	.	.	workman,	age 25
Foot and hip injured	.	.	.	workman,	age 35
Foot cut off	.	.	.	.	workman,	age 27

These injuries to railway workmen are more serious
than at first appears, for very few of the men who
are injured are over thirty-five, and most of them are
in the twenties. This period — between twenty and
thirty-five — is the most important period of a workman's life. It is the time when he is of utmost value
to his family, since the children are still too young to
take up the support of the family.

The responsibility of the railroads for poverty
resulting from injuries or casualties is of three kinds
at least. First: In many cases they overwork their
employees. Dr. Samuel McCune Lindsay says:
"Emergencies frequently occur due to accidents or
condition of weather when men may be required to
work continuously from twenty to thirty hours, and,
in exceptional cases, men have been continuously at
work in train service for thirty-six hours." [1] Second:
Many railroad systems have resisted and violated the
law compelling them to put on automatic couplers,
and they are now fighting the introduction of the
Block System, both of which improvements are
designed to prevent accidents and injuries. Third:
In case of accidents, "company" physicians and

lawyers hasten immediately to the place of the accident, and, if possible, persuade the workmen to sign contracts by which they agree, for some small immediate compensation, to release the company from any further liability. I have known many, many cases where workmen have, for a few dollars, signed away their rights to sue when their injuries have been as serious as the loss of a leg or arm. In the seventeen years ending June 30, 1902, 103,320 persons were killed and 587,028 injured by the railway industry.

The returns of those killed and injured in the mining districts are less complete than the ones given for the railroads. Dr. Peter Roberts, who has for several years studied with great care the industrial and social conditions of the anthracite regions, states that in certain sections of that community the non-fatal injuries are more serious now than they were in past decades. He says that "nearly half the employees have no provision for either the incapacitated through accident or for the maintenance of widows and orphans when death befalls those who provide for them in this hazardous calling. Many operators display generosity worthy of emulation ; others manifest criminal indifference to the sufferings of employees and their families because of accident. . . . To leave these men to the mercy of overbearing operators in case of injury and death is unworthy of the civilization of the century in which we live." [1] It is impossible to say how much of the existing poverty is caused by accidents, injuries, and sickness, due to industrial processes and conditions ; but such facts as we have would indicate that these poverty-producing causes are more active in the United States than in any other great industrial nation.

These various indications of poverty might be followed by many less significant ones.* The earlier age at which men are incapacitated in this country is but one of the more important. An inquiry made several years ago in New Jersey showed that workmen began to decline between the ages of thirty-five and forty-five, although in many cases they were not completely incapacitated until twenty years later.[2] Dr. Roberts shows that the average age of the deceased in the anthracite district was 24 for the female and 24.8 for the male, although the average for the country as a whole was 35.2 years.[3] But there are too many of such minor indications to be worthy of detailed examination. In lieu of definite, accurate figures concerning the extent of poverty, such figures as we have of distress, of insanitary housing conditions, of overcrowding, of deaths from tuberculosis, of unemployment and of accidents, indicate that the poverty in certain portions of this country is hardly less extensive than that of certain parts of England.

* See Housing, Tuberculosis, and Accidents, Appendix A.

From a different point of view, — from figures of
the ownership of wealth in this country, — another indication of poverty may be considered. Wealth and
poverty seem to be inevitably associated with each
other. In the report of the Royal Commission on
Labor, presented to the Houses of Parliament in
1894, the following sentences, succeeding an account
of the poverty and wretchedness existing in English
towns, show the relation which these two things —
poverty and wealth — bear toward each other. "It
is impossible to refrain from connecting this deplorable condition of the working class with the
fact that two-thirds of the annual product of the
community is absorbed by one-fourth of its members,
and that the annual tribute of rents, royalties, and
dividends levied upon the industry of the nation
amounts to nearly 500,000,000 sterling."[1] Here
again our figures are deplorably deficient when compared with English ones. There is a general impression that we have a widespread diffusion of property
ownership. It is, of course, natural that, with great
tracts of land opened within the last century to
millions of individuals, there should be an extent of
individual ownership of farms in this country far
greater than that existing elsewhere. But nevertheless, Mr. George K. Holmes, a cautious and conservative investigator, shows, on the basis of the census
figures for 1890, that over 34 per cent of our farmers

are renters and an additional 18.6 per cent have their
farms mortgaged.[1] All together there are over
52 per cent of the farmers in this country who have
only a partial ownership of their farms, or who are
propertyless.

The number of persons owning farms is an indication of the ownership of property in the rural
districts only; while the figures concerning the ownership of homes give us an indication of the number of
persons in cities, towns, and agricultural districts,
having no property interests. The census figures
for 1900 show that 8,365,739, or considerably over
half of the families in the United States, do not
own the homes in which they live.[2] In the cities
the ownership of homes is much less common than in
the smaller towns. Illustrations of this fact are seen
in the following percentages of homes hired in
various cities :[3] —

Boston	81.1
Chicago	74.9
Cincinnati	79.1
Fall River	82.
Holyoke	80.6
New York (Manhattan)	94.1
Philadelphia	77.9

The percentages show that of all the persons living in these cities a very large proportion do not own
the homes in which they live. Probably no wage-

earners in Manhattan own their homes, and in several other large cities probably 99 per cent of the wage-earners are propertyless. The significant thing in this lack of ownership lies in the fact that a very large majority, probably 90 per cent, of the workmen in the cities and industrial communities, are propertyless, and, furthermore, are involved in a weekly indebtedness for rent of from one-fifth to two-fifths of their earnings, regardless of whether they have work or not.

The estimates of wealth and of the distribution of wealth, made by Mr. Holmes, are less reliable than the aforegoing figures of ownership, but they indicate, nevertheless, that there exists in this country "an enormous culture bed for poverty." The entire wealth of the country was estimated by the census of 1890 at $65,000,000,000. Mr. Holmes concludes, on the basis of his inquiries, that three-tenths of one per cent of the families in this country own one-fifth of this wealth, that is to say, 20 per cent of the wealth of the country. Nine per cent of the families in the country own 71 per cent of the total wealth.[1]

Mr. Charles B. Spahr has estimated, with most painstaking care, the distribution of incomes in the United States. The results of his inquiries are very effectively set forth in the following tables and diagrams : —

THE UNITED STATES 1890 [1]

ESTATES	NUMBER	AGGREGATE WEALTH	AVERAGE WEALTH
The Wealthy Classes $50,000 and over . .	125,000	$33,000,000,000	$264,000
The Well-to-do Classes $50,000 to $5,000 . .	1,375,000	23,000,000,000	16,000
The Middle Classes $5,000 to $500 . . .	5,500,000	8,200,000,000	1,500
The Poorer Classes under $500	5,500,000	800,000,000	150
Total	12,500,000	$65,000,000,000	$5,200

From this table Mr. Spahr concludes that less than half of the families in the United States are property-less; nevertheless, seven-eighths of the families hold but one-eighth of the national wealth, *while but one per cent of the families hold more than the remaining ninety-nine per cent.*

Another table, based upon Mr. Spahr's inquiry, and accompanied by a diagram, is taken from Mr. John Graham Brooks' "The Social Unrest." [2]

DISTRIBUTION OF WEALTH IN THE UNITED STATES

CLASS	FAMILIES	PER CENT	AVERAGE WEALTH	AGGREGATE WEALTH	PER CENT
Rich . .	125,000	1.0	$263,040	$32,880,000,000	54.8
Middle . .	1,362,500	10.9	14,180	19,320,000,000	32.2
Poor . .	4,762,500	38.1	1,639	7,800,000,000	13.0
Very Poor .	6,250,000	50.0	. . .	. . . . . .	. .
Total .	12,500,000	100.0	$4,800	$60,000,000,000	100.0

DIAGRAMS SHOWING, BY PERCENTAGES, THE POPULATION AND
WEALTH DISTRIBUTION IN THE UNITED STATES

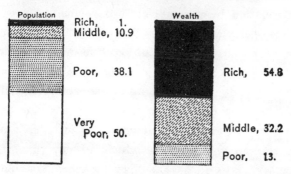

Mr. Brooks says regarding this latter table: "I do not personally believe that trustworthy statistical sources exist that enable one to make tables of this character that are more than mere guesses at the fact. Yet if it were known what the possessions of the one hundred and twenty-six thousand richest families in the United States are, the result would be all that any agitator need ask." How many liberties have been taken with Mr. Spahr's figures in order to construct this latter table I do not know; it can be said, however, that while neither his figures nor those of Mr. Holmes have escaped criticism, the critics have not, thus far, been able to make out a case against them which necessitates any material alteration either of the handling of the data, or of the conclusions finally drawn.[1] Without committing ourselves implicitly to them, we must acknowledge that they indicate an inequality of wealth distribution which should have before now received exhaustive investigation by our official statisticians.

A propertyless person is one without any economic reserve power. He is in no position to ward off the sufferings which must frequently come to most persons depending wholly upon their ability to labor and upon the demand, in the community, for their services. In an industrial crisis, for instance, a person without any property which he may convert, if necessary, into the means of sustenance, is unable to keep off distress until economic conditions revive sufficiently to require his labor. His family must suffer in case of his being unemployed or incapacitated or killed, unless there should be some one else in the family able to take his place as breadwinner. The loss of profits or earnings from property is a serious loss to thousands of families more or less dependent upon incomes from that source; but the classes who possess no property, not even a home from which they may not be evicted, must of necessity pursue that precarious livelihood which depends solely upon health and strength and upon economic conditions, which may, or may not, at any time, require the services of the worker. Security of livelihood in the present state of society comes only with the possession of property; and the large masses of people, whom this short summary of

wealth distribution indicates to be propertyless, have
no assurance whatever that they may not be at any
time, if indeed they are not already, in poverty.

Before summarizing the facts dwelt upon in the
aforegoing pages as indicative of widespread poverty,
let us consider one other important method of measuring its extent; namely, the number of persons, so
far as that can be determined, who are not receiving
an income sufficient to enable them to maintain a
state of physical efficiency. There are many, many
thousand families who receive an income adequate
enough to supply the necessities of physical life, but
who, for one reason or another, — drink, ignorance,
sickness, extravagance, misfortune, or weakness, —
do not manage to obtain the essentials for maintaining physical efficiency. There are also many, many
thousand families who receive wages so inadequate
that no care in spending, however wise it may be,
will make them suffice for the family needs. If every
penny were spent judiciously, the income would not
be sufficient to provide enough of the necessaries
to maintain in efficient working order the various
members of the family. Such wages are neither
"fair" nor "living" wages : they are poverty wages.

It is obvious enough that it is impossible to determine a sum which may be called a "fair" or "living"
wage, and which will apply with equal justice to the
various parts of the country. There are at least two

reasons for this. First, the prices of commodities
differ greatly in so large and varied a country. The
cost of necessaries is much lower in the South than
in the North, and lower in Boston than in New York,
and lower in Fort Wayne than in Chicago. When the
cost of living in rural and urban districts is compared, it
will be found that rents are perhaps responsible for the
most considerable difference, and the prices of food
and fuel also vary.   This variation in the cost of living renders any fixed estimate of a necessary wage
for the whole country practically valueless.   There is
a second element which is sometimes suggested as
important when making estimates of the necessary
cost of living.   If it were indeed an important
element, it would make any computation of a necessary income in this country almost impossible. The
foreign peoples represented among our working
classes are said to require various standards of living.   The Jews, for instance, seem to thrive in the
most insanitary tenements, despite poor food and
insufficient clothing.   The Italians and Hungarians
seem to do as well as the Irish on a much more
limited diet.   The Jews, who are most saving and
economical in their ways of living, do unquestionably
manage to live better on a smaller income than many
other races ; and in so far as this is true of any race,
that race, of course, will be able to live better than
another which is less wise in its economies.   The

same thing is true of different families. But the income of any family must increase with the increase of physical expenditure. And for all races the increase of physical expenditure in the industrial life of America, over what they were formerly required to make in their native countries, is the principal reason for an increased standard of living, and consequently for an increased income. The element of the exhaustion of the physical energies by work must enter into all calculations concerning a required income. It is therefore very doubtful if the Italian and other of the recent immigrants will be able to do as much hard, sustained, and intense work as the American or the Americanized Irishman or German, without a meat diet or, at least, without a much more ample vegetarian diet than that which the Italian, for instance, has been in the habit of having in the milder climate of Italy, doing a lighter and easier and a less sustained kind of work.[1] It is well known that immigrants are at first very easily exhausted in trying to keep pace with the intense, ceaseless rush of the American methods of work. Nowhere abroad is seen the same intense working activity which is customary in the United States.

The breathless and exhausting pace required in the workshops of this country is not seen in the workshops of Europe. For instance, the Jew in the Russian Ghettos runs a sewing machine as one would

E

expect a human being to run a machine, intermit-
tently, with brief periods of rest ; not as a sweated,
starving creature in New York or Chicago runs
one, never easing the twisted spine, never rising
to fill the half-closed lungs. In Russia a man
runs a machine in competition with other men,
and not in competition with the tireless, bodi-
less, and soulless power of steam or electricity.
The Italian, in a sunny climate, in the vineyards and
olive fields, needs little more to fit him for his work
than a limited vegetarian diet, a small supply of
clothes, and an indifferent house. But the Italian,
the Jew, or the Hungarian will need good food,
warm clothing, and a sanitary tenement, if he is
to be paced by the swiftest workman, and rushed by
a machine, which must be tended and cannot be
stopped to permit a full breath or a moment's rest
until the day's labor is done. The present industrial
life "takes it out of a man," as the saying is, and it
must be put back into a man, or the human machine
depreciates and degenerates. It is hardly to be
doubted that nearly all men, exhausting themselves
at the same rate, require very much the same
necessities to keep them in working order.[1] For
these reasons I do not consider that there should
be different wage standards established for the
different nationalities, although, unquestionably, the
standards for the varying parts of the country

should vary in relation to the varying cost of commodities, etc.

Without regard to these apparent differences in the standards of living required by different races and the varying costs of commodities, there are, nevertheless, a number of opinions concerning the necessary income for a family of average size. It was shown by the Massachusetts Bureau of Statistics that it takes $754 a year for a family of five persons to live on.[1] John Mitchell has said that a minimum wage of $600 a year is necessary in the anthracite district for a worker with a family of ordinary size.[2] The New York Bureau of Labor considers that $10 a week or $520 a year is inadequate for city workmen.[3] A prominent official of one of the largest charities in New York City thinks that $2 a day, or about $624 a year, is necessary for a family of five in that city. Granting that these estimates are above the amount necessary to supply only the strictest necessities for useful, efficient living, they are, nevertheless, the opinions of well-informed persons as to a fair wage. It is unnecessary to say that, if any one of these estimates were taken as the standard necessary wage, an enormous number of working people, practically all of the unskilled and a considerable percentage of the skilled, would fall under the poverty line. However desirable and however socially valuable an income of $754 a

year for each family would be, it is unquestionably
too high for a fair estimate of the minimum necessary one.   While $624 a year is probably not
too much for New York City, in view of the excessive rents (consuming in some cases 40 per cent
of the income) and other almost inevitable expenses
such as car fare, etc., it is, nevertheless, an estimate
which could not apply, with equal fairness, to all of
the industrial states of the North.   When one gets
below these figures, however, every dollar cut off may
mean depriving a family of a necessity of life, in
times of health even, and unquestionably in times
of sickness.*   But to estimate in the most conservative way possible, let us take more or less arbitrarily
$460 a year as essential to defray the expenses
of an average family, — a father, a mother, and
three children, — in the cities and industrial communities of the New England states, of New York,
Pennsylvania, Indiana, Ohio, and Illinois.   In the
cities the amount ought to be placed higher and
in the smaller towns the estimate would naturally
be lower, but on the whole the average seems a
fair one.   In the South about $300 a year would
probably cover the cost of like necessaries.   This
estimate of $300 for a family of average size in
the South, and of $460 for a family of average size
in the industrial states of the North, would approach

* See Appendix B.

very nearly a fair standard for the poverty line; that is to say, if any working-class family should be unable to obtain this wage, they would in all likelihood be unable to obtain the necessaries for maintaining physical efficiency.

Even if all were agreed upon these amounts, as fair estimates of necessary yearly wages in the North and South, there is still an obstacle in the way of measuring the extent of poverty by this method. This obstacle consists in the inadequacy of our wage statistics. It is hardly to be doubted that the mass of unskilled workers in the North receive less than $460 a year, or that the same class of laborers in the South receive less than $300.* But, unfortunately, that cannot be proved by any statistics obtainable. There are, however, some figures which show that a very large number of workmen are unable to obtain for themselves and families an average income equal to these standards. Testimony was given before the Industrial Commission showing that the 150,000 track hands, working on the railroads of the United States, received wages ranging from 47½ cents a day, in the South, to $1.25 a day in the North.[1] About half of these men are not employed in the winter, so that their yearly wages are further reduced by a period of idleness. But, leaving that out of account, the sum received

* See Appendix C.

in the South would amount to less than $150 a year, and the yearly wage in the North would amount to less than $375. The same witness testified that these wages were also paid to the carmen and shopmen in the North and South. There were 200,000 men employed in these latter trades.[1] Before the same Commission testimony was given concerning the wages of the street-car employees. For these workers the wages ranged from $320 a year to $460.[2] Mr. Elsas, of the Georgia cotton mills, confessed that the average wage paid his employees was $234 a year. Even men were given only from 75 to 90 cents a day for twelve hours' work.[3] Dr. Peter Roberts says that the average yearly wage in the anthracite district is less than $500, and that about 60 per cent of the workers do not receive $450.[4] According to the United States census for 1900, 11 per cent of the male workers over sixteen years of age, employed in the New England cotton mills, received a rate of pay amounting to less than $6 per week, or, in other words, about $300 a year.[5] This is the most they could have earned if they had worked every day in the year, which of course they were not able to do.* In the Middle states nearly one-third of all the

---

* Since the census was taken there have been two wage reductions in the cotton mills, one of 10 per cent in 1903, and a later one of 12½ per cent in 1904.

workers are receiving a rate of wages less than $6
per week, that is to say again, less than $300 a year;
and in the Southern states 59 per cent are receiving
less than this amount. This, it must be remembered,
is what the census terms the rate of pay, and will
only be received if employment is continuous throughout the year. An inquiry made in Massachusetts
showed that the average number of months during
which the cotton operatives in Fall River were
employed was 9.38.[1] If this proportion would apply
to the above operatives, whose wages were investi-
gated by the United States census, their wages
would be reduced nearly one-fourth; in other words,
their wages would fall to about $225 a year.
In the shoe-making industry 51 per cent of the
unskilled workers receive less than $300 a year.
In the Central states 80.3 per cent, and in the
Middle states 87 per cent of these workers receive
less than $300.[2] It is unfortunate that we are
unable to determine the total number ot workmen
in the country who do not receive the minimum
wage of $460 in the North and $300 in the South,
because in this way, if the standards were fair
ones, we should be able to obtain a very accurate
idea of the extent of poverty.

While the above figures are altogether too inadequate to permit us to base upon them any estimate
as to the extent of poverty, it seems reasonable to

assume that the wages of the unskilled laborers in this country rarely rise above the poverty line. A certain percentage are doubtless able to maintain a state of physical efficiency while they have work, but when unemployment comes, and their wages cease, a great mass of the unskilled workers find themselves almost immediately in poverty, if not indeed in actual distress.

It can be assumed, therefore, fairly, I think, that the problem of poverty in this country is in ordinary times confined to a certain percentage of the unskilled laborers who have employment, to most unskilled laborers without employment, and to many unemployed skilled workers. In addition to these workers in poverty, there are those who are weak, infirm, unfortunate, the widows, the families of the sick or the injured, and those who are too incompetent, drunken, or vicious, etc., to be reliable workmen. These are, in the main, the classes of persons in poverty in this country.

It is safe to say that a large number of workers, the mass of unskilled and some skilled workmen with their families, fall beneath the poverty line at least three times during their lives, — during childhood, in the prime of life, and at old age. Mr. Rountree, as a result of his inquiries in York, has made the following diagram which illustrates this fact : [1] —

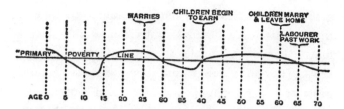

The ordinary increase of family numbers, and the increase or decrease in the family of the capacity for earning, forces the ordinary working-class family above and beneath this line at certain periods, despite their will. Some families may always remain beneath the line by reason of individual or social causes. The curve may at any moment drop to the bottom by reason of unemployment, infirmity, sickness, exhaustion, or accident. There are many observations of fundamental social importance that might be made upon the significance of this diagram. The things of real significance are, however, that the laborer in childhood, when he most needs upbuilding, is in poverty; the wife, when she is bearing children, — a time when she most needs good food and relief from want and worries, — is in poverty; the aged, when they should be in peace and comfort, are in poverty. The reason for this is that the wages of the ordinary unskilled workman are sufficient to support him and his wife, and perhaps one or two children. As more children arrive, the income

gradually becomes less and less adequate to meet
their needs. The family drops below the poverty
line. They are unable to get sufficient necessaries. They drop lower and lower as the children
grow and larger supplies of food and clothing and
more house-room are needed. Then as the children begin to earn, the family rises out of poverty
again, but it remains above the poverty line only
until the children leave home or marry, or for
some other reason may not continue to aid in the
support of the family. At about this time the
father's earnings are likely to drop off through
age or infirmity, and again the parents are in poverty. In this way laborers of the poorest class
pass backward and forward over the poverty line.
The coming of children, the leaving of children,
the periods of employment and of unemployment,
the days of health, the days of sickness, the coming of infirmity, the hour of death, — all of these
things either force the workers of this class backward, or carry them forward over the poverty line.
A large immigration, insanitary tenements, dangerous trades, industrial changes, panics and bankrupt-
cies — in a word, the slightest economic disturbance
or rearrangement — may precipitate them into
misery. The margin of life upon which many of
them live is so narrow that they must toil every
possible hour of working time, and the slightest

economic change registers its effect upon this class of workers.

Any one going carefully through the figures which have been given will agree that poverty is widespread in this country. While it is possible that New York State has more poverty than other states, it is doubtful if its poverty is much greater proportionately than that of most of the industrial states. Twelve years ago I made what was practically a personal canvass of the poor in a small town of Indiana. There were no tenements, but the river banks were lined with small cabins and shanties, inhabited by the poorest and most miserable people I have almost ever seen. About the mills and factories were other wretched little communities of working people. All together the distress extended to but slightly less than 14 per cent of the population, and the poverty extended to not less than 20 per cent of the people. I cannot say how typical this town is of other Indiana towns, but I have always been under the impression that conditions were rather better there than in other towns of the same size. In Chicago the conditions of poverty are certainly worse, if anything, than in the smaller towns, and that is also true of the poverty of New York City. On the whole, it seems to me that the most conservative estimate that can fairly be made of the distress existing in

the industrial states is 14 per cent of the total
population ; while in all probability no less than
20 per cent of the people in these states, in ordinarily prosperous years, are in poverty. This
brings us to the conclusion that one-fifth, or
6,600,000 persons in the states of New York,
Massachusetts, Connecticut, New Jersey, Pennsylvania, Ohio, Illinois, Indiana, and Michigan are in
poverty.[1] Taking half of this percentage and applying it to the other states, many of which have
important industrial communities, as, for instance,
Wisconsin, Colorado, California, Rhode Island, etc.,
the conclusion is that not less than 10,000,000
persons in the United States are in poverty.* This
includes, of course, the 4,000,000 persons who are
estimated to be dependent upon some form of public relief. While the estimate is unquestionably a
conservative one, it may be thought that, although
the percentage, as applied to the industrial states,
is fair, half of that percentage, as applied to the
states largely agricultural, is too high. I think,
however, that the figures concerning the number
of farms rented and mortgaged would warrant the
use of this percentage, if, indeed, there were not
many other facts to warrant an assumption of
that amount of poverty. Professor C. S. Walker
said in 1897, in a discussion before the American

* See Appendix D for other estimates.

Economic Association, "By using all available statistics, it becomes evident again and again that,
deducting rent and interest, the American farmer
receives less for his exertions than does the laborer
in the factory or the hired man on his farm." [1]
However, there can be no question but that the
estimate is within the mark. The fact that over
2,000,000 male wage earners in the United States
were unemployed from four to six months during
the year 1900 would alone warrant the estimate that
10,000,000 persons are in poverty.

The conclusion that about 10,000,000 persons in
the United States are in poverty is, of course, largely
based upon the figures of distress and of unemployment which have been given ; and it would be
warranted, were there no other indications of widespread poverty.   However, many indications lend
themselves to the support of this conclusion. A very
large proportion of the working classes are propertyless ; a very large mass of people, not only in our
largest cities, but in all industrial communities as
well, live in most insanitary conditions ; there is a
high death-rate from tuberculosis in most of our
states ; a large proportion of the unskilled workers
receive, even when employed, wages insufficient to
obtain the necessaries for maintaining physical efficiency ; from all indications, the number injured and
killed in dangerous trades is enormous ; and, lastly,

there is uncertainty of employment for all classes of workers. About 30 per cent of the workers in the industrial states are employed only a part of each year, and, in consequence, suffer a serious decrease in their yearly wages, which, in the case of the unskilled, at least, means to suffer poverty. Nevertheless, the estimate that somewhat over 10,000,000 persons in this country are in poverty does not indicate that our poverty is as great proportionately as that of England. But it should be said that a careful examination would, in all probability, disclose a greater poverty than the estimate indicates.

These figures of poverty have the weakness of all estimates. But even if it were possible to prove that the estimate herein given, of the extent of poverty, is in error, the fact for which I contend is not disproved. Poverty is already widespread in this new country, and knowing this to be true, it seems the height of folly that the nation should disregard so absolutely this enormous problem of misery that not even an inquiry is made as to its extent or as to the causes which add to its volume. Many people give as a reason for this apathy of the fortunate classes that poverty is irremedial. Did not the Lord say, "The poor always ye have with you"? But those who say this fail to distinguish between the poor, who are poor because of their own folly and vice, and the poor who are poor as a result of social wrongs.

The sins of men should bring their own punishment, and the poverty which punishes the vicious and the sinful is good and necessary. Social or industrial institutions that save men from the painful consequences of vice or folly are not productive of the greatest good. There is unquestionably a poverty which men deserve, and by such poverty men are perhaps taught needful lessons. It would be unwise to legislate out of existence, even were it possible to do so, that poverty which penalizes the voluntarily idle and vicious. In other words, there are individual causes of poverty which should be eradicated by the individual himself, with such help as his family, the teachers, and the preachers may give him. For him society may be able to do little or nothing. The poor which are always to be with us, are, it seems to me, in poverty of their own making.

But as surely as this is true, there are also the poor which we must not have always with us. The poor of this latter class are, it seems to me, the mass of the poor; they are bred of miserable and unjust social conditions, which punish the good and the pure, the faithful and industrious, the slothful and vicious, all alike. We may not, by going into the homes of the poor, be able to determine which ones are in poverty because of individual causes, or which are in poverty because of social wrongs; but we can see, by looking about us, that men are brought into misery by the

action of social and economic forces. And the wrong-
ful action of such social and economic forces is a preventable thing. For instance, to mention but a few,
the factories, the mines, the workshops, and the railroads must be forced to cease killing the father or
the boy or the girl whose wages alone suffice to keep
the family from poverty; or, if the workers must be
injured and killed, then the family must at least be
fairly compensated, in so far as that be possible.
Tenements may be made sanitary by the action of
the community, and thereby much of this breeding of
wretched souls and ruined bodies stopped. A broader
education may be provided for the masses, so that the
street child may be saved from idleness, crime, and
vagrancy, and the working child saved from ruinous
labor. Immigration may be regulated constructively
rather than negatively, if not, for a time, restricted
to narrower limits. Employment may be made less
irregular and fairer wages assured. These are, of
course, but a few of the many things which can be
done to make less unjust and miserable the conditions
in which about 10,000,000 of our people live.

Among the many inexplicable things in life there
is probably nothing more out of reason than our disregard for preventive measures and our apparent
willingness to provide almshouses, prisons, asylums,
hospitals, homes, etc., for the victims of our neglect.
Poverty is a culture bed for criminals, paupers, va-

grants, and for such diseases as inebriety, insanity, and imbecility; and yet we endlessly go on in our unconcern, or in our blindness, heedless of its sources, believing all the time that we are merciful in administering to its unfortunate results. Those in poverty are fighting a losing struggle, because of unnecessary burdens which we might lift from their shoulders; but not until they go to pieces and become drunken, vagrant, criminal, diseased, and suppliant, do we consider mercy necessary. But in that day reclamation is almost impossible, the degeneracy of the adults infects the children, and the foulest of our social miseries is thus perpetuated from generation to generation. From the millions struggling with poverty come the millions who have lost all self-respect and ambition, who hardly, if ever, work, who are aimless and drifting, who like drink, who have no thought for their children, and who live contentedly on rubbish and alms. But a short time before many of them were of that great, splendid mass of producers upon which the material welfare of the nation rests. They were in poverty, but they were self-respecting; they were hard-pressed, but they were ambitious, determined, and hard-working. They were also underfed, underclothed, and miserably housed, — the fear and dread of want possessed them, they worked sore, but gained nothing, they were isolated, heart-worn, and weary.

F

CHAPTER II

IT is hardly too much to say, in view of the foregoing chapter, that certain influences in society cast each year a large number of people into the most distressing poverty; and then, by an injudicious system of relief, miscalled charity, the poor are pauperized. The very administrators of the ruinous relief then become alarmed at the abject dependence of the poor and their repeated demands for assistance, and, while not permitting them to starve, endeavor as far as possible to withdraw all relief in order to prevent pauperism. This seems at first glance an intemperate criticism of both society and philanthropy. It has been made, however, after many years of work in this field of social effort and not without careful consideration. In the first place it is obvious to inquiring persons that society, as a result of its industries, its tenements, its policy of almost unrestricted immigration and its system of education, ill-adapted in so many ways to the needs of the people, causes a large part of the poverty which exists amongst us.

66

For instance, the aged, after years of honest and exacting toil, may find themselves at last thrown out of work, propertyless, and sometimes penniless. Dangerous trades cripple the bodies and undermine the health of large numbers of workmen, and almost unrestricted immigration helps to increase an already too intense competition for wages in the underpaid, unskilled trades, with the result that the whole mass is more or less in poverty all of the time, and a certain percentage finds it necessary actually to apply periodically for charitable relief. The greed for profits on the part of owners of tenement-house property has so interfered with the enactment and enforcement of laws establishing certain minimum sanitary standards that a considerable number of working people have their labor power diminished or destroyed by tuberculosis and other diseases. It would be impossible to question the responsibility of society for such common and widespread causes of poverty. After the economic independence of the family has been destroyed, so-called charity undermines the character of the poor either by private alms or by public outdoor relief. Charity has meant to be kind; private charity in particular uses every effort to prevent pauperism, but in the great mass of cases where relief is given it results in the degradation of the family and in the loss of self-respect. It is difficult to realize how much the loss of self-respect means. With it gone, there is little or no hope for the family to be anything but paupers for the rest of their days. Having come to this state, the pauper, if indeed he be not called undeserving, is given as little relief as possible, and the givers of relief endeavor to bring to bear upon him every agent of repression for the purpose of making pauperism intolerable to him.[1]

It is the pauper and the making of the pauper which interest us in this chapter. The pauper must be clearly distinguished from the poor. He is destitute not only of the necessaries for maintaining physical efficiency, but also of the necessaries for sustaining life, and must depend upon relief to supply them. There is no need now of speaking of professional paupers and vagrants who plead destitution for purposes of dishonest gain, and who constitute a special class in the great mass of paupers. In a legal sense a pauper is one who depends upon public charity for support, but pauperism, in its accepted sense, is a far more widespread and subtle thing than that expressed by these words. Men or women, who have the ability to obtain for themselves the necessaries of life and yet who, from some social or other cause, cannot do so, are often enticed into pauperism by relief given them during a time of temporary need. In nearly all cases, he who continually asks aid becomes a craven, abject creature with a lust for gratuitous maintenance. And he who becomes an habitual pauper undergoes a kind of degeneration. He loses his self-respect, the backbone of character; he develops a fawning and solicitous manner. In some cases he becomes almost incapable of self-support; he loses all capacity for sustained effort. As Mr. R. L. Dugdale has said, " The ideal pauper is the idiotic adult unable to help himself, who may be justly called a living embodiment of death." [1] Avoiding any useful effort, he becomes skilled in those activities which enable him the more perfectly to retain his state of dependence.

Pauperism, as the word has come to be used in Sociology, is analogous to parasitism in biological science. It is a disease of character; but, nevertheless, as is shown in " The Vagrant " on page 128 and also in the studies of the Jukes and Ishmaels, it may even result in certain forms of physical degeneration.[2] It is perhaps the most terrible outcome of poverty and its present treatment.

While poverty unquestionably is the soil, as it were, in which pauperism may most readily grow, pauperism itself is not peculiar to the poor; it is also a disease of the rich. Mr. C. S. Loch, the ablest student of this subject in England, considers that pauperism is a moral and not an economic question, and the first it unquestionably is. An important book written by two professors of the University of Brussels on " Parasitism, Organic and Social " gives instances of widespread pauperism or parasitism existing in all classes of society. The people of tropical countries have often been called the "Paupers of Nature " because life has been made easy for them, and means of livelihood have been supplied them at certain times and places without any effort on their part. The idle rich have also been called paupers. Professor Emile Vandervelde has given the following examples of proprietary parasites, " From the moment when you become a proprietor of the land, of houses, or of the machinery of production, you may, as Henry George says, sit down and smoke your pipe, you may lie about like the lazzaroni of Naples or the lepers of Mexico, you may go up in a balloon or dig a hole in the ground, and all the time, without any act of yours, the rent of house and farm, and the interest on your other capital, will keep dropping steadily into your hands." [1] There are, of course, many other forms of parasitism or pauperism, if one may so call it, existing among the rich.

Augustine Birrell says somewhere, " You may live like a gentleman for a twelvemonth on Hazlitt's ideas." I suppose that is a kind of intellectual pauperism. In the case of the rich, pauperism is at least a possible alternative. One may choose between a self-supporting existence and an idle life upon an unearned income; but for the great mass of the poor there is no alternative; they must at times become paupers in the legal sense at least. When eviction or hunger stares them in the face, they must seek aid. I have known men to weep like children when that hour came. After every other resource had been exhausted, after all the clothing that could be spared was sold, and at last the wedding-ring pawned, after friends and relatives and neighbors had lent all they were willing to lend, after food had been reduced to the minimum, leaving only tea and bread perhaps, the hour had come, and charity had to be applied for. It takes a long time to exhaust the reservoir of kindness and true charity which exists among the poor, for, as Maurice Hewlett says: —

> " Only the poor love the poor,
> And only they who have little to eat
> Give to them who have less."

But it is exhausted in time. The decision to apply for public aid is perhaps the greatest crisis in the life of the poor. Hundreds and hundreds of men at such times leave their families and become vagrants. It is always the woman who comes to ask for aid.

Rarely can the man be induced to do it. The fact that the givers of relief are likely to favor the deserted woman is perhaps the most important reason why so many men at such times desert their families. But this is not the whole reason. I have known many men to whom the ignominy and disgrace of receiving public charity were worse than death. When this crisis comes, the workless "wage-earner" may choose one of two ways to avoid starvation : he may become a pauper or a criminal. Mr. R. L. Dugdale, the most careful and thorough student of pauperism, and, perhaps, of crime, that we have had in this country, shows, in his study of the Jukes, that the more vigorous men and women become criminals, while the weaker ones become paupers. He clearly demonstrates that the pauper is of a less aggressive temperament than the criminal.[1] It is a common observation that during an industrial crisis, when great masses of men are unemployed, the number of crimes increases greatly in all large centres of population.

The study of the criminal, however, is somewhat afield. The thing which interests us here is the number of persons who must, at such times, become paupers. It was estimated in the previous chapter that not less than four million persons in the United States are dependent upon state or city relief funds for sustenance. This estimate does not include many thousands who are relieved by private charity only. In the cities pauperism is very much greater than in the rural sections of the country. To convey some idea of this city pauperism it is perhaps unnecessary to say anything more than what Mr. Riis has said in "How the Other Half Lives." It is almost impossible to believe the figures of distress which he places before you. "The reader who has followed with me the fate of the Other Half thus far, may not experience much of a shock at being told that in eight years 135,595 families in New York were registered as asking or receiving charity. Perhaps, however, the intelligence will rouse him that for five years past one person in every ten who died in this city was buried in the Potter's Field. These facts tell a terrible story. The first means that in a population of a *million and a half*, very nearly if not quite *half a million persons* were driven, or chose, to beg for food, or to accept it in charity at some period of the eight years, if not during the whole of it." The charitable societies "estimate upon the basis of their everyday experience that, allowing for those who have died, moved away, or become for the time being at least self-supporting, eighty-five per cent of the registry are still within, or lingering upon, the borders of dependence." This is worse than the "submerged tenth" of London; it is even worse than the statistics of Poverty prepared by Booth and Rountree for

England. Nothing is more astonishing than the number of pauper burials; for, as Mr. Riis says, "the Potter's Field stands ever for utter, hopeless surrender. The last the poor will let go, however miserable their lot in life, is the hope of a decent burial." [1]

A few years after this was written the dependents became even more numerous and the conditions in New York grew even worse. During the depression of 1893, besides the chronic cases of want and begging considered above, there was an increasing number of families, before that year independent of charity, who had reached the end of their resources; all their small savings had gone; there was nothing more to pawn, and the suffering of wife and children compelled the disclosure of need. These are almost the words of the report of the Charity Organization Society for 1894. [2] The United Hebrew Charities, in its report for 1901, declared that from 75,000 to 100,000 members of the New York Jewish community were unable to supply themselves with the immediate necessaries of life, and for this reason were dependent in some way upon the public purse. [3]

The amount of pauperism in certain parts of the city is graphically shown by the Poverty Map prepared by Mr. Lawrence Veiller for the Tenement House Commission of 1900. [4]

Each dot represents five families who have applied for charity in five years either to the Charity Organization Society or to the United Hebrew Charities. Mr. Veiller says, " It seems beyond belief, yet it is a fact, that there was hardly one tenement-house in the entire city that did not contain a number of these dots, and many contained as many as fifteen of them."

Now let us see what this pauperism means. A great number of reports have been made by various societies showing the kind of disposition which should be made of these cases of suffering. The United Hebrew Charities say that the poverty among their people is due largely to the inability to find opportunities to become self-supporting.[1] The Charity Organization Society shows that from 43 to 52 per cent of all applicants need work rather than relief. Nor is this peculiar to New York.[2] It applies equally well to Chicago and to some other cities. The thing most evident in these facts is that poverty, due to industrial derangement, is not a problem which charitable organizations are fitted to solve. They can, of course, relieve the distress which results from inability to find work, but the relief is almost sure to result in injury to the applicants. If half of the persons applying for aid need work rather than relief, then society must itself provide a solution of the problem. It is absurd for charitable societies even to accept such a burden, not because of inadequate funds for the purpose, but because support in idleness and dependence does an additional injury to a class already unfairly treated by society. The question of unemployment should be met by the state frankly and fairly.

For the purpose of determining how far charitable agencies are fitted to deal with dependents, the following table is introduced. It is not an exhaustive classification, but it is an attempt to show briefly the classes of persons appealing for aid and how the relief of each class must vary. It is, of course, needless to say that the classification is not a rigid one. Some of the insane can be cured, and in many cases crippled men and children may be made partially, if not entirely, self-supporting. The deaf, dumb, and blind can be made productive by proper education. The table is introduced merely to show that there are various kinds of treatment which must be applied to the different classes of dependents both by society and by philanthropy if any real progress is to be made in the treatment of pauperism.

DEPENDENTS AND THEIR TREATMENT

I. ABSOLUTE DEPENDENTS	TREATMENT
The Aged.	
The Children.	
The Crippled (incapable of work).	Proper care continued
The Incurable.	as long as may be neces-
The Blind.	sary in institutions or
The Deaf and Dumb.	elsewhere.
The Insane.	
The Epileptic.	
The Imbecile, Idiot, Feeble-minded.	

II. DEPENDENTS CAPABLE OF SELF-SUPPORT	TREATMENT
The Professional Vagrant. The Professional Beggar. The Morally Insane.	Industrial education, repression, confinement for protection of society.

III. TEMPORARY DEPENDENTS LIKELY TO BECOME CHRONIC	
The Sick; especially { The Convalescent. The Consumptive. The Inebriate. Those addicted to drugs, etc.	Complete cure in proper institutions to prevent infirmity of a permanent character.

IV. TEMPORARY DEPENDENTS	
The Unemployed. Widows with children.	To supply an economic existence free from any taint of pauperism.

For the sake of obtaining a clearer idea of what is now done for the various classes of dependents, we must trace hastily the history of the Poor Law system. It is part of our political inheritance from England. Dating back to the time of Elizabeth, it has remained unaltered in principle during every subsequent change of industrial or social life.[1] It began at the end of the feudal system, and it survived the industrial revolution in which steam, electricity, and the large factory displaced the hand-tool and the domestic workshop. It clings persistently even to the present day. In its method of relieving it has varied but little, although the weight of responsibility for poverty has been shifted very largely from the individual to society. In the early days of this coun-

try, when the pauper was himself largely responsible
for his own misery or degradation, because then, if
ever, equal opportunities existed for all men, the same
system prevailed which exists to-day, when but few
men can be held entirely responsible for their own
misery. This inherited system of poor relief consists of two institutions : the almshouse or Indoor
Relief, and the relief of the poor in their homes, the
latter called Outdoor Relief.

This bipartite system exists almost everywhere in
America. In early days all the classes of dependents
introduced in the foregoing table were cared for indiscriminately in almshouses, or, if it was necessary
or cheaper, by doles to the poor in their homes. It
has only been in recent years that the poor have
been classified in any way. In 1868, the poorhouses of New York State did not in every instance
separate the sexes in their sleeping apartments.
The aged, the children, the sick, the insane, the
epileptic, the idiotic, the blind, the able-bodied
vagrant, and the debased "mingled freely with each
other." A state report, speaking of this indiscriminate herding, says, "This, it hardly need be stated,
served to sink the depraved still lower, and tended
also to break down self-respect in the better class,
who, from sickness or other misfortunes, were compelled to seek public aid." [1] New York has made
great progress in its treatment of the poor since that

day, but in various other parts of the country conditions are much the same as they were here forty
years ago. Generally, however, there are now, in
the most advanced states, separate institutions for
the children, the deaf, dumb, and blind, the insane,
the feeble-minded, and the sick, and, of course, the
sexes are separated. The condition of the Ulster
County poorhouse of New York, recently under investigation, shows, however, that careful supervision
is still needed in order to prevent most outrageous
treatment of helpless dependents.[1] There are now
colonies in several states for the proper treatment of
epilepsy, and Massachusetts has a state hospital for
the treatment of inebriety. These various specialized
institutions have only gradually been established as
some grave necessity or abuse has manifested itself.
There is now everywhere a strong tendency to give
special treatment to those classes of paupers who
injure others, as well as to those classes who are
themselves injured by indiscriminate herding in
almshouses. The physical necessities of the dependents have perhaps been more generously dealt with
in the development of specialized care than the moral
necessities. Boston has, however, a special almshouse for the aged in which the self-respecting poor
are properly cared for.

The indoor treatment of the poor is a much less
difficult matter than the treatment of the poor in

their homes. Outdoor relief is the only public provision made for the various classes of poor who may not best be cared for in institutions. In most states it means a weekly sum or a dole of supplies given to some poor family by a township or county official. This part of the system of poor relief has itself come into such ill repute during recent years that, with the exception of some effort in Massachusetts, comparatively little has been done to improve it. Great efforts have been made to abolish it.[1] There is no question but that the gravest abuses have resulted from this method of relieving the poor. The Jukes and Ishmaels, two large families of paupers, were brought to their depraved condition largely by this system of public relief. It is estimated that the Jukes cost the state of New York not less than $1,225,000. This family numbered several hundred degenerates, most of whom were cared for, more or less, all of the time, by public funds. The tribe of Ishmael, an Indiana product, numbered over five thousand individuals, all of whom, like the Jukes, were paupers, criminals, drunkards, or prostitutes.[2] Mr. F. C. Montague has spoken of outdoor relief in the following words, " A legislation, inspired by just and humane feelings, yet more harmful than many of the worst enactments of selfish power ; a legislation which aimed at assuaging misery, yet chiefly served to make it more inveterate, hereditary, hopeless; a legislation which, in many instances, proved almost ruinous to the employer, whilst it everywhere depressed the wages of the workmen; a legislation which turned the peasant, for whose good it was designed, into a wretched dependent, too often into a lawless ruffian; a legislation directed to save the weak from overwhelming temptation, which filled the country with paupers and prostitutes."[1] It seems rather strong language, perhaps too strong, to use against the system, but there are times when it seems warranted by American as well as by English experience.

A few years ago, on one of the coldest mornings of winter, I saw a long line of shivering, half-clothed, hungry-looking men and women standing in front of the Cook County Outdoor Relief Department. They had come with bags and baskets to receive the doles of supplies. They were the public paupers gathered from the most wretched homes and districts of Chicago. Some were shamefaced, silent, and cowed; some were swearing, scolding, and quarrelsome; others were fearful, anxious, and hesitating; and some few gave evidence of decency, still holding fast to their self-respect. It was almost like a chain-gang marching under public gaze. Whatever there was of ignominy fell upon these unfortunates whose only crime was poverty. It is needless to point out the degrad-

G

ing, the levelling influence which this gathering together of the miserable exercises upon the more
sensitive and respectable of the poor. It is this
public system of indiscriminate doles which, nearly
every one is agreed, had better be abolished. It is
the only public relief given to the poor who must
be cared for in their homes. It is a common,
wholesale, degrading treatment of the poor which
ends by destroying their self-respect and in many
cases condemns forever the unfortunate applicants
to a position of disrepute in the community. This
is not true charity : it is brutality.

In this system of public relief, consisting on the
one side of institutional care, and on the other of
outdoor relief, there is too little variation in the
treatment of the poor either on lines of character
or on the lines classified heretofore. In consequence, a private system of charity has grown up
in the last fifty or sixty years which has endeavored
to lay down new principles of treatment. Whatever
reforms have been made in the treatment of the poor
result mainly from this voluntary movement; and yet,
after all, the United States, as a whole, has by no
means reached a high standard in the treatment
of the first class of paupers, and, with the exception of the persons who are sick with acute ill-
nesses, it has failed utterly to care for the other
classes adequately. Those of the first group are

obviously dependent. Almost every one in this class must be cared for either by relatives, by private charity, or by some form of public relief. Although a distinctly charitable problem, the reports of both public and private charities in all cities yearly appeal for larger funds and endowments to care for the needy of this class. This is true even of the East. The West and South are cruelly backward in the elemental humanity of providing fully for this class of unfortunates.

Having taken this brief survey of the history and workings of the Poor Law, let us now examine in detail the care of the dependents classified on pages 76–77. In almost every city the blind must be permitted to beg because there is no adequate public provision made for them. The incurable and crippled, wretched in their helplessness, are numerous in all large communities. In many places the epileptic and the feeble-minded are still left to the care of friends and relatives, however poor they may be. The aged poor, the most numerous of all, are insufficiently cared for in all cities — Boston possibly excepted.

"Scrubs" and "harpies" are the bitter names applied to the aged women who frequent the poorest furnished rooms of certain low sections of New York. For this class, the only provision made by the state is the almshouse. In this institution the worthy, temperate, and respectable poor may be compelled to associate intimately with the feeble-minded, the drunken, the fallen women, the consumptive, and the imbecile. A man entirely responsible for his own ills, after a vicious life, depraved in character and diseased in body, may be the associate, the room-mate even, of a man who has led an upright, honorable life of ceaseless industry, but who is compelled nevertheless in old age to accept public relief. As a consequence, it is to the credit of the aged poor that they would often rather die of starvation than go to the poorhouse. I have known old people to live almost wholly on tea and bread, to be half clothed and in poor, wretched rooms, and yet I dared not mention to them the poorhouse. I have known them to be slowly but surely starving, but if they were to be relieved it was only by means of some private pension, which can usually be obtained only with great difficulty. For this wholly dependent class, which we should most love to care for, the class of poor which should preëminently appeal to us, there is in many places inadequate provision.

It is interesting, even at the risk of diversion, to contrast with our common neglect the apparent stoicism with which certain savage tribes treat their aged, and the noble way in which the aged accept their fate. A well-informed writer gives the following account: "When a 'savage' feels that he is a burden to his tribe; when every morning his share of food is taken from the mouths of the children — and the little ones are not so stoical as their fathers: they cry when they are hungry; when every day he has to be carried across the stony beach or the virgin forest on the shoulders of younger people . . . he begins to repeat what the old Russian peasants say until nowaday: . . . 'I live other people's life: it is time to retire!' And he retires. . . . The old man asks himself to die; he himself insists upon this last duty towards the community, and obtains the consent of the tribe; he digs out his grave; he invites his kinsfolk to the last parting meal. His father has done so, it is now his turn; and he parts with his kinsfolk with marks of affection."[1] It is a noble way for the aged to face death; a burden to the tribe, they die for the benefit of all, pretty much as the older bees leave their hive for the benefit of the younger. It is a necessity in these savage tribes where food is scant and want constantly pressing. But it is not necessary for a rich and civilized people to leave their helpless ones to die from lack of care. At this moment in America, thousands of the aged — and not only the aged, but the crippled, the incurable, and the consumptive as well — are beggars on the streets, half-starving, half-clothed, in utter misery. There is no need of their suffering through neglect;

we can easily afford to care generously and tenderly
for the helpless and the destitute. They need not
die for the benefit of the tribe or of the community;
no other members of the community need suffer in
order that kindly and adequate provision may be
made for this class; no one would have to economize.
The price of a few luxuries would cover the expense
of all these dependents, wholly unable to care for
themselves, and yet all about us is the suffering, the
misery, the degradation of these pathetically dependent individuals. Some people find it difficult to
understand how the savage tribes can leave their
aged behind to die of starvation, but the "savage,"
it is said, is utterly unable to understand the cruelty
of those "civilized" persons who live in luxury while
neighbors and fellow-citizens die in want. "Consider
whether, even supposing it guiltless, luxury would be
desired by any of us if we saw clearly at our sides
the suffering which accompanies it in the world. . . .
Luxury at present can only be enjoyed by the ignorant; the cruelest man living could not sit at his
feast unless he sat blindfold." [1] This is what John
Ruskin once said.

Generally speaking, the aged poor beg more rarely
than other dependents. Of the first class, the blind,
or those who suffer from some other infirmity, are
most commonly found begging. The crippled are
incorrigible beggars. Every one has seen hundreds

of them crawling about the streets, or sitting on the cold pavements, on winter nights, with outstretched, appealing hands. I shall not soon forget one wretched little lad, whose legs had both been cut off by a railway train, sitting with his body in a pool of ice-water, forming from the slush of melting snow. He was begging from the working people as they came out of one of the cheaper theatres. He is a sample of many who endeavor to make more pitiable their condition in order to make more emphatic their plea to the givers of alms. The working people always give generously to such pitiable cases, but for those who have been trained in the modern ideas of relief-giving, there is consolation to their conscience, when withholding alms, in the belief that, for the sake of some vice, the beggar prefers to seek alms rather than to be properly cared for in some public institution. It is true that many of the crippled adult beggars seek alms solely that they may gratify their vices. A few years ago, at two o'clock in the morning I stopped in at one of the lowest dives, in one of the lowest districts, of Chicago. It was a " barrel house," corresponding to the stale-beer dives of New York. It was notorious as the resort of crippled beggars. The place was pandemonium with drunken men, all crippled in some way ; bandaged, maimed, diseased, they were prostrate on the floor, lying across tables, asleep in chairs, standing at the bar, yelling and howling. I have never seen a more fiendish sight. But what is the cripple to do? What can he hope to be? He is maimed for life. The only alternative to a life of begging and vagrancy which is offered him is an almshouse, the most dreary, terrible place for a sane man that one can imagine. I know nothing more depressing than a crowded mass of idle men, of almost every nationality, black and white, helpless through disease or vice, or suffering from some injury or infirmity. Because a man has lost his legs or his arms, the prospect for him of an entire life in such surroundings is no more tolerable than it would be to any of us.

This entire class of dependents must be cared for in some way. The responsibility cannot be escaped. In fact, in almost every state of the Union there is neglect to the degree of actual cruelty. I should think we could hardly, with easy conscience, be liberal in state grants or private gifts for benevolent purposes, such as libraries or even the higher schools of learning, until we had done our duty to the aged parents of our people, to the weak and to the helpless ones of our household.

Class two is so fully treated in the third chapter that nothing further need be said here. Those of the third class are mostly capable of being made valuable members of the community. I think it will be generally agreed that in the treatment of the con-

valescent out of hospital care, the consumptive, and
the inebriate, there is little else now done by the state
than to confirm them in pauperism. A prominent
physician of New York told me the other day, what I
have observed scores of times both in New York and
Chicago, that the hospitals are so crowded that there
is always the tendency to turn patients out before
they are cured, and that permanent injury doubtless
results, in many cases, from exposure and lack of
care in the convalescent period. So far as I know,
the same is true of every city in the country. This is
a most serious defect in benevolent provision, accompanied by painful consequences to the poor who are
underfed, underclothed, and forced by necessity to
work as soon as possible. It means in many cases
that they are never entirely cured and remain weak
all their lives.

The same inadequate care is at present about all
that is supplied the consumptive. There are several
sanatoria supported by private funds, and Massachusetts has an excellent state hospital; but there is at
present far too little provision. It is now generally
recognized that our failure to care properly for the
consumptive is the cause of thousands of needless
deaths and a great proportion of poverty. The victim of this curable disease is only beginning to be
considered by philanthropy.[1] It is a disease of the
masses, and is usually closely related to poverty; it

is infectious. In certain blocks and houses in the
poorer quarters it is epidemic. It is a long, lingering
illness which fast exhausts the resources of a wage-
earning family, and, when the bread-winner is the
sufferer, it almost invariably results in poverty for
the family. For the individual family to bear the
responsibility and cost of a disease which is distinctly
social, and for which the family may in no wise be
responsible, is the very height of social injustice.
As a matter of fact, the resources of few working-
class families are adequate to meet the heavy burden
laid upon them by this illness. Instead of the state
bearing itself, or compelling the industries to bear,
the cost of this tremendous burden of the working
class and endeavoring to save the lives of the workingmen for further productive uses and their families
from pauperism, it supplies merely a place in which
they may die, and cares for their families in such
a way as to confirm them in pauperism. The worst
of it, perhaps, is the decimation and degradation of
families which, under fair conditions, might have
become of precious value to the community. Any
state will, in the end, suffer which overlooks the
necessity of stamping out as soon as possible an
infectious disease which afflicts such large masses
of people.

In this same class of dependents, most of whom
might be saved from pauperism by proper treatment,

are the alcoholics or inebriates. The treatment of inebriety is a charitable problem rather than a criminal one. It is a disease which, in advanced stages, is very similar to insanity. While drunkenness is seldom treated as a crime, most drunkards are arrested sooner or later for disturbing the peace or for disorderly conduct. They are then punished by imprisonment. There are instances in almost every state of men and women who have been arrested and committed to various penal institutions, from a hundred to two hundred times. Alcoholics, in the most pronounced state, are thus periodically incarcerated and put to hard labor, and meanwhile, through neglect of proper treatment, their disease is becoming increasingly difficult of cure, and perhaps other even worse diseases are developing unobserved and unheeded. The jails to which inebriates are committed are not in the least fitted to give the medical or dietary treatment necessary for cure or even for improvement, nor do they pretend to do so. The inebriate, at the end of his period of imprisonment, comes out with an uncontrollable appetite for drink which he satisfies as soon as possible. This treatment of the inebriate, as a criminal instead of as a sick person, is bringing ruin to the homes of thousands and thousands of families. The root of pauperism in these families is the alcoholic. So long as the state fails to use its power in curing him and its resources in

providing hospitals for his care, just so long will the
private charities be powerless to save the family from
degradation. The mind of the inebriate may be
slowly degenerating, and his industrial usefulness
fast disappearing, as a result of the disease. The
woman may be bringing children into the world who
will be debilitated, alcoholic, idiots, and imbeciles, as
a result of their heritage.[1]   Despite this making of
paupers, there is at present little effort being made
anywhere to obtain on a sufficient scale the proper
medical treatment of inebriety. It is said by an
expert in this matter, that "the patient must be
placed in an insane asylum, or better, in a hospital
for inebriates, where total abstinence can be enforced.
Patients with delirium tremens especially need the
most careful hospital treatment. The principal directions are conservation of strength and cerebral quiet,
strong unirritating diet, and mild laxatives, etc.
Such in general is considered to be the best medical
treatment."[2]   While special provision is frequently
made in public hospitals for treatment of the acute
phases of alcoholism, the state of Massachusetts is, I
believe, alone in maintaining a public hospital exclusively for the treatment of this disease.

Drunkenness and sickness, according to studies
which the Charity Organization Societies have
made of the causes of pauperism, are responsible
for the distress of from 35 to 50 per cent of all

the applicants for charity.[1] Both of these causes
are in a great measure preventable and curable.
In no other field of social effort is there promise
of more satisfactory results than in the prevention
and cure of inebriety and of such diseases as
tuberculosis.

There are no more important problems than those
presented by (Class IV) the unemployed and
widows with children — two groups of the poor for
which there is, at present, in the main no other
provision than doles, public or private. It reflects
very grievously upon the justice of our social system
that so many men, willing to work, should be unable to find work to do. The history of the world
has perhaps never shown more abject victims of
chance than the modern propertyless workmen.
A man possessing his own tools or land may always
employ himself, and, although it may at times be
necessary for him to sell his products for a very
low price, he need not, except in extraordinary
times, become dependent upon others for relief.
The tools of the modern workman are the machine;
both it and the land are owned by others. He cannot work on the land or at the machine except by
permission of another. If the owner does not find
it profitable to employ him, the workman must remain idle. At certain seasons of the year this
idleness is compulsory to workmen by the tens of

thousands, and at times of business depression by the hundreds of thousands. Without savings adequate to supply his needs, and with his income wholly dependent upon an intermittent demand for his labor, circumstances are apt to arise sooner or later that will force him either to commit crime against property or to depend upon public relief for sustenance. If the state of dependence continues long, habitual pauperism or vagrancy is quite likely to result. In other words, these outcasts from industry have before them the choice of three evils, — starvation, crime, or relief by charity.

Some persons will doubtless maintain that the workers have the choice of saving enough to prevent themselves and families from depending upon charity. This, however, is by no means true. There is a large class of workmen who must spend every penny they earn if they are to have the necessaries of life. This is particularly true of unskilled workmen, who, I do not doubt, rarely average in wages more than $460 a year, and there are official studies to show that wages fall, for this class of workmen, even to $300 a year. But even supposing that a workman, with a family of ordinary size, received regularly $600 a year, — even then he could hardly be expected to plan deliberately, in spite of the rightful demands of his children for education and other advantages, as we call them, to save enough to protect his family in case he is killed by an accident, acquires an incurable disease, or is thrown for a long period out of employment. We may grant that a man should save for the period of old age, — most men do provide for it in some way, — but in the main they cannot provide for calamities of a sudden or unexpected nature such as the above. That is impossible on the wages which unskilled workmen at present receive. In regard to widows with children, it is now generally agreed, by all charity organizationists, that a pension should be provided for those who are unable to support themselves until the children have reached the age when they may properly be employed. The funds at the disposal of private charities, however, are so inadequate that it is usually quite impossible for them to carry this principle into effect. For those who are unemployed and in distress, some honest and useful work must be provided if justice is to be done. For them to depend upon charity is degrading and pauperizing, but, as work cannot be obtained by charitable societies for more than very few of this class of workmen, and then, often, only by pull and special favor and sometimes at the expense of a better laborer who might have secured the work unaided, there is no possibility under present conditions of being just to the unemployed

workers. There is no possibility because the problem of the unemployed is at present left to the
charitable societies to solve, and they are wholly
unable to cope with conditions of distress reaching
such immense proportions at certain seasons.

A brief summary of the treatment of the various
classes of poor will show how inadequate the charitable provision is. The dependents of the first class
have not as yet, by any means, been properly cared
for, although it includes only the helplessly dependent,
the aged, the children, the incurable, the crippled,
incapable of work, the blind, the deaf and dumb, the
insane, the epileptic, the imbecile, the idiot, and the
feeble-minded. The treatment of the second class —
the professional beggars, vagrants, and morally insane
— is perhaps rather a police question than a charitable one. As yet it has been given only local attention of an intermittent and spasmodic character.
Such repressive efforts as have been used in dealing
with vagrants have doubtless in no wise diminished
their number. They have simply been driven from
place to place. The third class — the convalescent,
the consumptive, and the inebriate, etc. — are given
very little, if any, consideration in certain portions of
the country. For the inebriate and the consumptive
as paupers very large sums of money are at present
spent from public funds, but, with two or three exceptions, not for the purpose of curing their disease, and

unfortunately with the result of rendering chronic and incurable a condition which might have been only a temporary disability. The fourth class, including the unemployed, widows with children, and others in temporary need, reach enormous proportions at certain seasons and especially in years of depression. As in the previous class, everything here depends upon treatment. This class, in particular, suffer poverty as a result of misfortune. Relief given them as paupers may do them infinite injury. They have, on the whole, the qualities of good manhood and womanhood. In the treatment of this class there is need of a social rather than a charitable policy. They are most unnatural paupers. Justice will not be done until the state supplies them an economic existence during the period when they are now necessarily dependent upon charity, and as soon as possible reëstablishes them in normal social relations. These, then, are some of the distressing social diseases and baffling problems which the charitable agencies, with their feeble powers, are called upon to face.

It seems an almost hopeless outlook; and it would be if there were not means at hand to meet some of these stern facts, other than those offered by the ordinary charitable activities. In the first place, there are many social reform measures which promise far-reaching results. The problem may be stated as

H

follows: If it be essential to the progress of society that these paupers be made, that every year great numbers of men be crippled, others afflicted with consumption, and so on — if this be inevitable, if every year so many poor must result from the present competitive strife, then the problem of the poor becomes merely a question of caring for the unfortunates in the most humane way possible; then it is merely a question of giving as generously as one can to private charities and of helping to develop public charities to relieve certain forms of distress. But it is not essential to society that paupers be made, nor is the only obligation one of caring for the injured as best one may. The poverty of to-day is in great measure unnecessary. It is due, in no small degree, to certain social evils which must be remedied and certain social wrongs which must be put right. The necessity of going back of the pauper and of attacking the causes which create him was once made unmistakably clear to me.

Several years ago I was living in a district of working people, numbering many thousand, employed in one of the largest industries of the country. They were all poor, all on the verge of suffering all of the time. The employer, one of the rich men of the country, was profusely generous in his gifts to charity. Those who knew him personally said that no one was more kindly or more humane than he. To the poor, known to him, he sent regular and generous gifts. When he died, there were columns of the papers devoted to his public philanthropies. To me the man was never a philanthropist. I knew him as an employer of men. Hundreds of his work people came to me for aid because their wages were insufficient to support them. I knew girls whose health had been broken down for life in the insanitary workrooms of his factory. Bread-winners of large families had acquired incurable rheumatism and consumption in the needlessly bad conditions in which they worked. In a way, this man personifies modern society. For society is inhumane, careless and thoughtless of the conditions which bring ruin into the homes of hundreds of thousands of people; heedless amid protests, apparently blind even to the existence of the destructive causes. But when ruin comes and the families become suppliant and ask for mercy and charity, relief is often given with generous hand.

The hopeful thing in present-day charitable work is the effort being made to attack the causes and to stop the carnage. The Charity Organization Society of New York has within the last few years carried through an important reform in the treatment of the housing problem, and more recently it has undertaken an effective crusade for the prevention of tuberculosis. The Child Labor Committees in various states are endeavoring to prevent those injuries to

childhood which result from premature work. It will
not be long until there are other movements along
purely reform lines to do away with still other social
causes of poverty. Shorter hours and higher wages,
steadier employment, improved sanitary conditions in
workshops, and protection in dangerous trades are
reforms which, in time, will materially decrease the
amount of pauperism. It will doubtless be some
time before it is possible to obtain for all workmen
wages high enough to enable them to bear out of
their own resources the cost of the suffering which
results to them in modern industry. Professor Edward D. Jones says, the necessity for higher wages
"is based upon the observation that, in the purchase
and sale of labor upon the market, all the necessary
and legitimate costs of producing labor are not provided for in the wages received. Such transactions
are not complete economically, and do not meet the
claims of social justice. Fair wages must include
more than enough to support the laborer while working, and must cover compensation for seasons of idleness due to sickness, old age, youth, lack of work, or
other causes beyond the control of the laborer. Skill
must be so paid for as to cover the expense of education and the risk of failure. The wages of those who
work should include enough to support that proportion of every normal society of human beings which
cannot or ought not to be earning wages. When one

pays for a vase he pays not merely for the one given him, but for a part of those which have been ruined in the making or broken in handling. So the cost of labor should include the expense of those who die in youth or who, in age, live to be a charge upon others. As the vase in fashion must pay for a part of a super-seded stock, so wages must take account of super-seded skill. If these elements in the social cost of labor are not provided for directly by wage payments, they must be surreptitiously added as public or private charity. If withheld entirely, the deterioration of the society concerned is certain." [1]

Perhaps the most important step in the direction of supplying some compensation to cover seasons of idleness, due to sickness, old age, lack of work, or other causes beyond the control of the workman, has been taken in the development of the Insurance Systems of European countries. [2] The German system of compulsory insurance is perhaps the most interesting and the most far-reaching in its results. In the United States the individual workman, how-ever blameless, must bear so far as possible the entire responsibility for whatever misfortune may befall him. If he is unable to bear it, he is classed as a pauper and becomes a public burden.

It is hardly humane, to say the least, for us to call a man a pauper who has grown old and vener-able by a life of vigorous, honest toil. It is brutal to call that man a pauper who has lost his labor power, in the form of limbs or eyes or health, while producing wealth for the world, and who must of necessity, after sustaining the loss, ask relief and respite until death. He has been exhausted in the service, and to call him a pauper is similar to calling a veteran a deserter when the latter has no more strength to march on; to call the unemployed, willing to work, actually seeking work and unable to find it, paupers is quite as unjust as to call widows with many children by the same term. The reason for our doing it to-day is not because we actually believe these men and women to be paupers or that we believe we are treating them justly when we offer them the choice between starvation and public pauperism. It is, I firmly believe, because we have never clearly established in our minds when the responsibility for poverty should rest upon the individual and when upon society. There is a variety of opinions, but no students of poverty have yet definitely shown exactly what persons are responsible for their own misery and what class or classes are in no wise responsible for theirs. In the German system of insurance there is an effort made to find out who is responsible for the poverty and to demand from him compensation for the injured. It is, of course, impossible to fix the responsibility for each case of poverty, but it is possible to fix the responsibility for poverty resulting from certain causes. Germany, as a result of statistics gathered in consequence of its system of insurance for old age, sickness, infirmity, and accident, has fixed upon society, and not upon the individual, the responsibility for a great mass of its poverty. It has been shown, for instance, that 80 per cent of all accidents in industry are due to the "professional risks" of industry itself, and that consequently, by this system of insurance, the industries of Germany and not the workmen must bear the cost of these accidents.[1] It is, of course, impossible to prevent all accidents, and in Germany the workman must still, when necessary, sacrifice his body; but he or his family need not, as a result, become paupers.

In addition to this fixing of responsibility in the case of accidents, the state has discovered that it is cheaper to save life than it is to lose it; or, in other words, it is more economical to preserve the productive forces wherever possible than it is to lose them. It is cheaper promptly and thoroughly to cure diseases which, if uncared for, may become a permanent infirmity to the workmen. It has discovered how really economical preventive measures are. A most significant thing in the system is the large sum spent each year in curing the consumptive, in building baths and model tenements, and in developing more sanitary conditions in homes and factories. Several millions of marks have been spent for the establishment of sanatoria for consumptives. Fifty-two million marks have been spent in improving and building new tenements. Thirty-six million marks have been spent for hospitals, convalescent homes, etc.[1] In addition to all these preventive measures, there has been a national museum established containing the various dangerous machines and showing appliances which will protect the workmen from injury. Scientists and investigators are now employed by the National Government to make mechanical inventions and to determine sanitary measures for the purpose of saving the lives of workmen in industry. The insurance already provides for the sick, the aged, the infirm, and those suffering injuries from accidents, and the plan will doubtless soon be extended to cover widows and orphans. The German Reichstag has even recently recommended the formation of a special commission to perfect some plan for the solution of the problem of the unemployed.[2] The crowning success effected by the insurance scheme has been to afford to workmen an *economic existence* when poverty has resulted from purely social causes. In consequence, it has relieved charity of a heavy burden and saved the self-respect of the workmen.[3] The whole system is administered by employers and workmen organized in groups.

This system of insurance is a palliative for much

of the most distressing misery resulting from this social problem. It encourages thrift, it involves no revolution in society nor in industry, and yet it is a beginning in justice. It does away, in part at least, with the abominable system and hypocrisy of making paupers on the one hand and of giving for their relief on the other. It relieves the charities of an unmanageable mass of distress which, in spite of their efforts, however generous, sincere, and kind, cannot be prevented from degenerating into pauperism. The retainment to this day for all classes of poor of a seventeenth-century system of relief, which degrades all alike without discrimination, is manifestly unjust. Its existence blinds us to the need of a broad and just social policy. It would be the height of folly to suppose that all poverty can be prevented by a social policy however wise, for no collective action can, or should, save men from the consequences of individual immorality ; but that poverty which is clearly due to social injustice, and not to the individual shortcomings of the miserable, can be in great measure prevented. I am not so pessimistic in regard to the moral state of our nation as to believe we shall much longer make the wage-earner bear upon his own shoulders the heaviest costs of progress and, in the painful struggle, become uncomplainingly the despised vagrant, pauper, prostitute, or criminal.

CHAPTER III

THE VAGRANT

THE vagrant is the modern nomad, drifting about, without aim or ambition. He emigrates to the country on the coming of spring. He returns, with the coming of winter, to the large centres of population and takes up a shifting residence in the various lodging-houses. In all cities there are special districts in which most of the nomadic vagrants as well as the habitual "town bums" are to be found. They usually furnish a considerable element to the flotsam and jetsam which constitute a large portion of the population in the districts of vice. New York has, among other such districts, the Tenderloin and the Bowery. Chicago has South Clark Street, Dearborn Street, and West Madison; Philadelphia, St. Louis, San Francisco, Denver, have similar districts, and so have all European cities. It is also significant that many cities, if not all, have districts of vice distinguished from each other on monetary lines; there is vice for the well-to-do, and there is vice for the poor. In the well-to-do districts are to be found hotels for transients, gamblers, perverts, and the sporty elements, and in the poorer districts lodging-houses for the vagrant population. In these districts the honest wayfarer seeking work, the clerk trying to live cheaply, and the young man from the country seeking employment in the city, become vicious and vagrant. Vices are added to their poverty.

Such districts have so large a population in certain cities, and wield so powerful a political influence, that the public officials have openly said at times that the vices of these districts could not be controlled. The mayor of one of the largest cities in this country said a few years ago that special privileges must be granted the people of these districts; they should not be governed by the more moral sections of the community; they should govern themselves in their own way. He was bold to say what other officials have, with rare exceptions, practised in their lax enforcement of the law. The mayor who made this declaration knows much more intimately than most people the grave and baffling problems presented by the slums.

The average American knows little of either the virtues or vices of any class in the community outside of his own clique of friends and associates. The well-to-do American may receive rents from those who might be called the entrepreneurs of the district; he may occasionally plan a "slumming tour," but it is very likely he will return to his clique with

ideas even more erroneous, if possible, than before.
Perhaps the most egregious error is the belief, which
exists in the minds of many, that the slum population and the working people are the same. It is true,
unfortunately, in many of the large cities that a certain number of the more poorly paid working people,
especially the ignorant and poverty-stricken immigrant, is obliged to occupy tenements and dwellings
inhabited at the same time by the vicious classes.
But the working people living in the slums, in most
cities, are comparatively few in number, and it is
rarely true that their association with the distinctly
slum population is more intimate than is absolutely
necessary. While the adults may become tainted and
their children contaminated by the vicious neighborhood, the real denizens of the slums can hardly be
classed as workers in any sense. Both the immigrant and the large class of floating laborers — the
accidental vagrants — must be kept distinct from the
vicious classes which constitute the life of the slums.*

If one were to classify the population of the slums
as broadly as possible, there would be the two groups,
— single men and single women. There is no family
life in the slums except that of the immigrant, and

---

* I try to use the word "slum" only in the sense of a vicious district. It has always seemed to me a great injustice to use it when
referring to working-class districts or to poverty-stricken districts free
relatively from vice.

he is there by necessity, not by choice. Except those of the immigrant, the children are in most cases illegitimate. Men and women are there who have shirked, by means of divorce or even more commonly by desertion, all family responsibility. They are now, to all appearances, single men and single women. The men crowd the saloons and lodging-houses; the women crowd the dance halls and brothels.

The vagrant is only one element in the population of the district. Every type of the needy individual, from the professional vagrant up to the wayfarer honestly seeking employment, can be found in the lodging-houses. Here is the debauched son of a good family (as he never fails to state), whose thin white hands and frayed coat of superior cloth reënforce his story. The cigarette, morphine, and opium fiends are here. The dipsomaniac shares at night the floor of the "barrel-house" with the working-man, who, by chance, is overcome with liquor; here are also the hobo, the dull-witted, the negro, and the petty sneak thief. The slender, youthful, well-dressed lover, whose sweetheart is supporting him by the wages of sin, waits about the poolrooms. The morally insane are here. Thousands are here who fail utterly in conceiving a single thought which is not vile, or an image which is not unspeakable. The man of every crime is here. The man of every vice is here also. The free lover, devoid of any philosophy on the subject, finds ample scope for his practice within the laws of the state. The bigamist and even polygamist tell stories to show how easily the marriage laws are evaded. In this social abyss, which exists in New York, Boston, Chicago, San Francisco, Denver, and other large cities, lives a great mass of single men and a great mass of women who avoid every social responsibility and yield themselves to every animal passion.

The food, the drink, the amusements, the interests, the flagrant vices, are unmistakable signs which indicate the characteristics of the population. In Chicago the district consists mainly of lodging-houses and brothels. Cheap restaurants, street stands with hot lunches, "barrel-houses" with free whiskey, saloons with free hot lunches, make up a large part of the business activity of the district. Five and ten cent museums with highly colored pictures, of an immoral sort, or illustrative of some horrible monstrosity, seem necessary to arouse the intelligence and interest of the jaded, callous, and deadened denizens and visitors of the district. Opium dens or hop-joints are hidden away behind Chinese laundries or in dark and apparently empty basement rooms under the pavements. Billiard rooms, run in connection with saloons, are extensively patronized. Shooting galleries are, for

some reason, always a successful part of the business of the district. The books and papers sold
reflect the mind of the community. They consist
almost entirely of blood-and-thunder stories of robbers, detectives, wars, pirates, and the outlaws of
the West. Sprinkled in with these stories of daring
are novels of a most degrading and immoral kind.
The latter, and the lewd pictures, which are sold in
packages and exhibited on the walls of saloons and
bawdry houses, minister to the vicious tastes of the
neighborhood.

One should not neglect to mention a class of
people, living in the district and supported by
serving the men and women, who are either "running" the dives, or who otherwise participate in the
showy life of "the Levee,"—negro errand boys,
children selling gum and cosmetics, young fellows
selling jewelry or millinery and ready-made garments
to the women, messenger boys running to and from
the brothels, the "Hot Wiener" man who begins
peddling at eleven or twelve o'clock at night and
continues on until morning. Most pathetic of
all are the laundresses and scrub women of the district. Their work is hard and disagreeable; they are
the servants of a class to which they are morally
superior. They live in a community where their
morality is abnormal and not respected. They bring
up their children with their own beliefs, to see them

at last resign themselves to the popular vices of the society about them. No less to be deplored is the life of the newly arrived immigrant. He moves into a street adjoining "the Levee" and rents rooms as soon as they are abandoned by the denizens. Rents are cheapest there. He shares the same house with immoral women who corrupt his children. He crowds his rooms to their utmost capacity; he is content with a basement room where the sun never enters; he is happy for rooms in a rear tenement. Nothing is too bad.

No description of the district would be complete without some mention of the politicians. To begin with, they have important property interests. They rent to the Chinese the house which he uses as an opium den; they own the finest houses of vice in the district; their saloons are loafing places for the boys. Competing saloon keepers are not foes, they are warm personal friends; even those who are not in politics themselves receive protection from the politicians. They are often given city jobs which involve no work, but which yield good salaries. In these districts the politician is king. Not only is a policeman not permitted to stop law-breaking when he sees it, he is even supposed not to see it. In certain cities he does not dare to enter places which exist in violation of the law. He would lose his job instantly if he were to do a policeman's duty —

without having definite orders from his superior. In a few cities the head of the police dares exercise but little more authority than the patrolman. He receives his orders from the Boss, and it is not without proof that the mayor receives orders also from the same source. The title "The Boss" is less ornamental than many others; but the Boss is the most powerful person in the municipal life of America.

The saloon-keeping politician is a feudal lord among his "boys." Among the "Franchise grabbers" he does a turn as Robin Hood, but in his district he is lord and master of his thousands. The habitual vagrants are an important part of his constituents. They eat at his bar and drink as his guests; they have a "corpse reviver" or an "eye-opener" every morning, — a "schooner" of beer or a glass of whiskey. What they beg, steal, or earn they spend with him. They vote as he says. In return he cares for them. If they are arrested on a petty charge, he has the court dismiss the case. If the charge is too serious, he arranges to have them sent to a jail instead of a penitentiary. In certain cities, when he chooses to do so, he has the mayor issue a pardon. He sends the sick to hospitals, obtains jobs, gets railroad passes; in short, in so far as he can, he does everything his drunken, diseased constituents ask. In return he asks but one

I

thing — power to do more for them; power which they alone can give.

It is in these slum districts that many of the vagrant unemployed find lodging. Wayfarers seeking work, many of whom have temporarily left wives and children, doubtless have as little as possible to do with the vicious element which constitutes the life of these sections of our cities, but they cannot fail to come in frequent contact with it. However much the more self-respecting classes of unemployed keep themselves for a time from sharing in the vice, they are, nevertheless, contaminated by its sensualism and debauch. There are few lonely, disheartened seekers of work who altogether withstand the temptations of good-fellowship, the attractions of drink and vice, which dominate the life of a community in which no one seems to work and every one lives for pleasure.

The lodging-houses of the largest cities are numerous and most varied in their sanitary condition. There are small hotels here and there which accommodate, on the whole, decently, men and women, many of whom have regular work. There are the meeting rooms of the Salvation Army and the Volunteers of America, where men are sometimes permitted to sleep on chairs and on the floors. These religious organizations have also regular lodging-houses, where hundreds of men are fed and sheltered. There are the lodging-houses conducted for special

religious, dietetic, or sanitary reasons. There are the
police stations in some cities gathering in swarms of
the most wretched and destitute vagrants, and saloons,
such as " Hinkey Dink's," " Bath-house John's," and
" Fink's," the gravitating centres of Chicago's homeless army. There are lodging-houses for women and
assignation houses for unmarried couples. In addition to the large and extensive lodging-houses " downtown," where hundreds, and in some cities thousands,
congregate, there is a vast number of smaller tran-
sient homes in various parts of the city, as well as of
" furnished rooms" in tenement houses, which accommodate a nightly gathering of transients and boarders,
in this manner often endangering domestic privacy
and decency.

The larger houses, often, as in Chicago, with a
thousand lodgers nightly, have an extensive range
in the matter of cleanliness, decency, and comfort.
Some of the better ones, which charge 25, 35, and
50 cents a night, usually accommodate, with fair
comfort, a class of clerks and other workmen who
get a reduced rate as continuous lodgers. The Mills
Hotels of New York City are of this kind. In the
ordinary lodging-houses of the better class there is
a separate apartment for each person, and often a
separate locker for valuables. There is a common
lavatory on each floor. The air is generally good
and the conditions sanitary.

The next lower grades are the 15 and 20 cent houses, followed close by even cheaper grades. Each floor, in these lodging-houses, consists of several rooms, which are little more than small boxes made by partitions. Lines are hung across the rooms to support the clothes of the lodgers. Across the top are wire screens to prevent a pillaging neighbor from "lifting" a suit of clothes in the night. On each floor there is usually a lavatory. The ventilation is nearly always bad, although it is, of course, much worse in the poorer grades of houses. The worst aspect of these places, however, is in the general lounging room. On almost any night one may find in the large houses of this class, one or two hundred men, sitting about the room in groups, talking, smoking, spitting tobacco juice, playing cards, etc.

In the better class of lodging-houses the men show by their appearance that they are capable of doing hard work. They are mainly wayfarers who are seeking employment during the day. They are, in many instances, taking their first step toward vagrancy. Whether the men are employed or unemployed, the lodging-house life is bad, devoid as it must be of the wholesome restraints of the home. I think it was Mrs. Charles Russell Lowell who spoke, a few years ago, of the evils inherent alike in the lodging-houses and in the uptown clubs, — both encouraging the vices of an irresponsible and unnatural

single life. The same criticism has often been made
of the Rowton houses of London. These "models"
have been called the "Houses of the Gray Lives." I
was told recently, by one who knows, that about the
lowest type of man in New York is the well-dressed,
unambitious habitué of the Mills Hotels, whose aims
in life are satisfied by 50 cents a day.

These, however, are the better lodging-houses.
The one adjoining may be lower in tone and in price.
There is the same room crowded with men, some
joking and laughing, others swearing, some telling
vile stories, others nodding in drunken heaviness.
The men here are not only not employed, they are
mostly habitual idlers, and they show evident signs of
degeneration. Some are old, with faces showing the
ravage of dissipated lives; others are broken-down
laborers, who refuse to stay in the almshouses
because of habits of drink and vice too pleasant to
give up. The whole aspect is worse than that of the
former lodging-house. There one saw the beginning
in the irresponsible life of single men; here one sees
the evil effect of a life divorced from every restraint.

There is a class of lodgers even below this, — the
vagrants sleeping on the floors of police stations or
in and about saloons and "flop-houses." These conditions are rarely permitted now in the larger Eastern
cities. I shall never forget a "flop-house" which I
inspected a few years ago in Chicago, and in which

I witnessed the most despicable animalism I have
ever seen. It was a large, four-story building, formerly used as a warehouse. The sign over the door
read " Lodgings, 10, 15, & 20 cents," but I found on
entering that the prices were 2, 3, and 5 cents.

On the first floor there were certainly a hundred
men sleeping on the floor itself, without mattresses
or bedclothes. They had taken off their shoes and
rolled them in their coats to make a bundle which
they then used for a pillow. They were sleeping on
newspapers which they had spread on the floor, and
were without any covering whatever. There was a
stove in the middle of the room blazing away, sending out a sickening heat, hardly sufficient, however,
to keep warm the men sleeping in the corners of
the room. The price of these "beds" was 3 cents.
Just before the stairway was a small lad huddled on a
box, doubtless for the purpose of keeping free from
the vermin which infested the floor. The second and
third floors were partitioned off into small rooms not
more than half as large as a stateroom on a small
lake steamer. The beds were covered with rags
and dirty, ill-smelling quilts. Beds 5 cents. On the
fourth floor, having to economize floor space, broad
shelves, fifteen feet wide, had been built from each
wall. There were two shelves on each side, one
above the other, running out almost to the middle of
the room, with an aisle crossing from end to end of

the room. There were certainly not less than two hundred men sleeping as close as possible to each other on these shelves and on the floor. The shelves had been introduced merely for the sake of adding, as it were, to the floor space, and the men slept on the bare boards without covering. Beds 2 cents.

The air throughout the entire lodging-house was indescribably bad, but in this last room it was foul and suffocating. I made a thorough search for a place to sleep, but, not being successful in finding an unoccupied spot, I decided not to remain for the night. The air made me faint and weak, and I hardly had strength to pick my way out of the room. As I passed a large stove, red with heat, the thought of fire struck me. What a trampling to death of some for the safety of others would inevitably result! Only men who had made themselves drunk, by stale beer and by the poisoned stuff sold for whiskey in these districts, could have found it possible to sleep in such a pest-house. The animalism and despicable foulness and filth made one almost despair of mankind. It is impossible to describe adequately the depths to which this submerged class descend. This lodging-house was not the only one that presented the problem of vagrancy and of unemployment; there were a hundred others filled with men; the police stations were full of men; the prisons full of men; the poorhouses overcrowded with men; the poor authorities rushed with applicants; the private charities caring for thousands. More men than the inhabitants of a large city, workless, vagrant, mendicant, drifting about from place to place, drunken, petty criminals, and beggars! These men could be of great value to the world as producers, as employed workmen. But as it is, not one of them gives form to a single piece of raw material. They eat, sleep, drink their idle lives into oblivion. It would be impossible to make any one, who has not seen with their own eyes these conditions, realize the utter waste of life, as I realized it, when I closed the door of this lodging-house and stepped into the cold, fresh air of that winter's night.

It is a prevalent impression that vagrants are usually criminal. Of the class just described that is not true. In fact, there are very few criminals of a really predatory type in the poorest lodging-houses. Of course, every one steals when he has a good chance, but the habitué organizes no plans or schemes to accomplish theft. These vagrants are now and then petty thieves and hold-up men, of an occasional sort, but there is rarely a burglar or skilled thief among them. A frequenter of the lowest lodging-houses may occasionally, when desperate, take a gun and hold up some one; but it is not in him to plan or outline a successful burglary, a daring theft, or an unusual bit of pocket picking.

One must be a person of considerable capacity to be a successful rogue, and no one expects to find in the lowest lodging-houses of America men who are in condition to make a success of anything. Occasionally one finds in these great hotels men who have had capacity of a high sort. I remember a man who had occupied the first position with a large and first-class publishing house. The books of some of the best American writers received his approval before they were published. To-day he is a pitiable wreck. Except for common laborers and a few skilled mechanics, one seldom finds in lodging-houses of this class men who could now be relied upon for much of anything. They are cowards; they steal because opportunities for stealing something without being caught are plentiful. They have no originality and no capacity. They have vices, and live to satisfy them. They steal each other's clothes; they rob a guttered drunkard. They would rob their benefactor; they would steal a newsboy's earnings or rob a chewing-gum girl of her returns as readily and greedily as they would sip stale beer from the keg. They are wrecks, they are cranks, they are loafers, they are drunkards, but they are seldom, if ever, criminals that any one need fear.

Nor can it be said that all vagrants are absolutely unemployed. Those who obtain their information concerning vagrants from *Puck* or *Judge* are likely to believe that they never, under any consideration, work. A vagrant once exclaimed to a friend of mine: "Work? Work? I have no time to work. I've got to hustle around in order to get enough to eat." This is the typical vagrant, as we think of him. But despite our jokes, the tramp has a large number of petty occupations — so many, in fact, that one cannot begin to enumerate them. These employments have, as a usual thing, one characteristic — they do not compel early rising and one can "knock off" work at pleasure. An important field of casual employment is the doing of odd jobs about private houses, cheap hotels, and restaurants. The putting in of coal, the cleaning of steps, the washing of dishes, the peeling of potatoes, the raking of grass, the cleaning off of snow, etc., are a few of the various odd jobs which a tramp relies on in an hour of dire need.

A large number of business firms who sell novelties of all sorts employ a semi-vagrant element living in the lodging-houses to sell wares on commission. There are probably thousands of acknowledged vagrants who are employed in this fashion as "fakirs" or pedlers. The "Mush Fakir," one of this class, is in many ways the most interesting of all vagrants. He relies upon a ready wit for his success. A tramp friend of mine once said of the Mush Fakir: "He is like Autolycus in 'A Winter's

Tale' — his 'revenue is the silly cheat.' He is
eminently 'a snapper-up of unconsidered trifles,' as
Shakespeare says." If opportunity offers, he may
steal something; if you are sympathetic, he will
permit you, after he has told a pathetic story, to
give him money. If you are poor and need many
things, he will sell you something absolutely worth-
less and take your pennies; perhaps you may buy a
combination of muriatic acid, white crocus and chalk
to clean silver, and after he has gone you remember
that you haven't any silver. The "Mush Fakir" is
by nature a psychologist of no mean order. He
doesn't much care what he sells, provided only that
it brings a good price and has no value. He can sell
to a woman, who never makes calls, a package of
calling cards. He will fascinate a poor washer-
woman into the disastrous purchase of an easel,
although she may have no use whatever for it and
may never have possessed a picture.

One can hardly explain such transactions, yet they
frequently occur. Whether or not it is the desire
on the part of poor people to treat kindly a gentleman who has troubled to talk so long and so inter-
estingly, it is difficult to say. One rather thinks it
may be the overwhelming desire which all people
have to possess a luxury or two, something which is
above the dead, dull level of things. For a poor
person to wish for something which doesn't go into

a hungry stomach, or which is not "kicked out on the children's feet," or which is not given to the landlord, is a worthy ambition. The poor are saved much unhappiness by not having time to look about the shops or to read bargain advertisements. But the "Mush Fakir" brings the shop to the home, and the poor housewife has a sorry time in resisting her temptations. Mostly she does not succeed, and fancy driven, she purchases whatever useless thing he chooses to have her buy.

There are still other employments which occasionally engage the vagrant. Even confirmed mendicants have been known to work as common laborers, and some work in the skilled trades. But it is spasmodic with them. The very considerable class of accidental vagrants work whenever possible, but they are not, as a rule, included in any of the descriptions of the vagrant which have preceded. They would be classed better under the head of Unemployed, as it is force of circumstances alone which prevents them from rising above this occasional vagrancy. The true vagrant, on the contrary, is compelled at times, by force of circumstances, to rise into the class of casual laborers.

It must be said, however, that when vagrants work they are as parasitic as when they beg. It is even probable that they do more harm to society as casual laborers than as beggars. They are satisfied with very little, and they are, as a rule, well able to supply their needs and gratify their vices upon the alms which people give them. As drones and idlers they are an injurious class in society, who do more harm negatively than positively ; but as casual laborers their injury is positive, and more or less serious according as work is plentiful or scarce and their numbers great or small. During an industrial panic, when laborers are plentiful and work places few, the fact that several thousand vagrants will accept work for a period of a few days is a serious detriment to bona fide laborers with families. At all times their influence is felt, however imperceptibly, upon wages. Even in good times employers, who find it advantageous to have a short working season, take advantage of the over supply of laborers and reduce the season to the shortest possible working space and lengthen the hours as much as human endurance will permit. Mr. R. M. Easley of the National Civic Federation was once told by a superintendent, "It is true, the way we have to rush things now makes it necessary for us to get in a batch of men, work them out, and then get a fresh batch." The habits of the vagrant are often suited to the requirements of these employers. The tramp wants a short period of employment, and finds it therefore easy to supplement, and in part displace, the laboring men in those trades which are subject to seasons of great and small activity.

Vagrants injure the bona fide workmen in at least two other ways. I saw two vagrants, not long since, who gave me an account of how they worked in a gang which went about the country for the purpose of breaking strikes. They said proudly that they were "professional strike breakers." A criminal, lately out of a Colorado prison, convicted of an unspeakable crime, told me the other day that he and "two hobos" had made "good money" by "scabbing" in several recent strikes. It may surprise most people to learn that vagrants were enlisted as members of the Coal and Iron Police during the recent strike in Pennsylvania. Men were actually taken from the Bowery lodging-houses and sent to the anthracite mines for the purpose of policing those properties. It is largely due to this vagrant element that there is so much destruction of property and loss of life in some of the most prolonged and bitterly fought battles between employer, and employee. Both the scabbing and the violence do serious injury to the genuine workmen. These are also examples of the curious and interesting fact that vagrants often do more harm to society by their employment than by their vagrancy.

There is a class of vagrants who never work. It is with them a matter of principle. They take vagrancy seriously; it is a profession, having its own peculiar code of ethics, and work is not mentioned in any of its sections. This vagrant has as much ability as the " Mush Fakir," but he has no inclination to peddle and no commercial ambitions. He is often interesting. He may know Shakespeare by heart; he may be a good companion; he may delight us with delicious wit; he may be gentlemanly and clever, but he is a parasite, and for this kind of an idler there are few apologists. He may have a fondness for the country and speak of the smell of the earth in springtime and the odor of new-mown hay. He may say, as one said to me once: " There is no time like the spring. Ugh! I hate cities, honest I do, and like to feel the road under my feet and hear the brook babbling along at my side. I like the noonday of summer and the long, restful sleep at a river's edge under the shadow of a tree." He is the most interesting of his kind, valiant and sturdy as he is; but we have no respect for him, and look upon him as we look upon the idle rich. He takes to himself always; he gives nothing. To have a good stomach is not a sufficient equipment for manhood.

Habitual vagrants, to which those who work even occasionally are often exceptions, show a variety of traits which result from their peculiar life. What productive and creative work has done for man it would be difficult to say, but what the lack of work

does for a man is a thing every one may observe.
E. Ray Lancaster, writing on "Degeneration," says,
"Any set of conditions occurring to an animal
which renders his food and safety very easily obtained, seems to lead, as a rule, to degeneration."[1]
Certain physical signs of degeneration strike one,
as one sees even casually, as I have, night after
night in the Chicago Municipal Lodging House,
several hundred vagrants taking spray baths. They
are pot-bellied and pigeon-breasted; they have asym-
metrical shoulders, often curvature of the spine,
flabby muscles, and a generally poor muscular development; their legs are thin with blue veins, their
finger nails are long, soft, and dirty, and their hands
long and sweaty; their hair is often deficient. One
can readily see the meaning of these physical characteristics. They are the result of lack of work and
of purpose. They are the effects of sensualism and
debauch. The tramp, instead of developing himself by struggle to overcome the obstacles of poverty, has evaded responsibilities and duties, and has
travelled the line of the least resistance. Whatever
he may have been at first, he is now one who dis-
likes regular work; he is physically incapable of
sustained effort; he has a misdirected and almost
childlike love of petty adventure; he possesses no
energy; his will is gone. His physique would be
proof enough of these mental deficiencies if there

were no other means of recognizing them. Perhaps the most fundamental of the morbid mental states common to vagrants is the absence of inhibitory power. It is sometimes tragic to see vagrants promising to use self-control; dreaming dreams of a more respectable livelihood, yearning to overcome a vice and to attain a virtue, but as unable to carry out the programme as an insane person is unable to will himself sane. The habitual vagrant has gone beyond the point where self-recovery is possible.

Intellectually, tramps manifest a variety of characteristics which bear a striking resemblance to those of the savage.[1] They possess no foresight; they are rarely retrospective. Dreams of the future they sometimes have, maudlin and remorseful glances into the past they permit themselves; but beyond this they never go. To-morrow must take care of itself. It is characteristic. They live for the present; their associations are ever shifting; their habit is ever to move on; they have a passion for fields ever new. They rarely argue from a rounded experience; their habits of living rob them of systematic memory. As much as possible they leave the past to the past. They have learned from it but two things: how to avoid danger and how to live without work. However facile mentally, they are erratic. Their mind is " reminiscent only, not constructive."

K

They sometimes have a flow of superficial ideas. They love to tell stories. But one is baffled when one tries to have them construct a statement, however simple and crude, of their philosophy of life. Their minds are strikingly concrete; most of them cannot grasp an abstract idea. To test them, I have read to those vagrants with whom I have been most friendly, some simple generalization or abstraction in the study of their own lives, but they seemed never to grasp the meaning. I have had vagrant friends who have coöperated with me in my effort to learn of the life of their class. They told me everything they could concerning their lives, but a collected reasoning, a generalization, an abstract statement, was not only never given me, but never appreciated, when, as formulated by students such as Flynt or Wyckoff, I gave it to them. Abstraction, furthermore, wearied them ; they were unable to concentrate their thought. Vagrants have in certain matters a very keen power of observation. As the Nomads of uncivilized days learned the physical aspects of the earth which were favorable to their lives, so the Nomads of the present learn quickly the things which are to-day favorable to them. Beggars know just when, how, and whom to ask for alms. Marks on the gate posts are but crude indications. They learn by continued experience to distinguish the person who will give alms from the person who will refuse.

The vagrant learns this, as Browning's Lippo Lippi did when a waif of the street by "watching folk's faces to know who will fling the bit of half-stripped grape-bunch he desires and who will curse or kick him for his pains." But beyond these mental judgments, which are drilled into their lives by necessity, they possess little discrimination or critical capacity. It is as true of the tramps as it is of the savage Australians, "they are incapable of anything like persevering labor."

I have made no attempt in this description of the vagrant to follow any classification. I have purposely dwelt upon the degenerate and habitual vagrants, to the exclusion almost of those vagrants who may be, for one reason or another, merely temporary vagabonds. There is an enormous number of such hopeless, drifting persons. When the unemployed become, through vice or drink, unemployable, when they associate for long time with this lowest element in the abyss, they degenerate into the fixed status of an habitual mendicant. They never rise out of it. Every student of the unemployed, whose works I have seen, emphasizes the fact that degeneracy, physical and moral, follows unemployment more often than it precedes it. There is a down-draught drawing the unemployed class into a chronic condition of dependence, making them lazzaroni incapable of regaining their manhood. The power of the down-draught is conditioned by the number of persons in any community to whom vagrancy presents an infinitely easier course than the bitter, hopeless struggle to keep alive the manly qualities of independence and industry, when as workless workers those qualities are valueless. Positive proof of this suction force tugging at the unemployed could be established beyond any question if any careful statistical study had ever been made of the numerical rise and fall of the vagrant class. The nearest approach to a study of this kind is the work of Professor J. J. M'Cook of Hartford, Connecticut. He shows from the returns of the tramps in Massachusetts that "the figures leap forward by almost their own length," in the two years of industrial depressions, in 1873 and 1893.[1] Vagrancy maintains, as a rule, a definite relation to unemployment. The figures continue to grow until the industrial machine gets back into working order. The exciting cause then disappears, and the figures remain stationary or decrease. But a very large proportion of the vagrants made during these crises are not again absorbed into industry. They go on as professional vagrants until the end of their days.

An English investigator, Mr. Geoffrey Drage, has observed the same tendency among the casual workers and unemployed of Great Britain. He says in his book on "The Unemployed": "The hopeless, hand-to-mouth kind of existence into which

they thus tend to drift is of all things least conducive to thrift ; self-reliance is weakened, and habits
of idleness, unsteadiness, and intemperance formed.
It has been said that in many trades the prevalence
of drunkenness is in direct proportion to the extent
of the irregularity of employment. The effects of
such casual work are even more marked in the next
generation. Apart from inherited tendencies, the
children of this class grow up without any training,
technical or moral, such as would fit them to enter
a trade, or, if they entered it, to remain in it. They
are forced to join the ranks of unskilled and casual
labor, and thus, under the same influences which
beset their parents, they not only become incapable of regular work, but cease to desire it, preferring to pick up a precarious living by means of
odd jobs and charity." [1] The habitual vagrant is the
result of this process. To confuse the evils which
are associated with that result, with the causes
which produce it, is a common error of judgment.
Our eyes deceive us as to the true causes of
vagrancy when we look for them in the vagrant.
Our first thought is that vice and drink have
brought him into misery. This judgment is made
because the vagrant, at the time when we see him,
is vicious and drunken. But such a conclusion
may be in fundamental error. Go back to the unemployed, and the sources of the evil stand out in un-

mistakable clearness. The unemployed, from which
the vagrant class is so largely recruited, are
brought into existence by many other causes than
the occasional depressions in business. There is
at all times a reserve of labor which may in the
nature of the case be only casually employed.
Charles Booth is but one of many students to
observe that "the modern system of industry
will not work without some unemployed margin,
some reserve of labor."[1] The cost to society of this
unemployed or casually employed reserve is vagrancy
and its accompanying vices. The cost to the men
who make up this reserve, and to their wives and
children, is not a thing one wishes to contemplate.

Until some social remedy is found which will
make it profitable for industry to absorb this reserve
of labor, vagrancy must continue to be an important
and distressing social problem. It is idle to expect
the charitable societies to accomplish any fundamental reform in the conditions which create
vagrancy. But even their efforts might be directed
to an end which would aid much in clarifying the
problem.

There has been a great deal said abroad about
the process of "social dredging," by which means
the vicious, criminal, and unemployed vagrants may
be drawn out of the cities and forced into colonies.
John Burns, a member of Parliament and a labor

leader, indicated the necessity for some such undertaking, when he said a few years ago: "In spite of
what some advocates of work for the unemployed
may say, I contend, as a Socialist, basing my
belief on an unequalled experience of the largest
meetings of unemployed that have ever been held,
and as spokesman on every occasion for deputations
on this subject to Government departments in the
past ten years, that until the differentiation of the
laborer from the loafer takes place, the unemployed
question can never be properly discussed and dealt
with. Till the tramp, thief, or ne'er-do-well, however pitiable he may be, is dealt with distinctly
from the genuine worker, no permanent benefit
will result to any of them. The gentleman who
gets up to look for work at midday, and prays that
he may not find it, is undeserving of pity." [1] In
this work of discrimination the charities have a field
of immediate usefulness. In order merely to point
out a possible beginning in this work, a classification
of vagrants is necessary.

A large mass of vagrants may be classed as Indi-
gent and Infirm. They are an unemployable and
dependent class, incapable of ever being restored
to industrial usefulness or economic independence.
A second group could be classed as Professional or
Voluntary Vagrants, and a third group, including at
times in the United States several hundred thousand

men, may be classed as Accidental or Involuntary Vagrants.

The first class presents a purely charitable problem very similar to that of the first class of paupers. It includes the aged, the defective of all classes, the incurable sick, the dipsomaniac, the morally insane, in so far as they are not curable, and the permanently infirm, etc. They are the invalids of labor and the outcasts of industry; they are the invalids of vice and the victims of heredity and of evil home environment. The second class includes the professional vagrant, who is not infirm, and has no physical or mental weaknesses which excuse his dependence. He is willing to be a vagrant. He prefers vagrancy to work. He is not ashamed to think of mendicancy as a profession. He is a "Moocher," a "Jocker," a "Mush Fakir," and will be in the end, very probably, a "Tomato-can Vag"; but it is a matter of choice so far as one can determine. In this country the vagrants of this class are largely English, American, and Irish. They are above working, so they say, with the dagoes and other foreign laborers.

These two classes of vagrants, — the dependent, inebriate and defective, etc., and the mendicant, loafer, semi-criminal, etc., are particularly the ones who should be dredged out of the slums. A large number go to the almshouses in the coldest weather, but in the spring they issue forth to join again the

vicious elements of our cities. It is not possible to
accomplish anything by the ordinary repressive measures. Even if these vagrants could be forced back,
by such means, into the working class, they would
only augment the distress which always exists in the
mass which makes up the reserve of labor, — the
casually employed margin. But they cannot be
forced back into this or any other wholly or partially self-dependent class. Repressive measures
merely drive them from state to state. As some
one has said, it is like sitting down on the edge of a
cushion; they have the same effect upon the tramps
that sitting down has on the feathers. They are
useful in driving them from any particular spot, but
that is all. They probably do not diminish vagrancy
in the least. In the cities any action which can be
taken to prevent men from sleeping on the floors of
saloons, and from having free lunches, will have the
same repressive effect. The poorest and most insanitary lodging-houses should, of course, not only for
repressive, but for other reasons as well, be closed
by the State or City Boards of Health. All lodging-
houses should be under sanitary supervision. Beggars
should, of course, be arrested, but they should be
placed in some agricultural colony where they will
be compelled, whenever possible, to support themselves. The present method of arresting vagrants
and putting them at hard, useless labor is cruel and

abortive. It acts in precisely the same way as "that monstrous folly of sending men (inebriates) over and over again, fifty, seventy-five, a hundred and twenty-five times to a jail where there is not a single reformatory influence." Nor is there, it may be added, a single curative or medical influence. These vagrants are at present being supported by private alms, or by state funds;* and it is inhumane, unreasonable, and uneconomical that they should be thus maintained in vice and idleness when reform and cure are possible. In those cases where reform and cure are impossible, they should be segregated in self-supporting colonies.

The accidental vagrants are the floating element of "the reserve of labor," or, in other words, of the unemployed classes. They are waiting to be used by the employer. Their vagrancy consists of a restless, agonizing search for employment. The class is a very large one. Upon the basis of the statistics gathered in the census of 1890, Dr. Washington Gladden estimates that "there must have been an average of 1,139,672 persons unemployed during the whole of the year ending May 31, 1890." [1] The census of 1900, as before stated, shows the number unemployed some part of the year to have been 6,468,964. Over 2,069,546

---

* Professor M'Cook estimates that there were in 1895 in the United States, 85,768 such vagrants, supported by the community at a cost of $17,000,000 a year. [2]

males were unemployed from four to six months, and about half a million males were unemployed practically the entire year.[1] If one were able to determine the proportion of these unemployed persons, who find it necessary to go about from city to city in search of employment, it would show the total number of accidental vagrants. The number changes from year to year in direct relation to the activity of industry.

So long as the wages of certain classes of workmen are only sufficient to keep them during the period when they are employed, so long as there is an ebb and flow of industrial activity, so long as certain trades employ men at certain seasons only, so long as those who close the factories continue to have no responsibility for the outcast workers, so long as the laws of competitive industry make industrial depressions necessary, and so long as the system of industry demands a surplus of labor which may be but casually employed, so long, indeed, as there is such a thing as enforced unemployment, — just so long will the sources of vagrancy be ever active. Neither artificial employments nor charitable provision can remedy the evil. The worker is himself helpless. He is a wastrel, begging to be used in a competitive industrial system which in its present form requires his continued existence.

CHAPTER IV

THE SICK

ONLY in times of severe epidemics, when nearly all lives are threatened, do we realize the meaning of sickness. At such times our conception of sickness becomes a social one. We are forced to rise above ourselves and to give our hearts and minds to the sorrow of others, — the thousands, outside of our own family, or circle of friends, who are in distress of mind and in agony of body. In ordinary times sickness is an individual thing related to some one whom we know and love. The sick no longer gather together in public places as they did at the pool of Bethesda. The "great multitude of impotent folk, the blind, halt, withered," are still amongst us, but they are in their homes and in the hospitals, and no longer awaken public compassion by an assembled presence. Occasionally, as for instance when the great Austrian surgeon came to America, they come into public view again. It was thought that one hundred crippled children would seek relief. Two thousand made application, and over eight thousand were

brought to light in one city.[1] For the time we for-
got individual sickness, and eight thousand homes,
each with its crippled child, passed before our
eyes.

But sickness is so multiform that only an incomplete and partial conception of what it means in
any great city is possible. It is so terrible in its
worst forms that the mere mention of the names
by which these more distressing diseases are known
is abhorrent. The ills which deform, wither, and
disfigure the human form, which paralyze and cripple the body, which consume with internal fires
helpless children and strongest men, are painful
even to contemplate. It is more than enough to
know in one's own family the dreadful suffering
which attends disease, without making the additional effort to conceive sickness *en masse*. But
the sickness of one's self or of one's family is only
as a wave in an ocean of waves. The long, weary
night of anxiety and care is the night of many,
many thousand troubled hearts. To-night—half a
million people in this great city are either themselves
sick or are anxious in mind about some dear one
who is sick.[2] Many are to watch and care the
whole night through. Nearly two hundred of the
sick are to die before another nightfall. Twenty
or thirty thousand are to linger on, to grow weaker
and weaker, coughing and choking, night after night,

until breath refuses to come. In the great houses of pain, with doctors and nurses and long rows of white beds filled with bandaged bodies and writhing forms, eighty thousand sick souls will pray for relief before the year is gone. Nearly a million more will pass through the doors of the dispensaries to have pains allayed and bodies healed.

The homes also have their burdens of the sick. All together in New York City — in the mansions, tenements, and hovels there are constantly a quarter of a million who are sick, and two-thirds that number are absolutely disabled.* In the home of the rich a child lies burning up with fever. All are watchful and awake the whole night through. Doctors, nurses, servants, with a thousand appliances, make every effort to ease and comfort that little life. In the big tenement a light burns all night, and a tired workman watches every movement and listens for every breath of his hot, restless little one. At dawn he goes to his work. He kisses the feverish lips. It may be for the last time, — he knows not; and all day long his heart is heavy and anxious. In the filthy hovel, a drunken woman becomes sober, and her flushed face white — when the doctor shakes his head over the starved baby in the bundle

---

* William Farr estimates that to one annual death two persons are on the average constantly suffering from severe sickness and three persons are ill enough to require some medical relief. " Vital Statistics," pp. 512–513.

of rags. These are but three homes — imagine a
quarter of a million. This sickness, which, as Emerson
says, "eats up all the life and youth it can lay hold
of," comes with its message of pain and destruction
to every home, and for every one visit to the man-
sion it comes twice to the tenement and thrice to
the hovel.

Source as it is of so much pain and of so much
else that racks the poor old body of humanity, sickness forces upon thousands and thousands of struggling families an almost greater misery — poverty.
But poverty is both a cause and a result of sickness.
No one knows how many thousand families of workingmen, through this cause alone, are brought to
distressing poverty and even to miserable pauperism.
The charitable organizations say that about one-fourth
of the distress which manifests itself is caused by
sickness.[1] It is a fertile and lively cause of poverty,
constantly active and supremely powerful. When
it afflicts a wage-earner, it stops earnings, and lays
at the same time heavier burdens of expense upon
the home. How often one hears a workman say, "I
am all right so long as I keep well and have work."
A man may be a drunkard and yet able to earn
something; but unemployment and disabling sickness may shatter every assurance the workman has
of food and shelter for himself and family, and for
these things he may be in no wise responsible. Upon

the chance of the bread-winner's remaining well and having work depends the livelihood of several million people in this country. The insecurity, the chance, the day by day uncertainty of livelihood among the wage-earning classes encourage many workingmen, half truthfully and half cynically, to call themselves wage-slaves *whose owners have been freed* from caring for them when sick or unemployed. At any rate, the workman, even when sick or unemployed, must now care for himself and family. The insecurity of livelihood caused by sickness increases with the increase of poverty. The highest classes of workmen have less sickness than the next highest, and so on down to the poorest, among whom sickness, in one form or another, is almost universal. Among 10,000,000 well-to-do persons the number of yearly deaths is probably not more than 100,000; among the highest class of wage-earners the number is probably not less than 150,000; and among the poorest, or those in poverty, the number is probably not less than 350,000.[1] These are rough estimates for the purpose of indicating how widespread sickness is among those in poverty, what heavy burdens it lays upon those who can least afford to bear them, and how much of the sickness of the poor is excessive and unnecessary. Poverty and sickness form a vicious partnership, each helping the other to add to the miseries of the most unfortunate of mankind.

This close relationship between poverty and sickness helps to make sickness in the tenements a misery which the more fortunate cannot understand. The sorrow which accompanies disease and death is a sorrow which almost any human being can understand. Both of these ills of mankind all men must some time suffer. The rich may escape some of the miseries which accompany all sickness in the tenements, but the sorrow and the pain all men must some time know. The well-to-do may have the best medical attention and nurses; they may be free from crowding and from hunger; they may escape from irritation and noises and street disturbances; they may cease work and need not return to it until they are quite well; they may have a change of climate and all other things that money can buy, and these things are much, but they can neither escape illness nor avoid death. The poor of the tenements must be sick oftener; they must die earlier; more of them must die in youth and in their prime. To the poor sickness means more than illness. It means misery of the severest kind. From those who have already sacrificed too much, new sacrifices are demanded. I have known mothers working in the sweatshops who have been " on their feet" for over one hundred hours, watching over the sick-bed, sewing and watching, sewing and watching. I have been through the tenements in the " dog days" of summer when the " infant

L

torches " go out. " Be quiet," a woman said to me
one day, as she tiptoed along a tenement hall; "there
is a sick child in there; I think it's dying." All
people are not thoughtless of others in the tenements; but in the days of summer, when the windows are open, no amount of consideration and
thoughtfulness can prevent annoyances. The crowd
on the streets, the yelling, the shouting of pedlers,
the continuous hum, the odors, the lack of conveniences, the noise and the bang, the flies, the heat,
and the overcrowded rooms, make sickness in the
tenements a hellish thing.

One day I visited the family of a man who had
been prostrated by heat while at work with a street-
paving gang. They were a family of seven, living
in a two-room apartment of a rear tenement. The
day was in August, and the sun beat down uninter-
mittently and without mercy. The husband had
been brought home a few hours before. The wife,
in a distracted but skilful way, found pathways
among the clamoring children. The air was steamy
with a half-finished washing, and remnants of the
last meal were still upon the table. A crying baby
and the sick husband occupied the only bed. I had
known before of five people sleeping in one bed;
but I learned here that the father and oldest child
usually slept on the floor. As I watched the woman
on that day I understood a little of what it meant to

live in such contracted quarters. To cook and wash for seven, to nurse a crying baby broken out with heat, and to care for a delirious husband, to arrange a possible sleeping-place for seven, — to do all these things in two rooms which open upon an alley tremulous with heated odors and swarming with flies from the garbage and manure boxes, was something to tax the patience and strength of a Titan.[1]

In this instance the man had broken down, and sickness is most serious when it attacks the bread-winner of a working-class family. The sickness of wife or child is far less terrifying. However painful the disease or distressing the consequences, the family's peace of mind is not shattered by the fear and dread of want. The man is not kept from his work, and his earnings, made more necessary by the sickness, may still supply the family's needs. The diseases which kill or undermine the health of the adults, especially the men, are the ones which strike terror to the heart of working-class families. Those which almost invariably cause death, — such as cancer, phthisis, Bright's disease, diabetes, — as well as those which permanently incapacitate a workman, — such as apoplexy, paralysis, etc., — the many accidents in industry, which cripple the body, and the diseases, arising from certain dangerous trades, which permanently undermine the health, are the forms of sickness which generally mean for wage-earning families poverty and often pauperism. Such diseases affect the welfare of the whole family. They stop all earnings unless the wife is able, or one of the children old enough, to become a wage-earner. Sickness assumes a new and more terrible meaning when one realizes that the mass of wage-earning families are pathetically dependent upon some one person's health. Any one familiar with the poor knows with what grim determination half-sick workmen labor under this heavy responsibility. An Italian workman dying of consumption once said to a friend of mine, who was urging him as a last hope to quit work and go to a sanatorium, "No! No! Me die not yet at all! Me gotta bringa de grub to ma chil'."

Wives suffer from the ordinary forms of sickness which afflict men, and, in addition, have to go through the serious trial, periodically occurring, of childbirth. The unnatural disease, puerperal fever, so often due to lack of care, insanitary conditions, and overcrowding, is perhaps the greatest ill which the women in poverty have to suffer. The quack doctors and the untrained midwives, in the poorer districts, even more than the conditions of poverty, make this disease an ever menacing misery. The most terrible neglect is frequently observed during such critical periods. I have often tried to forget the story of one case of illness and death which came under my observation several years ago. The little girl and a "neighbor-woman" told it to me when they came to apply for enough money to bury the mother and the baby child. The mother, a recent widow, had finished a hard day of labor; she came home tired and ill. The little girl, used, even at her early age, to household cares, prepared the supper for herself and mother. During the night a baby child arrived. The little girl helped her mother as best she could, but hers was not the skill required. The mother and baby died. During the previous week they had been evicted from their former house, and the little girl knew no one in the new neighborhood. In fear and despair, she locked the door and sat with the dead mother and sister all that day. Again and again she kissed the mother's face, but, as the child told me, "she would not wake up." On the following day she went out, locked the door, and walked several miles to their former house and found there the neighbor-woman who brought the child to me. When we talked of burying the mother, the miserable little girl, who had, up to that time, seemed almost heartless, broke into sobs. For a long time she refused to give up the key to the rooms, and all the time she besought us not to take her mother away. It would not be possible to describe the misery and wretchedness which I have seen in the homes of the poor, and none is more painful to remember than the sickness of women.

And yet whatever the ills of mankind, they seem to weigh heaviest upon the children. The enormous number of deaths in certain parts of our largest cities has been referred to as the " Massacre of the Innocents." In certain rear tenements, in dark rooms and in the most insanitary portions of the "double-decker" tenements, and especially in certain insanitary and pestilential blocks, the death rate of children under five years of age is a matter of public disgrace. The death rate of children under five years in those places where there were both front and rear tenements, ran up as high as 204 per thousand. In other words, four or five times as many babies die in these houses as in the houses of the well-to-do districts. If this same rate were maintained among all the poor (which is not probable), of 1,000,000 babies under five years, 200,000 would die annually; while of 1,000,000 babies in well-to-do districts only 50,000 would die.[1] The Tenement House Committee of 1894 called these rear tenements "veritable slaughter-houses."

Excessive death rates among children, as among men and women, are, of course, largely unnecessary and preventable. William Farr said many years ago, " When any city experiences a higher rate than the average, it should always be a matter of serious inquiry and concern to its citizens." [2] The same may be said of any one section of a city as compared with other sections of the same city. It is said that the number of unnecessary deaths in London is as great each year as the total number of deaths in the English army during the three years of the Boer War.[1] The reduction in the year 1903 of the death rate in New York from 20 per thousand to 18.75 per thousand meant the saving of 4500 lives and the prevention of about 10,000 cases of severe illness. It saved the work of one or two great hospitals; it saved some wives from being widows and some children from being fatherless, and it also saved some from poverty. This is the work of prevention. We shall never know whose lives were saved, but that 4500 lives were saved — that we know. The same saving can be made again and again. This year, if perfect sanitary measures could be put into effect, probably 20,000 or 25,000 lives could be saved in New York City alone, and 40,000 or 50,000 cases of severe illness prevented. Many of the men, women, and children who are sick and who die unnecessarily, live in insanitary homes, and some of them work in insanitary mills, mines, offices, and factories, and the work of prevention lies in enforcing, in so far as is possible, a collective standard of cleanliness and sanitation upon every home and workshop.

So far as preventive measures are concerned, the greatest improvements of recent years have been those health measures compelling sanitary conditions in homes; and these improvements strike at the root of many of the foregoing evils. It would not be possible, in limited space, to go into details concerning either the bad conditions which still exist, or the many wise and humane measures which have been undertaken, in many of our cities, to stamp out the worst evils in tenements and work-shops. A few years ago there existed a frightful death rate among the people of a certain section of Glasgow. The municipal authorities, after becoming acquainted with the conditions, demolished the houses in that section and built new tenements to take their places. By this act the death rate was reduced from 55 per thousand to a little over 14 per thousand. An adjoining slum still had a death rate of 53 per thousand. Here were two groups of houses, sheltering practically the same classes of people, one with a death rate of a little over 14 per thousand, the other with a death rate nearly four times as great.[1] The discovery of similar conditions in all great cities, both in this country and abroad, has given a new impulse to the development of sanitary measures, in some cases involving the expenditure of millions of dollars.

We are still very much behind European countries both in our knowledge of the facts and in our remedial measures. Our housing question has

never been carefully studied in its relation to the
death rate or in its relation to sickness and to
various forms of debility and exhaustion. The
Tenement House Committee of 1894 made an effort
to get at the facts, and Dr. Roger S. Tracy's work
was and still is of value; but the last Tenement
House Commission of New York almost ignored
the subject. Even a study of the death rates was
not made, because of the difficulties involved.[1] For
this reason we cannot marshal the same array of
facts in support of housing reform which give
terrible force to the arguments of German, French,
and English advocates of improved housing. It is
also for this reason that we must use English data
to indicate some of the worst evils of insanitary
housing. There is, however, every reason to suppose that we should arrive at the same conclusions
if a careful study of American conditions were
made.

The evils of overcrowding are perhaps the most
important. The Royal Commission of 1884 gathered a great amount of facts and took extensive
testimony on this subject. The general summary
showed that pauperism, immorality, perverted sexu-
ality, drunkenness, and many other forms of de-
bauchery were caused in some instances, in others
abetted, by the indecent overcrowding which existed.
The testimony further showed most distressing physi-

cal results due to overcrowding. High death rates;
a pitiful increase in infant mortality; terrible suffering among little children; scrofula and congeni-
tal diseases; ophthalmia, due to dark, ill-ventilated,
overcrowded rooms; sheer exhaustion and inability
to work; encouragement of infectious diseases; a
reduced physical stamina, causing consumption
and diseases arising from general debility, were
some of the evils of overcrowding.[1] Similar, but
less definite, conclusions regarding the evils of
overcrowding were arrived at by the New York
Tenement House Committee of 1894. The secretary, in his report, says that overcrowding has evil
effects of various kinds, for example: "Keeping
children up and out of doors until midnight in
warm weather, because rooms are almost unen-
durable; making cleanliness of house and street
difficult; filling the air with unwholesome emana-
tions and foul odors of every kind; producing a
state of nervous tension; interfering with the sepa-
rateness and sacredness of home life; leading to a promiscuous mixing of all ages and sexes in a single room
— thus breaking down the barriers of modesty and
conducing to the corruption of the young, and
occasionally to revolting crimes."[2] The conclusions
drawn by both commissions concerning the physical, the mental, and the moral degeneration which
results from overcrowding, constitute a most seri-

ous indictment of the living conditions in which hundreds of thousands of working people live both in this country and abroad. Even if one ignored the cost to the community of disease and vice, the heavy burdens which these conditions force upon the individual families of the working people show the vital necessity of those preventive measures which society alone has the power to initiate.

Probably no other city in the world has so many dark rooms and other insanitary conditions, which act as exciting causes for the spread of tuberculosis and similar diseases, resulting from broken vitality, as New York City. Light and sanitary homes are probably more necessary to our working people than to those of any other city or country. Recreation and recuperation are vital necessities to the man whose work is hard, intense, and spurred on by the feverish competitive spirit of American life. It is needless to point out that the particular insanitary conditions which prevail in the New York tenements are in many cases the very ones which most effectually deny this needed recuperation.* It would be of great value to know to what extent the working classes suffer from debility and exhaustion due to these conditions of work and living. In addition to knowing more of the ordinary diseases resulting from occupations, contagions, and other causes of serious

* See Appendix A.

illness, it would be well to know to what extent over-crowded and badly ventilated homes are responsible for broken vitality, debility, and exhaustion. Some light has been thrown on this matter by inquiries in England. The Earl of Shaftesbury said before the Royal Commission on Housing : "When we were at The Board of Health some years ago we instituted inquiries in these low and miserable neighborhoods to see what was the amount of labor lost in the year, not by illness, but by sheer exhaustion and inability to do the work. We found upon the lowest average that every workman or workwoman lost about twenty days in the year from sheer exhaustion " . . . and the wage thus lost "would go a great way toward paying an increased rent for a better house." [1] That deterioration in health which often does not figure in the death rates is one of the most serious and least observed of the evil results of bad housing.

While New York's conditions are worse than those of any other American city, the remedial efforts here have been the broadest and best. In many other cities also an awakening has taken place which promises to advance housing reform. However partial and ineffectual our efforts have been up to the present, we can look forward to a slow improvement in the living conditions of the people. But any advance in sanitary living conditions is, at best, but a partial advance. Improvement of conditions in which the people work should go hand in hand with the improvement of living conditions. In this field we have done almost nothing. There is no other nation, comparable industrially to the United States, which is so backward as this country in its knowledge, in its legislation, in its administrative machinery for dealing with the insanitary conditions in factories, mines, and workshops, and in preventing or regulating those dangerous processes in industry which are responsible for a very large number of unnecessary diseases, accidents, and deaths. We have been limiting the power for harm which may be exercised by the individual landlord; but no other country has so much as our own permitted individuals to disregard, to a criminal extent, the health and welfare of employees. I dare say no other nation has so many needless deaths or so many cases of illness wholly due to preventable industrial causes as the United States of America. It is perhaps needless to repeat that these insanitary conditions of home and factory have a mighty bearing on the extent of poverty. The field is one which offers the greatest opportunity for humane and merciful legislation. The workmen who are crushed, crippled, or killed, who contract incurable diseases, who are poisoned, or who are incapacitated by carelessness, insanitary conditions, or dangerous machinery, are so numerous in this day that in a very few decades we shall look back upon this period as one of downright barbarism.

Social action is almost more necessary in order to improve the sanitary conditions in workshops than to improve those of the tenements. The individual workman is powerless. He cannot bargain for a sanitary workshop. The best third of his life is spent at work. He must work in mine or factory however injurious to his health, however menacing and however preventable the dangers of the employment. He usually accepts them without complaint. If there be poisons, or dangerous machinery, or disease-producing dusts which he must inhale, he may hope that he will escape injury, but he may not refuse to work. He may know that phossy jaw, plumbism, tuberculosis, rheumatism, palsy, or sudden death may at any time be his fate. But he must accept the conditions as they are if he wishes the work. He can, to a certain extent, choose his tenement, but he is, as an individual, almost powerless to choose his factory or a kind of employment which is without dangers. As Mr. and Mrs. Sidney Webb say in their book on Industrial Democracy:[1] "The wage-earner sells to his employer, not merely so much muscular energy or mechanical ingenuity, but practically his whole existence during the working day. An overcrowded or badly ventilated workshop may exhaust his energies; sewer gas or poisonous material may undermine his health; a badly constructed plant or imperfect machinery may maim him or even cut short his days; coarsening surroundings may brutalize his life and degrade his character: yet, when he accepts employment, he tacitly undertakes to mind whatever machinery, use whatever materials, breathe whatever atmosphere, and endure whatever sights, sounds, and smells he may find in the employer's workshop, however inimical they may be to health or safety."

Few realize that a very slight injury or breakdown may incapacitate certain workmen from further usefulness in a trade for which they may have been especially trained. A hernia (or rupture) may render a workman employed in moving heavy materials incapable of further usefulness in this employment. Continuous, intense, laborious work demands of the workman a strong constitution and good health. It often happens that one part of the body may be broken down by heavy lifting or over-exercise, and, while the general health of the laborer may not be impaired, such a breakdown, though apparently slight, may compel him to learn a new trade. As a matter of fact, excessive strains usually result in the breakdown of precisely those muscular organs by which a workman is enabled to earn his living in any specialized trade.[1] Let us take a few examples. There are many well-known diseases which are recognized as "marks of trade." Typesetters, telegraphers, tailors, writers, etc., suffer frequently from muscular cramps and similar afflictions. Such breakdowns may at first prevent only a free muscular action, but they are likely in the end to result in palsy and paralysis of the over-used muscles. The latter, for instance, happens very frequently to sewing-machine operatives. Shop girls are likely to suffer, as a result of their occupation, from a narrow, contracted pelvis. Varicose veins and ulcers result from continuous standing. Curvature of the spine results almost inevitably from certain employments. These are but a few among many of the physical ills which result from certain specialized occupations.

Even these comparatively slight afflictions are serious to the workman, because he must work or become a pauper. The more terrible and loathsome diseases of occupations, which utterly destroy the workman's health or which cause death, are too many to mention in detail. Those diseases which result from handling or coming in contact with the poisonous materials used in the chemical industries are the ones most generally known. Lead is a commonly used poison. A very large number of workmen are employed in many different industries where they are subjected to the dangers of lead poisoning. The early symptoms of the disease are blue gums,

followed by a loosening and coming out of the teeth;
but blindness, paralysis, and death in convulsions
finally result.[1] Miscarriages, still-births, and convulsions occur frequently to women lead-workers who
are with child. This is one of the worst of the so-
called poisonous trades. The dust-producing trades
cause various respiratory diseases, such as miners'
asthma, and consumption. Mining, street-sweeping,
and file-grinding are the ones most generally known.
Bakers, laundresses, tailors, and dressmakers are
also subject to certain diseases, resulting from their
work and from insanitary conditions, which cause
repeated breakdowns and a high death rate. The
dangers of work on the railroads have been spoken
of elsewhere.

These problems of unnecessary and preventable
sickness, whether of home or of factory, cannot be
solved by the individual. The individual who suffers is in the main powerless to alter conditions. On
the other hand, the landlord and the manufacturer
not only do not, as a rule, voluntarily improve the
conditions, but they are at times even active in preventing humane legislation for bettering sanitary
conditions. Dr. J. T. Arlidge, a great specialist on
diseases of occupations, says: " When visiting manu-
factories, the visitor is almost invariably informed
that the particular manufacture therein pursued is a
very healthy one. Even in cases where the con-

M

trary is a matter of general knowledge, and demonstrated by statistics, it is no uncommon thing to find the matter treated as of very little moment. If undeniable, the evils are minimized, and the masters and managers are prone to close their eyes to conditions of labor that loudly call for a remedy, and cast the blame more or less upon the workpeople." [1] Again and again in England and Germany, where many studies of injurious employments have been made, the employing class casts all the blame for high death rates and excessive disease upon the workers, and the landlord class does likewise when opposing sanitary measures for the improvement of tenement-houses. Even in those industries where the workers are degenerating and would become extinct, were it not for new recruits, the employers manifest the same unconcern for their health and accept with great unwillingness any proposed sanitary improvements. So far is the greed for profits carried. The deterioration of an entire people may result if this greed be not restrained.* From these facts alone it is fair to assume that, if the sanitary evils of home and factory are to be stamped out, it must not rest with the employers or landlords : it must be done by the community itself.

Any one will realize how fragmentary and incomplete this brief survey is of preventable disease

* See Appendix B, p. 347.

and of preventive measures. We have hardly
made a beginning in certain of the fields which
have been mentioned. Within the last few years,
however, a movement has developed which promises to arouse our people to the wisdom of preventive measures. Within the last decade there
have been a multitude of societies formed for the
purpose of stamping out the most serious disease
which afflicts mankind. Tuberculosis is the great
modern plague, more subtle and less generally
feared, but far more deadly, than any other plague
the world has known.

There was once a Great Black Plague. It was
the consternation of the people of the time when
it grew and flourished. Those who were able to
do so fled from the cities which it ravaged. It
lived a year and caused the death of two or three
million people. It was probably the result of filthy,
undrained streets and vile tenements. "The Great
White Plague" has lived for centuries and centuries; it was known before the time of Christ.
It has caused the death of millions and millions of
people; it will this year cause the death of over
one million more. One hundred and fifty thousand
people in the United States alone will this year die
of the disease. Within the next twelve months not
less than fifteen thousand of the people of New
York City, some of whom will be our neighbors,

friends, and even perhaps our relatives, will bow down before the Great White Plague. It is a needless plague, a preventable plague. It is one of the results of our inhumane tenements; it follows in the train of our inhumane sweatshops; it fastens itself upon children and young people because we forget that they need playgrounds and because we are selfish and niggardly in providing breathing spaces; it comes where the hours of labor are long and the wages small; it afflicts the children who are sent to labor when they should yet be in school; the plague goes to meet them. It is a brother to the anguish of poverty, and wherever food is scant and bodies half clothed and rooms dark, this hard and relentless brother of poverty finds a victim. It is more kind to the old, who have every reason for dying, than it is to the young, who have no reason for dying. It takes, as it were, an especial delight in mowing down the bread-winners of wage-earning families at the sweetest and most treasured period of their lives, — at the time when they are having the first joys of married life and bringing into the world their little ones. More than one-third of all deaths that occur between the ages of fifteen and thirty-five are due to the Great White Plague. It is a waste of youth prepared for life and labor, cut off by needless death as life and labor begin. For it is a wholly needless and preventable cause of death and of inestimable mourning and anguish among the widows and the fatherless.

The extent of the White Plague is one of the best tests of a high or low state of society; in many ways it is the truest and most accurate of social tests. The number of its victims will indicate the districts in which sweatshops flourish, and the streets in which the double-decker tenement, the scourge of New York, is most often found. Where the death rate from the Plague is greatest there ignorance prevails; drunkenness is rife; poverty, hunger, and cold are the common misfortune.

A prominent physician said a few years ago: " This is a disease which has claimed more victims than all the wars and all the plagues and scourges of the human race. Even in the few short years since Koch's discovery over two million persons on this continent have succumbed to its fatal infection. . . . The annual tribute of the United States to this scourge is over one hundred thousand of its inhabitants. Each year the world yields up one million ninety-five thousand, each day three thousand, each minute two of its people, as a sacrifice to this plague. Of the seventy million individuals now peopling these United States, ten millions must inevitably die of this disease if the present ratio is kept up." [1]

Tuberculosis is more common in the cities than in the country. The death rate from this disease in the cities of over twenty-five thousand inhabitants is about twice that of the rural districts of the state. The tenement districts suffer much more from the disease than do the well-to-do districts. In Paris the death rate is three times as great in the poorest quarters as it is in the well-to-do quarters. In Hamburg the proportion is almost the same. In the First Ward, near the Battery in New York City, fourteen times as many people die from tuberculosis, in proportion to population, as in a certain ward adjoining Central Park.[1] Obviously it is a plague which exists much more among the poor than among the rich.

Certain tenements become infected with the disease. We have recently heard of the " Lung Block " with its frightful death rate. We have also heard of the " Ink Pot " with its many deaths from tuberculosis. Mr. Ernest Poole, in describing the conditions in this tenement, says : " It has front and rear tenements five floors high, with a foul, narrow court between. Here live one hundred and forty people. Twenty-three are babies. Here I found one man sick with the Plague in the front house, two more in the rear — and one of these had a young wife and four children. Here the Plague lives in darkness and filth — filth in halls, over walls and floors, in sinks and closets. Here in nine years alone twenty-six cases

have been reported. How many besides these were
kept secret? And behind these nine years — how
many cases more?

"Rooms here have held death ready and waiting
for years. Up on the third floor, looking down into
the court, is a room with two little closets behind it.
In one of these a blind Scotchman slept and took the
Plague in '94. His wife and his fifteen-year-old son
both drank, and the home grew squalid as the tenement itself. He died in the hospital. Only a few
months later the Plague fastened again. Slowly his
little daughter grew used to the fever, the coughing,
the long, sleepless nights. The foul court was her
only outlook. At last she, too, died. The mother
and son then moved away. But in this room the
germs lived on. They might all have been killed in
a day by sunlight; they can live two years in darkness. Here in darkness they lived, on grimy walls,
in dusty nooks, on dirty floors. Then one year later,
in October, a Jew rented this same room. He was
taken, and died in the summer. This room was
rented again in the autumn by a German and his
wife. She had the Plague already, and died. Then
an Irish family came in. The father was a hard,
steady worker, and loved his children. The home
this time was winning the fight. But six months
later he took the Plague. He died in 1901. This is
only the record of one room in seven years." [1] Miss

Brandt of the New York Committee for the Prevention of Tuberculosis is authority for the statement that one house in Chinatown has a record of thirty-seven cases in nine years; another house has a record of twenty-five, and still another of nineteen.[1] A house in the Syrian quarter has had thirteen deaths from tuberculosis.[2] In the " Lung Block " there have been two hundred and sixty-five cases of tuberculosis reported to the Board of Health in nine years. Mr. Ernest Poole, who knows the conditions in this block also, says that this is probably not more than half the actual number. In other words, there have probably been over five hundred cases of tuberculosis in this one block during the last nine years. The disease is one which affects especially residents of the tenements and the workers in certain trades, as, for instance, printers, tailors, bookkeepers, dressmakers, bakers, cigar-makers, potters, stone-cutters, file-grinders, dyers, wool-carders, etc.[3]

To know why these classes of people are affected, let us for a moment consider how the disease is spread. A person having consumption can, it is said, expectorate in a day seven billions of germs or bacilli. These germs or bacilli are the only cause of the disease. The sputa or expectorations from the diseased lungs dry and afterward become a pulverized dust which is blown about through tenements, theatres, street cars, railway trains, offices, and factories. In fact, the infection is disseminated wherever tuberculous sputum becomes dry and pulverized. The germ is killed by sunlight and lives but a short time in the open air, but it will live for months in darkness or in places artificially lighted. Every consumptive, therefore, who is careless about his sputa — and most consumptives are careless who have not been trained to discretion by having lived for some time in a sanatorium — becomes, in consequence, a centre of infection. Those about him are very likely to contract the disease ; those living in the same rooms or working in the same factory or office, are the ones most liable to the infection, especially when they are delicate, overworked, underfed, or underclad.

Dr. Hermann Biggs, the General Medical Officer of the Board of Health, says that there are thirty thousand persons in New York City suffering from tuberculosis.[1] There are therefore about thirty thousand centres in the city disseminating the infection. Where conditions are favorable, as, for instance, in certain offices, factories, sweatshops, and tenements, the disease is constantly spreading. As a result, there are " Lung Blocks," and, doubtless, if it were known, " lung factories " and " lung sweatshops " also. This dry, pulverized dust is the most important of the means of spreading tuberculosis throughout all parts of the city, so that, I do not doubt, a consumptive of the sweatshop, spraying the garments he sews by sneez-

ing or coughing, may convey to some delicate lad or
girl in a far-distant part of the country or in a wealthy
part of the city the disease which the sweatshop has
given him. A virulent cause of consumption is the
spray discharged from the nose, lungs, or mouth
of the consumptive invalid. As before mentioned,
those near the person suffering from tuberculosis
are very likely to contract the disease. Children
playing about on the floor, kissing or embracing the
diseased mother or father, taking the milk from a
tuberculous mother, so often contract the disease
that the mass of people have an almost unshakable
belief that it is inherited. Eminent physicians, however, say that the disease is not inherited. Professor
Koch, who twenty-two years ago discovered the cause
of tuberculosis and thus opened the way for saving
millions of lives, says in an instructive interview on
the subject: " The last three or four weeks of life are
the most deadly in the spread of infection. . . .
His every cough, sneeze, or effort at speech sends
forth a spray laden with bacilli in virulent form
deadly to the poor wife and children around him. . . ."
He speaks further of the dying consumptive who
sets "this terrible spray in operation." In another
place he says, " it is not cruelty to isolate these cases;
it is the truest and highest kindness. . . .

" In all other infectious diseases we attack infection
at its source; cases of small-pox, of leprosy, of diph-

theria, of plague, are isolated, but cases of tuberculosis in their last stages, the most deadly stage of the most deadly disease of all, are still allowed throughout Europe to spread further infection broadcast in the midst of their already destitute families. This fact does not yet seem to be learned. When it is, and when we have these homes for the hopeless cases adjoining every city, then tuberculosis will pass from the midst of us." [1]

Let us consider whether it is an economy on the part of society to ignore the spread of tuberculosis and to do little more than to furnish the consumptive with a place in which to die. The state has gone little farther than that in this country. We need not, for the moment, consider what is kind, what is humane, what would be doing unto others as we would have others do unto us if we had consumption. We need only consider cold figures and the economics of the disease. Dr. Hermann Biggs, who has spent a good part of his life in doing invaluable work for New York and is one of the few physicians of this country who have carefully studied the social consequences of individual diseases, has recently said in an important lecture on tuberculosis that the average cost to society of preparing a man for usefulness is $1500. This is in the nature of a grant from parents or state, which the child, when he becomes a man, is expected to return to the community by his labor.

Considering that 10,000 people every year die of tuberculosis in New York, the natural conclusion is that New York loses annually about $15,000,000. The cost of their nursing, food, medicines, attendance, as well as the loss of productive labor, adds a further loss to the municipality which Dr. Biggs estimates at $8,000,000. Upon the same basis it is estimated that the annual loss in the United States from tuberculosis alone is $330,000,000.[1] It should be noted that this is an annual loss. Each consumptive uncared for infects some one near him; he passes his disease on to others; he leaves a legacy of death to friends and neighbors. The 120,000 consumptives who die this year yield 120,000 consumptives who are to die next year, and so on continuously. It is cheaper in every way to cure a consumptive in a sanatorium than it is to let him die in a hospital or in a public institution of some kind, but to let him die in a hospital or institution of whatever kind is cheaper than to let him die in his tenement. What we are doing now is just the wrong thing. As Dr. J. H. Pryor has said, "We must care for the consumptive in the right place, in the right way, and at the right time, until he is cured; instead of, as now, in the wrong place, in the wrong way, at the wrong time, until he is dead." It is cheaper and it is infinitely more humane.

It is unquestionably the duty of society to care for

the victims of this disease. It is a social disease. Society is responsible for its continuance. If I contract the disease when in a theatre, a factory, or a public building or when riding in a street car, or if I move into a tenement which has just been vacated by a consumptive, or if I live in a tenement where a consumptive was permitted to spit on the floors in the hall, or if I am compelled by poverty to live in a dark, unventilated room, which the law should everywhere prohibit, I know that society is to blame for my having contracted the disease, because society alone through its board of health and governmental agencies, can prohibit careless expectoration, can disinfect tenements, can compel notification of diseases, can confiscate sweatshop garments. It alone can remove centres of infection by powers which it alone has.

Many years ago I was engaged in taking into the country a great many small children from one of the poorest districts of one of our largest cities. The little ones were gay and active and could hardly be kept quiet or in hand during the journey. One little girl, in a condition of extreme anæmia, with bright eyes and a very delicate little frame, found herself so easily exhausted in play that she came to sit by me and talk. I discovered from my short conversation with her that her father had been ill for several months, that he "coughed and coughed"

and lay in bed most of the day. She and another
little one slept with the father; the mother and two
babies slept in another bed in the same room.
The mother earned the living, and in the evening
when she came home, the little girl said, "she
would just weep and weep." Upon my return I
called upon the father and told him how he was
endangering the lives of the children by remaining
at home, and especially by his extreme carelessness
in spitting about the room. I urged him to go to a
hospital, but he refused, saying that, as he had to die,
he was going to die with his family. The rooms
were cold and dark and bare, and I knew what the
result would be if he were left to continue at home.
Failing in all efforts to persuade him, I urged the
Board of Health to compel him; but the Health Board
responded by saying that, according to the law, tuberculosis was not an infectious disease and that therefore
the man could not be forcibly removed. I remember
with what despair I worked for two or three weeks in
trying to persuade him to be just and fair to his family.
Finally I left the city and was gone for somewhat
over two .years and a half. Upon my return, I inquired concerning the family from a charity agent
who had visited them frequently. She said they were
no longer dependent upon charity : they were all
dead. One seldom sees a more perfect, nor indeed
a more terrible, example of the helplessness of the

individual, and of the need of social action, to stop the spread of the disease.

The following measures, if carried out in every part of this country, would stamp out the Plague in twenty years.* First, the disease should be declared in all states and in all cities "infectious." Second, there should be compulsory notification of all cases of tuberculosis. The necessity for this need not be argued. The reasons for it have been fully presented by Dr. Biggs and others, and a form of it is in operation in New York City, in Prussia, and in Norway.[1] Third, the advanced cases should be given care in institutions suited to their need. Professor Koch says : " Let their days be made as pleasant as ingenuity can make them ; let them in some airy ward, or in an open *Liegehalle*, receive visits from their friends, even in these last days ; but let them go to the grave with the consolation of knowing that they are not handing on a legacy of tragedy to those they leave behind."[2] Fourth, the establishment and maintenance of sufficient sanatoria and dispensaries for the treatment in the earlier stages of every case of consumption. Fifth, careful and complete disinfection of all houses and rooms in which consumptives have died and from which consumptives have been removed, etc., etc.

* Professor Koch says that he sees "no reason why" in England and in Germany tuberculosis should not be banished "from our midst in, say, ten years . . . without any exorbitant outlay on the part of either State."

Sixth, the construction of decent tenements, and the destruction, or satisfactory renovation, of every house known to be a source of infection, the demolition of "Lung Blocks," and the establishment of breathing spaces in the poorer districts of the cities. Seventh, a crusade of hygienic education among all people and the punishment of promiscuous spitting.

"The Great White Plague" is the result of our weakness, our ignorance, our selfishness, and our vices; there is no more need of its existence on the earth than of the existence of the Great Black Plague, the plague of typhus fever, the plague of dysentery, the plague of Asiatic cholera, the plague of leprosy, or the plague of small-pox. These other plagues have been driven from the western world, and so, too, will the Great White Plague have been, when the crusade against tuberculosis shall have enlisted a larger army of competent physicians, and of other public-spirited citizens who will give generously of their time and wealth to the prevention of this disease; or when, as in Germany, the state itself and the municipalities in the state provide the needed sanatoria for the care of its victims. It will be stamped out when the humane work of the Tenement House Department and the Health Department of this city, and of every other city, is victorious over opponents; when there is established in the mind of every one that vital principle of an advanced civilization, namely, that the profits of individuals are second in importance to the life, welfare, and prosperity of the great masses of people. It will disappear from that community which demands the destruction of an insanitary tenement regardless of inconvenience to individuals and which also demands that there shall be no dark and windowless rooms within its boundaries under any condition whatsoever, as a result of any plea, or as a favor to private interests great or small.

Tuberculosis has continued so long in the world because the individual man, and communities made up of men, thinking individually, cannot in their hearts appreciate the wickedness and the sorrow which are both cause and result of the White Plague. Ruskin truly says : " People would instantly care for others as well as themselves if only they could imagine others as well as themselves. Let a child fall into the river before the roughest man's eyes; he will usually do what he can to get it out, even at some risk to himself; and all the town will triumph in the saving of one little life. Let the same man be shown that hundreds of children are dying of fever for want of some sanitary measure which will cost him trouble to urge, and he will make no effort; and probably all the town would resist if he did." When we are told the following story by one who has worked among the consumptives of our largest city, and who knows that it is typical of hundreds

N

and thousands of wretched, poverty-stricken people, .
have we no incentive to do all that we can, individually
and in association with others, to stamp out so devastating an affliction as that of the needless and preventable Great White Plague?

"THE PRAYER OF THE TENEMENT [1]

"'Breath — breath — give me breath.' A Yiddish
whisper, on a night in April, 1903, from the heart
of the New York Ghetto.

"At 18 Clinton Street, back in the rear tenement,
a young Roumanian Jew lay dying of consumption.
I had come in with a Jewish doctor. With every
breath I felt the heavy, foul odor from poverty, ignorance, filth, disease. In this room ten feet square
six people lay on the floor packed close, rubbing
the heavy sleep from tired eyes, and staring at us
dumbly. Two small windows gave them air, from
a noisome court — a pit twenty feet across and five
floors deep. The other room was only a closet six
feet by seven, with a grated window high up opening on an air-shaft eighteen inches wide. And in
that closet four more were sleeping, three on a bed,
one in a cradle.

"'Breath — breath — give me breath.' The man's
disease was infectious; and yet for two long weeks
he had lain here dying. From his soiled bed he
could touch the one table where the two families

ate; the cooking stove was but six feet from him; the cupboard, over his pillow; he could even reach one of the cradles, where his baby girl lay staring frightened at his strange position. For his wasted body was too feeble to rise; too choked, too tortured, to lie down. His young wife held him up while the sleepers stared silently on, and that Yiddish whisper came over and over again, but now with a new and more fearful meaning. 'Breath — breath — breath. Or kill me; oh, kill me!'

"Two years ago this man had come to America — one of the four hundred and eighty-eight thousand in 1901. He came young and well and hopeful, with his wife and their baby son. Two more had been born since then. It was to be a new country, a new home, a fresh start, a land to breathe in. 'Breath — breath — give me breath.' He had breathed no air here but the close, heavy air of the sweatshop from six in the morning until ten at night. Sometimes — he whispered — he worked on until eleven. He was not alone. In New York to-day and to-night are over fifty thousand like him working. And late in the night when he left the feverish labor, at the hour when other homes are sleeping, he had come in through the foul court and had sunk into restless sleep in the dark closet six feet by seven. There are three hundred and sixty-one thousand such closets in the city. And this was his home.

"'Luft — giebt mir luft.' He spoke only Yiddish. The new country had given the Plague before the language. For the sweatshop and the closet had made him weak; his weakened body could make no fight; the Plague came in and fed swiftly. Still on through the winter he had worked over the machine in the sweatshop, infecting the garments he sewed — feverish, tired, fearful — to buy food and coal, to keep his 'home' alive. And now, on this last day of life, ten times he had whispered to his brother, begging him to care for the wife and the three little children.

"The struggle now is ended. The home is scattered. The smothered whisper is forever hushed. 'Breath — breath — give me breath.' It speaks the appeal of thousands."

Unquestionably the responsibility, whether for the sanitary conditions of the tenements, the sanitary conditions of the workshops, or for the rendering of industrial processes less dangerous, is definitely a social one. The individual alone is powerless. Fevers and plagues will continue to afflict mankind until the community itself is aroused to demand wise and humane legislation, providing for the most thorough preventive measures. The individual cannot make laws for the community; he is very greatly dependent upon the common water supply; he is dependent upon the action of the

community to insure to him and to others pure air,
an abundance of light, cleanliness of streets and
surroundings, the provision of good sewerage and
efficient plumbing. Society must protect him from
poisonous vapors and odors, arising from decompos-
ing animal and vegetable matter and from offensive
trades, such as slaughtering, etc.; he must depend
upon the sanitary authorities to prevent adulteration
and to guarantee to him and to others pure food.
The sanitary authorities alone can prevent dangers
to health from those insanitary conditions arising
as a result of street excavations, privies, stables,
accumulated garbage and dead animals. The community alone has the power to compel an individual
to keep the tenement he owns in a wholesome and
sanitary condition; it alone can legislate and it
alone can enforce sanitary conditions in mines,
workshops, and factories. The individual of the
present day is dependent upon society for all of
these preventive, sanitary measures. Whatever may
be the weaknesses in socialism as applied to industry, socialism is now demanded by every one to
protect the health of the community and to make
wise and far-reaching provisions for the physical
welfare of all the people.

There is now a pretty general realization of the
necessity for social action to stamp out disease
whenever it is epidemic and to employ preventive

measures whenever a disease threatens to become epidemic. Social action has already extinguished a long list of epidemic diseases which in former times caused a dreadful mortality. The great epidemic diseases of the Middle Ages, which destroyed nations almost, have been exterminated. Cholera, typhus fever, small-pox, and dysentery have been so reduced that they now affect but small numbers of people. Even yellow fever has been reduced and can be practically stamped out by proper sanitary measures. A reduction, within the last few decades, in the number of deaths due to tuberculosis is one of the striking achievements of modern sanitary science. All of these diseases are contagious or infectious, and, perhaps for that reason more than for any other, the community has been spurred to lively and associated action. There is still, however, a formidable list of preventable diseases, such as scarlet fever, diphtheria, measles, whooping-cough, and summer diarrhœa, which cause widespread sickness. In addition to the crusade against these forms of sickness, the prevention of accidents in industry and of certain diseases resulting from dangerous trades and insanitary homes and work-places are fields of promise for the sanitarian and for community action. These latter forms of sickness are, however, not as a rule contagious or infectious, and therefore reform moves slowly, held back as it is by the many obstructions set in its path by selfish landlords and manufacturers. Such greed is plainly responsible for high death rates and for much sickness and poverty.

Unnecessary disease and death are mainly active in bringing misery to the working classes and especially to those in poverty. The well-to-do classes are relatively free from preventable, disease-producing conditions of work and of living. It is questionable whether, in the long run, the well-to-do classes, who own the tenements, the mines, and the factories, are really adding to their profits by resisting sanitary improvements, and by refusing, whenever possible, to remedy conditions which undermine the health and increase the death rate of the working people. To put it upon this criminally low commercial basis, even that is questionable. An increase of population is profitable to the owners of tenements; they see this very clearly when they support, as some of them do, unrestricted immigration. A large immigration means an increasing demand for tenements; but so does a decreased death rate. And yet, for the sake of profits, they often support unrestricted immigration and oppose measures for decreasing the death rate. The cost of sickness, now a loss to both landlord and tenant, might go toward an increased rental for a more sanitary tenement. The financial burden of sickness

is considerable even among well-to-do people. The
workmen, with their smaller purses, must bear far
heavier burdens. But the loss to the world of productive laborers, and the financial loss by sickness,
are after all as nothing compared to the crime of
unnecessarily and unconcernedly adding to the number of widows and to the number of the fatherless.

The entire matter sums itself up very easily. In the
first place, we put property before human life; we
unconsciously estimate it more highly and foster
it more tenderly; we do it as individuals and we do
it collectively. The railroads consider the Block
System of signals and automatic couplers unwarranted luxuries because profits are valued more
than the lives of the workmen. " The sanitary
improvements which this law forces on us will ruin
us," the landlords and manufacturers say, when a
law is proposed to remedy the insanitary conditions
of home and workshop. They will not, of course.
Such laws never have, although many of the most
important sanitary measures of the last hundred
years have been opposed on these grounds. But
suppose they did? Must we then withdraw our
sanitary measure and continue to sacrifice certain
human beings in order that other human beings
may make profits? A few years ago I urged that
a certain tenement be destroyed because it was vile
and insanitary and caused about eight unnecessary

deaths every year. An officer answered my complaint in these words: "To demolish this tenement would do a great injury to the widow woman who owns it. It is her only property." Now murder is murder — whether the killing is done by a tenement or carbolic acid, whether in hatred and revenge or in cold blood, for a certain price or for profits, for the benefit of a rich man's purse or for the last crust which a widow may ever hope to have. As I understand it, THOU SHALT NOT KILL admits of no exceptions. It applies to the man who makes profits by the killing as truly as it applies to the hold-up man.

This evil, as indeed most evils, is rooted in the old, old sins and in the old, old crimes. They are merely in new guises. Murder, Adultery, and Thievery have so disguised themselves that we do not recognize them. No one can help knowing that sickness is caused by vile tenements, by dangerous employments and insanitary workshops; every one must know also that much poverty and misery inevitably result from unnecessary sickness; furthermore, no one can fail to know that an excessive number of deaths occur among the work-people employed in certain industries and living in certain tenements. The cause and effect are clear. Then why does not the owner or employer remedy the cause of the sickness, poverty, and death? "He

probably does not know it exists," is the ordinary
answer. But it is no answer. Attempt to remedy
the evils by legislation, or by enforcement of the
laws, and then you begin to realize that you are in
a fight, and that, for one reason or another, the
landlords and employers are against you. Every
movement you make is watched and attacked.
Even bribery will be used to defeat sanitary measures; that is to say, measures to save life. Now
the conclusion one is forced to draw from an experience of that sort is not a pleasant one, but the logic
by which one reaches the conclusion seems clear
and certain. These men are murderers.

Mr. Jacob A. Riis says, "You can kill a man
with a tenement as easily as you can kill a man with
an axe." But in the one case there is no concern.
The newspapers do not mention the murder and no
one is indicted or sent to prison. In the other case
the whole town is more than likely to be in a fever
of excitement. By preventing legislation, or by
using influence or bribes to prevent enforcement,
a man may kill thousands of human beings and still
be considered perfectly respectable; he may remain
a member of the best uptown clubs, and free to go
on repeating his crimes; but Heaven help the man
who uses the axe! We are deceived by the use of
new methods in killing. One is a social method for
the sake of profits; the other the use of individual

physical force. It would seem as if we had arrived at the point where a social act may be understood. Almost every important act to-day is a social act and the most important crimes are social crimes. Ruskin has put the whole matter into powerful words : " A great nation, for instance, does not spend its entire national wits for a couple of months in weighing evidence of a single ruffian's having done a single murder; and for a couple of years, see its own children murder each other by their thousands or tens of thousands a day, considering only what the effect is likely to be on the price of cotton, and caring nowise to determine which side of battle is in the wrong. Neither does a great nation send its poor little boys to jail for stealing six walnuts and allow its bankrupts to steal their hundreds or thousands with a bow, and its bankers, rich with poor men's savings, to close their doors ' under circumstances over which they have no control ' with a ' by your leave '; and large landed estates to be bought by men who have made their money by going with armed steamers up and down the China Seas, selling opium at the cannon's mouth, and altering, for the benefit of the foreign nation, the common highwayman's demand of ' your money *or* your life,' into that of ' your money *and* your life.' Neither does a great nation allow the lives of its innocent poor to be parched out of them by fog fever, and rotted out of them by dunghill plague, for the sake of sixpence a life extra per week to its landlords ; and then debate, with drivelling tears, and diabolical sympathies, whether it ought not piously to save, and nursingly cherish, the lives of its murderers." [1]

These are terrible words, and we are just awakening to their awful truth. We ourselves, and especially our penal laws, put most things on an individualistic basis, because our thoughts, our moral principles, and our laws have been moulded in an individualistic society which has largely passed away. Only an individual man killing an individual man, or an individual stealing from an individual, or an adulterer injuring an individual, is censured and punished. The injustice lies in the killing, the stealing, or the degradation of a human being, and not in the method by which it is done. The evils of gambling are not less evil because a "public service" corporation makes it possible, nor is killing less terrible because it happens in a Southern cotton-mill owned by Northern capital, or in a tenement owned, but perhaps never seen, by one of our wealthiest citizens. Public property obtained by grab-bills, or by bribery, is not less stolen property than the revenue of a pickpocket. A man who causes adultery by paying his working-girls starvation wages, which must be increased, if in no other way, by sin, is not less injurious to the community than the procuress. I do not believe that the mass of the men who are responsible for these things know what they are doing. But most of our present-day social ills are due to these old sins and old crimes masquerading in unfamiliar guise.

This loss of life, so much of which is unnecessary, these heavy burdens which sickness lays upon the wage-earning classes in particular, and this bitter poverty of the widows and the fatherless, which follows so often upon sickness,—these are things which point to terrible social crimes and also fortunately to remedies which are immediately at hand and obvious.

CHAPTER V

THE CHILD

" Sweet are the uses of adversity,
    Which, like the toad, ugly and venomous,
    Wears yet a precious jewel in his head."

THIS adversity is necessary to men. Difficulties
and struggles, simple fare and simple living, are good
for men; but poverty — the poverty of which we
have been speaking — is without its jewel and is both
unlovely and venomous. And this is more true of
the child of poverty than it is of the man. However sad and miserable that poverty is which undermines the power and usefulness of men, it is a slight
thing compared to that poverty which blights and
ruins childhood. It will be recalled that in those
streets and courts and alleys in which the inebriate,
the blind, the crippled, the consumptive, and the
aged — the ragged ends of life — live, there also live
the half-starved, underclad beginnings in life. The
poverty which kills, which makes terrible the end
of life, is not so terrible as the poverty which
blackens and stifles childhood and casts a shadow
over all the after life. Poverty degrades all men

who struggle under its yoke, but the poverty which oppresses childhood is a monstrous and unnatural thing, for it denies the child growth, development, strength; it robs the child of the present and curses the man of the future.

And yet wherever there is a man in poverty there are several children. There are more children than adults in the world, and the same holds true of those in poverty. If there are indeed ten million persons in this country underfed, underclothed, and badly housed, the great majority are children who have neither violated social laws nor committed any sin. There are children in every stage of poverty — from the lowest and most vicious, to the highest, most clean, and self-respecting. The child product of the lowest is the street Arab, the waif, or gamin, — the child who is stunted in body and crooked in mind. He belongs to a type which is almost universal, and, when Shaftesbury describes the London waif, or Hugo the gamin of Paris, we recognize in him the tramp-child of our own cities. " He lives in bands," Hugo says, "roams the streets, lodges in the open air, wears an old pair of trousers of his father's, which descend below his heels, an old hat of some other father, which descends below his ears, a single suspender of yellow listing; he runs, lies in wait, rummages about, wastes time, blackens pipes, swears like a convict, haunts the wine-shop, knows thieves,

calls gay women *thou*, talks slang, sings obscene
songs, and has no evil in his heart." But these
children are waifs, many of whom have severed their
connection with home life.

There are others, many above the waif and some
perhaps even below him, the beaten, cowed, and
starved child of the inebriate, for instance, — all of
whom suffer the evils of poverty. It seems to me
sometimes that all children from the tenements, and
even from many apartment houses, should be classed
in poverty, not because they are underfed, underclothed, or badly housed, for the majority are not,
but because they have been forgotten, their play-
space has been taken up and no excuse made, nor
has any substitute been supplied. When the city
came to be the abode of men, the child was given
the common to replace the fields; as the city grew
in size, the child was pushed from the common into
the small yard, and from the yard he has been thrust
into the street. And now the street life is the most
conspicuous and universal thing in the child life
of New York City. There are not less than half
a million children in Greater New York whose only
playground is the street. As the most widespread
evil of child life in the largest cities, and as a kind
of poverty, — since play is a necessity to childhood, —
let us consider what this lack of play-space means in
the way of injury to the child.

There has been a great deal said in recent years about the importance of play as a powerful educative influence in the development of children. Not only, of course, is play recognized as a necessity to the child, but it has been proved, beyond reasonable doubt, that the child in play cultivates naturally his mental, moral, and physical life. The widest and most varied opportunities for play have surrounded the child for centuries in the country life. In the last century the growth of large cities has deprived the child of these opportunities. Except for a few parks and playgrounds, the street is all that is left to the playing child, and the street gang is his organization for purposes of play. This gang is the really vital influence in the life of most boys in the large cities. Every street and neighborhood in the tenement districts of New York has such a gang. Mr. Brewster Adams, formerly of the University Settlement, has recently published a very instructive paper on "The Street Gang as a Factor in Politics." He points out the "Chrysties," the "City Halls," the "Cherry Hills," the "Elizabeths," the "Leonards," the "Mott Streets," the "Mulberry Bends," the "Catherines," the "Pearl Streets," and many other gangs with names which indicate their preëmpted playgrounds. They have no purpose except to play, and this means, with the children in these districts, to "steal, to destroy, even to stab or

o

shoot . . . if done in a worthy (?) cause, in the name of the gang." To illustrate the type of children in these gangs, Mr. Adams says: "'Little Spec,' who lives in a tenement down on James Street, has suffered violence at the hands of the 'Mott Streets,' the most dangerous gang of boys under fourteen in lower New York. 'Dere's a guiney over at de Points [Five Points] what cut me wid a knife,' he tells his friends on James Street. 'Us kids will get togedder and go over dere, and we won't do much but make circles around dat gang,' responds Hiteye, his friend, who lives in the next flat, and Hiteye leads the gang." [1]

It is the life of the street, in a city which has forgotten the child, that develops, as Mr. Jacob A. Riis says, "dislike of regular work, physical incapability of sustained effort, misdirected love of adventure, gambling propensities, absence of energy, and untrained will, carelessness of the happiness of others." Dr. Elisha Harris referred to the same matter as early as 1866 when he said, before a New York Legislative Committee: "The younger criminals seem to come almost exclusively from the worst tenement-house districts. When the great riot occurred in 1863, every hiding-place and nursery of crime discovered itself by immediate and active participation in the operations of the mob. Those very places and domiciles, and all that are like them, are to-day nurseries of crime, and of the vices and disorderly courses which lead to crime. By far the largest part, 80 per cent at least, of crimes against property and against the person are perpetrated by individuals who have either lost connection with home life, or never had any, or whose homes have ceased to be sufficiently separate, decent, and desirable to afford what was regarded as ordinary wholesome influences of home and family."

It is the great, homeless, yardless tenement — the nursery of crime, Dr. Harris has called it — which causes the greatest injury to city children. The collapse of home life in the vicious districts, and the necessity which compels both mother and father, among the poorest classes of working people, to work early and late, bereave the child of every good influence except that of the school, or, by chance, that of the settlement. The little ones are left to range at will in the tenements and streets. This freedom can hardly be good for them; for in the crowded quarters of the yardless tenement the children suffer manifold restrictions and are in contact with conditions, physical and moral, which predispose them to criminality. Because of these and other reasons the extent of juvenile crime in these districts is enormous. Crowded in the tenements where the bedrooms are small and often dark, where the living-room is also a kitchen, a laundry, and often a garment-making shop,

are the growing children whose bodies cry out for
exercise and play. They are often an irritant to the
busy mother, and likely as not the object of her carp-
ing and scolding. The teeming tenements open their
doors, and out into the dark passageways and courts,
through foul alleys and over broken sidewalks,
flow ever renewed streams of playing children.
Under the feet of passing horses, under the wheels
of passing street cars, jostled about by the pedestrian,
driven on by the policeman, they annoy every one.
They crowd about the music or drunken brawls in
the saloons, they play hide-and-seek about the garbage boxes, they "shoot craps" in the alleys, they
seek always and everywhere activity, movement,
life.[1]

This using of the main open spaces as playgrounds
is critically called "the street habit." But both it
and "the gang habit" are at first perfectly innocent
and natural results of the crowded tenements and
of the universal necessity for play. Now a healthy
expression in play of the mental, physical, and moral
faculties of the children of the tenements is at present almost impossible. In consequence they break
windows, they ring door-bells, they steal, they especially rejoice in "making it warm" for the unpopular
neighbor who displeases them. They annoy every
one because they are not reckoned with in the city's
scheme of things. Only within the last few days one

child was crushed by a truck, another killed by
an automobile, and still another child, while playing with her kitten on the roofs of some tenement
houses, fell into a chimney and was buried alive.
Every day brings its horrors because children must
steal their play-space from a thoughtless and selfish
community.

The newspaper reports of crimes, immoralities, and
death often bear with them evidence of how little
provision is made to satisfy this play-hunger of childhood. Our gardens are given a place apart; flowers
and plants are tended and drawn out by wise hands,
which supply unobtrusive and safe guidance; but the
childhood of our city is without its place, without its
tending, and without its guidance, and, in innocent
play, tangles itself up in the shaftings and cogs of our
business.

In the failure to satisfy this need of the children
with properly equipped municipal playgrounds, the
street habit and the gang habit become the causes,
not only of many unnecessary deaths, but also of a
large percentage of juvenile crimes. Sneak-thievery
and many other forms of vice and wickedness run
their course in these gangs of the tenements with
epidemic power; for to contagious diseases of all
sorts, moral and physical, tenements furnish the line
of least resistance. Without the saving influence of
an attractive home or playground, whatever mental

and moral food they get, they obtain from the life of the streets. It impresses itself upon them, and they reproduce it all; gambling, drinking, the vaudeville, the fighting, the torchlight processions — whatever they see, good and bad alike, they imitate.

It is in this spirit of play that the children commit most of their petty crimes. When one of them is caught stealing, he is brought to the Children's Court. He is taken away from father and mother and the tenement and sent to a Reform (?) School, where, in certain cities, he is put behind iron bars and uniformed guards are placed over him just as if he were a wild animal. And this is often the innocent beginning of a life of crime. Sir Thomas More asked several centuries ago, "I pray you, what other thing do you than make thieves and then punish them?" This was never so pertinent a question as now. The city child becomes criminal because it can almost be said that in these districts the only things to do worthy of a boy's spirit are those things which are against the law. At any rate, the victim of overcrowding sees little difference between the laws which prevent him from "flipping" on and off street cars or playing ball in the streets, and those which prohibit truancy, stealing, etc. He does see that whatever depends upon bravado, which all boys love, is looked down upon by the policeman. The causes of crime are many, but among the most important ones are the evil associations of the tenement, the bad sanitary conditions, the collapse of home life, and lastly, the yardless tenement itself.

These evils of child life are doubly serious and dangerous because the mass of people in poverty in our cities are immigrants. The children of immigrants are a remarkable race of little ones. They are to become Americans, and through them, more than through any other agency, their own parents are being led into a knowledge of American ways and customs. All the statistics available prove that vice and crime are far more common among the children of immigrants than among the children of native parentage, and this is due no less to the yardless tenement and the street playground than it is to widespread poverty.[1] In a mass of cases the mother and father both work in that feverish, restless way of the new arrival, ambitious to get ahead. To overcome poverty they must neglect their children. Turned out of the small tenement rooms into the street, the child learns the street. Nothing escapes his sharp eyes, and, almost in the briefest conceivable time, he is an American ready to make his way by every known means, good and bad. To the child everything American is good and right. There comes a time when the parents cannot guide him or instruct him; he knows more than they; he looks upon their advice as of no value. If ever

there was a self-made man, that man is the son of
the immigrant. But the street and the street gang
have a great responsibility; they are making the
children of a hundred various languages from every
part of the world into American citizens.

These present-day problems of the child — the
cities, the coming of immigrants, the collapse of
home life, the yardless tenement — are all due to
one underlying cause. There has been an entire
revolution in industry during the last century, and
nearly all the social problems of child life have
grown up as a result of this revolution. The best
thought of this entire period has been given to
industrial development, — to economy, wealth, profits,
and wages. That the needs of the child have been
overlooked, if not entirely forgotten, in the readjustment of society to the new conditions, cannot be
questioned. At the risk of a slight interruption in
the discussion of the problems of child life, perhaps
it would be well to trace the recent changes in life
which have occurred, for the purpose of showing
their effect on the child and the present necessity
of important readjustments of old institutions to
these changes and of new social institutions to satisfy
the needs of the child.

A few decades ago in England and America,
practically the entire life of parents and children
— whether working, playing, or learning — was in

and about the home, and even now in certain backward industrial countries this is likewise true. The
mass of people lived in small towns, or hamlets, as
they might better be called, since that word in itself
conveys the idea of home. There were a few large
towns, but most of the population was grouped in
these small rural communities. Nearly all work was
done by hand, — manufacture. Horse-power, water-
power, and hand-power were the bases of industry.
The home fields raised the foodstuffs; killing, brew-
ing, cooking, baking, smithing, forging, spinning,
and weaving were home occupations. The home had
its own water supply; the home supplied its own
defence; the home took precautions against disease
and cared for the sick and even the insane. Social
gatherings took place in the fields near the home or
in the house itself. The children received practically
their entire education either in the home or in the
adjoining fields. Certainly in those days the child
received his best education under the supervision of
his own parents. The entire schooling, which was
necessarily restricted to the teaching of the three
R's, did not average in 1800 more than eighty-two
days for each person.[1] The children were nearly
always in the sight of their parents. Both parents
worked, and the children worked also; but the
parents could stop in their work at any time for the
purpose of instructing the children. In a word,

the home was the centre of the moral, educational, industrial, and social life.

In most of the countries of western Europe and America this is now all changed. Except in a few belated industries, the domestic workshop no longer exists, even in the country; industrial processes, except, of course, agriculture, are now carried on by large, well-organized groups of employees, in offices, factories, mills, and mines, sometimes of enormous size. Steam and electricity have displaced hand-, water-, and horse-power as the motive forces of industry. The individual workshop has given way to large coöperative methods of work. Hamlets have grown into factory towns, and the towns into cities. Millions of people in all parts of western Europe have emigrated from their homes and fields in the rural districts to the crowded centres of industry. We have now, on an enormous scale, coöperative production, a minutely organized division of labor and great aggregations of working people, laboring together in the houses of industry and dwelling together in the huge tenements of our cities. No revolution was ever before known that so completely and rapidly revolutionized the life and work of the people as this one of the last century.

When this revolution brought into the world large cities and a new industrial life, it, at the same time, destroyed what has been described as the Home.

In our largest cities *this* home no longer exists. The economic development of the last hundred years has destroyed it and left in its stead a mere shadow of what once was the source of all things essential to the world. The mills, factories, abattoirs, breweries, and bakeries took from the home the various trades ; the state supplied the defence, and the city the water supply ; the sanitarian, the surgeon, and the alienist took precaution against disease and replaced home remedies by skilled practice and medical science; the sick have hospital care, the schools undertake the instruction of the child, and the factory, etc., the technical training. The home is now a few rooms in a crowded tenement or apartment house. The fields have diminished to commons, the commons to yards, and the yards to courts and light shafts ; the tenement has become yardless. Little or nothing has replaced the social losses of the home, and the same may be said of the possibilities for recreation, which were lost with the fields and commons. A few settlements have endeavored to supply opportunities for keeping alive the neighborhood feeling; a few playgrounds have come to supply the recreative needs ; but the losses have been serious and as yet there are no sufficient substitutes. The rapidity with which this revolution has occurred is almost unbelievable. There are men now living who have seen the working out of the whole industrial process.

Every one of these changes has had its effect upon
the child. Although, in the working out of this
process, the child was never once thought of, the
revolution has vitally changed the environment and
conditions of child life. We are in an era of great
cities, and in a few years the mass of our population
will live in cities. In these changes from the home
to the factory, from the cottage to the tenement, and
from the country to the city, the needs of childhood
have been forgotten. Imagine a child in a great
city, cities that are, as Ruskin has said, "mere
crowded masses of store and warehouse and counter;
and therefore to the rest of the world what the larder
and cellar are to a private house; cities in which the
object of men is not life, but labor; and in which all
chief magnitude of edifice is to enclose machinery;
cities in which the streets are not the avenues for
the passing and procession of a happy people, but
the drains for the discharge of a tormented mob, in
which the only object in reaching any spot is to be
transferred to another; in which existence becomes
mere transition, and every creature is only one atom
in a drift of human dust and current of interchanging
particles, circulating here by tunnels underground,
and there by tubes in the air." [1]

In the scramble to readjust ourselves to the cities
and to this new industrial life, built up as a result
of steam and electricity, the child has been for-

gotten. To a very large extent he has been left to readjust himself, and the result is a series of really appalling problems. His father now leaves the home and goes to the factory; he may not watch his father at work or work with him — and it would not be good for him if he could — until he himself is old enough to become a laborer. He is in the city instead of in the country. He has lost the playgrounds which nature lavishly furnished, — the hills, valleys, and woodland, the thousand varieties of plants and animals, the streams, the blue sky over all, even the starry night. Bored by the homeless tenement, he finds himself on an asphalt pavement, in a crowded street, amid roars of excitement, — in a playground alive with business with which he must not interfere. But he plays; the street is interesting, garbage boxes and lamp-posts have a place in his games, and the child is happy, God bless him.

These changes in the living and working conditions of the people and these changes in the environment of the child demand new agencies for the care of the child and a series of important readjustments of the social and educational institutions to the altered economic conditions. Certain social institutions have already readjusted themselves, but the distinctly educational institutions have been slow to change. All institutions for the common good undertaken by the community have developed more slowly than those institutions which have been initiated by individuals for the purpose of gaining profits. Parks, playgrounds, baths, recreation centres, athletic fields, gymnasia, social halls, play centres, crèches, the social use of schools and school excursions to the country, have developed more slowly than saloons, theatres, public dance halls, rapid transit, etc., because there is no possibility of large profits in developing the former institutions, so necessary especially to the children. The great cities need social statesmen who, seeing the evils of child life, will bring about, through public agencies, the new institutions required to save the rising generations from crime, street life, physical degeneration, and all the other evil results of the worst phases of city life.

If the school were to assume a larger responsibility for the child, it would find it necessary to begin with nurseries to care for those smaller children whose parents must go out to work. One evening, in an effort to visit a blind man whom I knew, I felt my way up the stairs of an old tenement in one of the poorer districts of New York. Those to whom I spoke seemed not to know him, so I inquired from door to door. Finding a door open, on one of the upper floors, I walked in and lighted a match to see my way. Directly in front of me lay a small baby

half covered with rags. It startled me. No one was
about, and the room was almost bare. I knocked
at an adjoining door and inquired where the mother
of the child was. A youngster of twelve years came
to the door, and in answer to my question said,
"Ah, de mudder of de kid cleans offices downtown,
and me sister goes to de kid when it yells." "Where
is your sister?" I asked. "I dunno! Say, mudder,
where's Maime?" cried the boy. "She's gone out
for the evening," the mother responded. Nothing
else is required to show the necessity. There are a
thousand similar cases.

In Paris the *Écoles Maternelles* and the *Classes de
Garde* have been formed for those children whose
parents are employed during the day. In the latter
the children are kept as long as necessary both day
and night.[1] However much we may deplore this
annihilation of the home caused by both parents
finding it necessary to become wage-earners, it is at
present far too common among the poorest workers,
and, until economic reform makes it unnecessary, the
school must be looked to as the one social agency
having power to save the children from the neglect
which the poverty of the parents necessitates.

Following upon these educational institutions for
assisting in parental care, another development is
necessary, — the furnishing of recreation, play, and
social centres for all the children of the street.

There has been a small and almost unworthy beginning in these developments of the social use of schools. This latter work has been pressed upon the authorities. It has not developed from a spirit within. The settlements, the women's clubs, and other organizations have been continuously holding up to the school its obligation to the child of the tenement. Even the proposals of Mr. Jacob A. Riis, supported by his knowledge of conditions in the poorer districts, have received too little consideration from the municipal authorities and even from the teachers themselves. The schools of New York City, the most important and vital instruments for advancing social welfare, are closed from one-half to two-thirds of the time between eight in the morning and ten at night. Here is a social plant, owned by the people and valued at close to $60,000,000, which is out of use during a majority of the available time. It is the use of the schools during this idle time that is demanded by those interested in the street boys and their gangs in the tenement districts. It is absolutely necessary for the social losses of the home to be replaced by the school if the children are to be saved from the worst evils of city and street life. Let the municipal authorities who are responsible for the proper financial support of the schools bear in mind what the great educators have said about play as an educative influence in the development of children. If what they say is true, it is inexcusable to permit the schools to be closed when the children have time to play. If the schools will not guide the play, it is one of the ironies of city life that play will do more than they to educate the child.

These problems of child life are school problems. They sum themselves up in the questions: Are we to have the school ignore this larger work of education and remain a sort of dispensary of learning — an inflexible missionary of the three R's? Will it, because of financial embarrassment, be forced to give itself only half-heartedly and slovenly to these new problems of education, or is it to take, as its responsibility, the entire problem of child life and master it? If the school does not assume this responsibility, how shall the work be done? The reason for the present neglect of these vital matters is, it seems to me, ignorance rather than unconcern. The city fathers do not appreciate the new social needs, and the teachers, as a class, are lacking in a knowledge of industrial history and social evolution. They have not realized that the home is passing away and that, unless the school takes the child, he is left to the street. They have specialized in philosophy, pedagogy, and psychology. They have isolated themselves from contact with those in poverty. I could not wish for a better example of these facts than that

P

furnished by a principal, who said recently (according to the daily papers): "With all the play centres provided by the Board of Education, crime is on the increase. The parents are anxious for some agency to take their children day or night. Don't mistake this for love of education. It is *parental selfishness that is throwing the burden, and the righteous burden, of the home upon the schools.*" It is almost inconceivable that a principal in our schools should know so little of the problems of the city child. He apparently does not know the tenement, — the yardless, homeless tenement, — and one fears that he may not know the rudiments of his obligations as an educator. But if he were the only one in ignorance, we should be fortunate indeed. As a matter of fact the Police Magistrates, the Board of Education, the Board of Estimate and Apportionment, as well as the teachers seem to be entirely unconscious of this industrial revolution which has entirely altered the conditions of child life, and they look upon these new problems as a result of parental selfishness, and upon the increase of juvenile crime as a result of parental neglect, and so on, never seeming to realize that the whole thing is a product of social evolution, and that the charge of neglect must rest upon the community and the school, and not, in most cases, upon the parent.

There are many other illustrations which I could

give of this ignorance of the teachers concerning
those problems of childhood which arise as a result
of changed social conditions. One more will suffice.
The problems of education differ widely in the various sections of our large cities. The education of
the well-to-do children is a different problem from
the education of the children of the poor. And
a similar difference exists between the educational
requirements of the native and the foreign children.
The schools have not, however, made an effort to
adapt themselves to the peculiar needs and abilities
of the various classes and nationalities. At present
the same system of instruction prevails for the
Italian, the Irish, and the Jewish children. The his-
torical background of their lives is given little or no
consideration. To most members of public school
boards all children are much the same; a child is a
child; he is to have so much instruction of a certain
kind, whether he be the result of the peculiar psychi-
cal, social, or physical conditions of Italy, Roumania,
Scandinavia, Russia, or Syria. One familiar with the
homes abroad from which the immigrants have come,
and familiar, as well, with the parents and the environment of the child here, knows that the child of
one of these races may be almost as unlike the child
of another as Caliban is unlike Prosper. But, even if
the school were able at present to adapt itself to the
varying needs of the children of these many different

races, there would still be other adaptation needed.
The environment of children living in different sections of the city causes still other problems to be presented to the schools. The child of good food, of
happy and educative home surroundings, of adequate
opportunities for recreation, of freedom from night
work and from early morning toil before the opening
of school, of relief from crowded streets and saloon
brawls, is not the same child as the one born in the
poorest tenement with its degraded environment. It
does not seem possible that a child may be well
educated by a system which does not take into consideration these racial differences and these varying
conditions of environment. It is not enough for
the teacher to know the child isolated from all else.
However well he may be trained in school and college in abstract pedagogy, the teacher must also be
familiar with some of the social and industrial conditions out of which the child comes to receive his
education in school and into which he must return
when his education is finished. The isolation of the
school administration and of the school teacher from
the life of the people, from a vivifying knowledge of
the whole child and his environment, is so great as to
prevent a wise adaptation of our educational system
to the needs of the child. Education should treat
children as individuals, not as an indiscriminate mass
who must be put through a certain routine, wholly

regardless of the past of the child, and with little regard for its present or future in the life of the world. There are no specifics arranged by educational experts which will apply equally well to children of all nationalities, of varying home conditions, of varying prospects in life, of varying prospects of work, of varying material resources. There are probably no other people in the country, of equal importance to the country, who, as a class, need to be brought back to the people so much as do the teachers.

I do not mean, of course, that one race or class of children should be given a quality of education inferior to that given another race or class of children. My point is that social position, past training, environment, and heredity have contributed to the development in different races and classes of certain aptitudes, manual and mental, artistic, mechanical, commercial, and administrative, which should be directed and cultivated by those who are responsible for the education of children. In other words, each race and class has, in more or less degree, a certain peculiar essence or flavor of mind, discoverable by a discerning and wise teacher, which, if given its proper bent and lovingly cultivated, would yield to the world untold values in specially powerful aptitudes. This is an aspect of education which is peculiarly important to America with its mixture of races. An intensive cultivation of childhood would yield untold values. But, while this is true of the education of races and classes, it is even more important when applied to the training of individuals. The Italians might give to us more artists and the Poles more musicians than other races, but the individual child of whatever class or race should be given every opportunity to yield the best in any walk of life which his natural gifts make possible.

These criticisms of the educational methods now in vogue are perhaps severe in view of the fact that the school authorities have had enormous burdens thrust upon them by the rapid growth of population and especially by immigration. As a matter of fact the schools have not only been unable to assume the new responsibilities; they have also to a certain extent been unable to fulfil their primary obligations. Unfortunately no one knows to what extent. A careful estimate has been made for New York City showing that 14 per cent of all children of eleven and twelve years, considerably over one-fourth of all children of thirteen years, and more than one-half of all children of fourteen years of age are not in the public schools.[1] I am informed by the Superintendent of Schools that about two hundred thousand children are in private and parochial schools, but, as their ages are unknown, the number of children who elude the truant officers cannot even be estimated. However, the en-

forcement of the present child-labor laws has brought
out facts which show that a certain class of children,
largely, doubtless, those of immigrants and poverty-
stricken parents, receive a most inadequate education.
Several hundred children in New York City of fourteen years of age have been refused working papers
because they were unable to pass the simple literary
requirements which a child of eleven or twelve years
of age should be able to pass easily. A trade school
in New York which accepts no children under fourteen
years of age has found it necessary to teach almost
every child how to spell and how to do simple sums.
Even these beginnings in learning have not been
acquired during the several years of training in the
schools. These facts alone show that there is something radically wrong. But I am sure that the fault
does not lie altogether with the schools. There are,
no doubt, faults in the curriculum. Some of the inef-
ficiency may be due to overcrowded classes and to the
part-time classes. But these faults and shortcomings
will not alone explain the difficulty which the public schools here, and the public and church schools
abroad, have in giving even the most elementary learning and mental training to a certain class of children.
These children come from those homes of poverty in
which the irregular, hand-to-mouth existence of the
parents exercises a blighting influence over the lives
of the children. The effects of poverty are nowhere

else so clearly seen.   Poverty's misery invariably falls
heaviest upon the weakest.   The poorest children are
several inches smaller, considerably lighter, and in all
ways less developed than the children of well-to-do
parents.   The half-starved, beaten, and neglected
child of the inebriate, the physically weak child of
the consumptive, — these are most to be pitied.   But
the poverty of any family is likely to be most serious
at the very time when the children most need nurture, when they are most dependent, and when they
are obtaining the only education which they are ever
to receive.*   Guidance and supervision of the parents
are impossible because they must work ; the nurture
is insufficient because there are too many hungry
mouths to feed ; learning is difficult because hungry
stomachs and languid bodies and thin blood are not
able to feed the brain.   The lack of learning among
so many poor children is certainly due, to an important extent, to this cause.   There must be thousands
— very likely sixty or seventy thousand children — in
New York City alone who often arrive at school
hungry and unfitted to do well the work required.
This curse which poverty lays upon innocent children
is an awful one, for it means that they may not grow,
that they may not learn, and therefore that they may
not be strong enough mentally or physically. to overcome the cause of it all, — poverty.

* See Chapter I., pp. 56–57.

Many cities in England, France, Germany, Switzerland, Belgium, and Italy have been for several years feeding at the schools the poorest children, because they have discovered that underfed children cannot be taught the simplest sums or the most elementary spelling. I have just been reading a large volume — an English report of several hundred pages — on "Underfed School Children." [1] It is doubly sad reading to an American who knows that we have not even made inquiries in this country concerning this aspect of poverty. It is utter folly, from the point of view of learning, to have a compulsory school law which compels children, in that weak physical and mental state which results from poverty, to drag themselves to school and to sit at their desks, day in and day out, for several years, learning little or nothing. If it is a matter of principle in democratic America that every child shall be given a certain amount of instruction, let us render it possible for them to receive it, as monarchial countries have done, by making full and adequate provision for the physical needs of the children who come from the homes of poverty.

This child problem is the greatest of all problems. No manifestation of it is unimportant. No age and no nation has a greater responsibility nor a supremer duty than the training and education of the child. This is true even of Russia, ruled as it is by a

privileged class; but it is nowhere so true as here
and now in this democracy. The masses must and
will control a democracy. And the school must ever
be one of the most important influences in moulding the
masses. Is any man niggardly and miserly when it
comes to the question, How shall I educate my child?
Does he seek to buy education in the cheapest market
and have it supplied by machine methods? The problem of each individual parent is collectively the problem
of the nation. "My child" becomes "our children"
when we consider education socially. Is it then
possible for a good and great nation to starve and
beggar the schools, to be niggardly in the appropria-
tions for their support and advancement? President
Eliot of Harvard has written a book called "More
Money for the Public Schools," in which he shows
the need for more ample funds to enable the school
to do well the work it has now in hand. It will cost
ten times as much as it costs now to do what must be
done if the problems of child life, which arise as a
result of the factory and the tenement house, are
to be solved. There must be instead of a Board of
Learning, such as we now have under another name,
a Board of Education, which we do not have, —
whatever our school authorities call themselves, —
and the work of the new board will cost vastly more.
But what difference can that possibly make? What
is of more worth than the work which it has to do?

The instinct most to be treasured in men is the willingness to slave, to starve, and even to annihilate one's self for one's children. This is an individual virtue ripe for being socialized. As the earth — wealth, art, property, all — must, in a few years, be given over to these little ones, now learning their A-B-C's, may we not wisely use a large proportion of its income to make them worthier than ourselves to possess it ? Will learning alone make them worthier ?

Poverty, the problem of city life, the homeless and yardless tenement, the street gang, and the many other influences outside of the school, are too powerful to be overcome by a little learning. Nothing less than education is powerful enough to save the child. And " *to prepare us for complete living* is the function education has to discharge." The city child needs, as no child ever before needed, everything that education has to give, and all things that may wisely be included in the term. To make education synonymous with learning is to rob the child of the sweetest blessings of education. When we come to value education more than we value learning, the school will be the world of the child, whether working, playing, or learning.[1] In the school he will be prepared to enter fitly the world of men.

I have intentionally dwelt upon the lack of playspace in the modern city and upon the resultant evils, because " character," as Goethe says some place, " is developed in the stream of life." This stream of life is for the child the field of play. Justice or injustice, patience or impatience, kindness or cruelty, generosity or meanness, humility or vanity, courtesy or brutality, selfishness or unselfishness, good or ill temper, sincerity or insincerity, — these roots of character and of the soul of man are first grown in the play of childhood. Put learning beside character, and how unimportant, in comparison, it becomes. But the roots of character, the foundations of society, are neglected by society, while for learning, millions are spent. The provision we have made for the lesser thing is a great American institution, — the school; for the infinitely greater thing, — the street, the gutter, and the garbage box.

I would not, of course, have the community spend less for learning, — that is not the burden of my argument, — but rather that this great American institution should be developed further, so as to become also a great social institution which will feed the children hungry for play, as well as lead them in this, and in many other ways, to become trained and useful men and women. In order that the school may be given larger funds to do this greater work of education, and in order that it may not do it partly, or weakly and ineffectually, the community must see that the street life of our great cities is not the result of parental neglect or of childish viciousness, but of economic progress. I was standing one day watching some boys who were being driven from the only vacant lot in a thickly populated tenement district. The boys were protesting, and some were throwing stones at the man who was "firing 'em off" their last remnant of play-space. I spoke to a group of them gathered on the sidewalk to find out what the trouble was. "De'se goin' to put up a tenement, and den we ain't got no place to play ball," he said, and I noticed tears in his eyes. This was all very typical. Even the vacant lot, which is a great institution in most American cities, has disappeared from New York. The problems of the child which have arisen as a result of economic progress are problems for the school — the broader school for education — whose interests lie in the whole child, night and day, at work and at play. It is commonly said nowadays that the school is the one power which can save democracy. To destroy it may not be difficult, but to save it the school cannot ignore the new problems which were brought into the world by steam and electricity.

There are in the common schools of this country sixteen million children — a young American nation — the great mass of whom are never to enter the higher schools.[1] Considerably less than one per cent of our population will finally reach the university. The problem of the thorough training of these future

men and women is stupendous. The institutions,
commerce, industry, statesmanship, — all things of the
years immediately to follow, — will depend upon these
little ones, now learning their A-B-C's, and forming
their street gangs. The great and the nameless unknown, the rich and the poor, of the present generation must make way at the advent to maturity of
these children. The universities are great and powerful in their way; but how much greater and more
powerful are these common schools, training the
hearts and minds of these millions. The head of the
greatest university in New York has five thousand
students to make into men; the head of the common
schools of New York has nearly half a million children to make into citizens. If there be a great man
in this country, let us put him at this task; let us then
look up to him and support him, and call him our
foremost man, for he and those of his profession
are making the nation.

The aforegoing evils of child life result, one likes
to believe at any rate, not from any ill will, but from
poverty and from the lack of adjustment of city life to
the needs of the child. We have not realized that
the little ones need the school not only for the hours
of instruction but also for the hours of play. We
have forgotten that there must be breathing spaces
and trees and plants and flowers and gardens — for
these too must come one day. In these things the

child has suffered through our neglect, and not through brutal or premeditated actions.

The nation, however, is engaged in a traffic for the labor of children. By the introduction of the little ones into mines, factories, and mills, we do a direct evil for which we are definitely responsible. You cannot rob children of their play, any more than you can forget and neglect the children at their play, as we now do in the tenement districts, without at some time paying the penalty. When children are robbed of play time, they too often reassert their right to it in manhood, as vagabonds, criminals, and prostitutes. There is a time for work and there is a time for play. A well-known educator has said: "Play is the first and only occupation of our childhood and remains the pleasantest our whole life long. To toil like a beast of burden is the sad lot of the lowest, the most unfortunate, and the most numerous class of mortals, but this is contrary to the intent and wish of nature." [1] Whether or not it is contrary to the intent and wish of nature, at this moment, after one hundred years of war has been waged for the abolition of child slavery, over 1,700,000 children under fifteen years of age are toiling in fields, factories, mines, and workshops.*

These figures may mean little to most persons, for, as Margaret MacMillan has said, " You cannot put

* For detailed figures see Appendix E.

tired eyes, pallid cheeks, and languid little limbs into statistics; " [1] and neither can any one, by any effort of the imagination, call up before the mind's eye the human units in census figures. But if our legis-lators could, by any means whatever, be brought to see clearly the meaning of these eight words, — one million seven hundred thousand child wage-earners, — the evil would once for all disappear from this country. But they are figures which we see, and not children, and figures come before the eye and are forgotten. We should never forget one sight of a hundred of these little ones if they were marched out of the mills, mines, and factories before our eyes, or if we saw them together toiling for ten or twelve hours a day or a night for a pittance of wage; but that we do not see, and we forget figures. New York City has not so many children; all the thousands of the streets are not so many as these children of the workshops; even the massed crowds in the evening at Brooklyn Bridge are few compared with this million seven hundred thousand working children. But it is all figures again, and not tired eyes, pallid cheeks, and languid little limbs, and we forget figures.

This evil of child labor is a new evil. It was brought into existence by the factory system, as the street child was brought into existence by the tenement.* It is little more than one hundred

* Child labor now beginning in Japan, see Appendix E, p. 357.

years old. I do not mean, of course, that children never worked before the factory made child labor an evil. Children have always worked; but their labor was not an evil, but rather it was a good thing, in the earlier days. When the race was young and the battle of life was directly with nature; when the world was poor and the securing of even the most meagre livelihood meant constant struggle; when there was no other method of doing the world's work but by hand and with the aid of the simplest instruments, — inexorable necessity forced man, woman, and child to labor in order that life might be maintained. There was then need for child labor, a valid excuse for its existence. And even more than that, — for even extreme want would not have excused the child labor of that time if it had meant the ruin of the child, — the labor of the children in the days of the craftsman and artisan was educative, and the processes of learning how to weave, spin, and brew, to do the work in the fields or home, were not such as to overburden and break down the little workers. With the advent of the machine this period of harmless child labor passed away. And now in this day of steam and electrical power, when the mere force of one's hands is the most insignificant part of production, and when numberless machines are able to turn out a hundred and a thousand fold more than it was possible for men to do when aided only by the simple

Q

hand-tools, child labor has become an evil, — superflu-
ous and wicked, — a shame to our civilization and
an inexpiable crime against humanity.

Child labor has been synonymous with "child
slavery" during the entire last century. Any one
reading the literature of the previous centuries will
see that child labor was never so thought of before.
In the days of home industry it was a most natural
and proper thing that the child should be a "little
helper" to father and mother; "little brother" once
meant that, I believe. In the home fields the child
was learning how to do the work of the world, and
there was both wisdom and kindness in teaching his
little hands to master the simple industrial processes.
The work was neither dangerous nor confining,
neither a monotonous, uneducative routine, specialized, as it now is, to a hundredth part of a man, nor
was it injurious to those of tender years and tender
bodies. It was the source of the child's real and
vital education, and, as a little helper or apprentice,
the child was given attention, direction, taught the
uses and value of materials and skill of hands, so
that, in a few years, he was graduated a craftsman
with a joy-giving and dignified calling. The workshop was his school, and it was a good school, with
able and competent teachers. But what was a bless-
ing in this age became a curse in the next.

An old French writer gives us a picture of a

workman's cottage in the days of the home workshop. After telling of the good brown bread, the
milk and the honey, the wine, and the open fire on
the hearth, he says the home "flock . . . clothed
with its wool, now the women and now the children; my aunt spun it, and spun also the hemp
which made our under-dress; the children of our
neighbours came to beat it with us in the evening by
lamplight, (our own walnut trees giving us the oil,)
and . . . by the fireside, . . . while we heard
the pot boiling with sweet chestnuts in it, our grand-
mother would roast a quince under the ashes and
divide it among us children."[1] This was a home
workshop of the eighteenth century, and these children, working with the wool, were the child laborers. Compare with this picture the prison-like
factory of to-day, with great chimneys, and huge
volumes of smoke blackening the sky, the walls
trembling with the ceaseless, regular throbs of great
and intricate machines, the maze of shaftings,
pulleys, cogs, the humid artificial air, the odor of
oil and perspiration, the yelling of one operative
to another, which the din of steel jamming steel
makes it impossible to hear, the alert, strained look
of the working children, rushing from one machine
to another, from lever to roll, back and forth,
hour after hour for ten or twelve hours, day after
day, from year's end to year's end. To this and

to a thousand other like factories gather in from
the fields and streets, tens of thousands of children,
strong and happy, or weak, underfed, and miserable. Stop their play once for all, and put them
out to labor for so many cents a day or night,
and pace them with a tireless, lifeless piece of
mechanism, for ten or twelve hours at a stretch,
and you will have a present-day picture of child
labor. One other thing is essential to a realization
of the evil; the child must do one thing which is
neither of educational value nor fitted to develop
him, but on the contrary, much more likely to
dwarf and brutalize him. A vagrant whom I
once knew had for five years — from the day he
was eleven until the day he was sixteen — made
two movements of his hands each second, or
23,760,000 mechanical movements each year, and
was, at the time I knew him, at the age of thirty-
five, broken down, drunken, and diseased; but he
still remembered this period of slavery sufficiently
well to tell me that he had "paid up" for all the
sins he had ever committed "by those five years
of hell." But there is yet one thing which must
be added to the picture. Give the child a tenement
for a home in the filthy and muddy streets of an
ordinary factory town, with open spaces covered
with tin cans, bottles, old shoes, garbage, and other
waste, the gutters running sewers, and the air foul

with odors and black with factory smoke, and
the picture is fairly complete. It is a dark picture,
but hardly so dark as the reality, and if one were
to describe "back of the yards" in Chicago, or
certain mill towns or mining districts, the picture
would be even darker than the one given.

For several reasons child labor has become an
evil. From a national point of view it is a waste of
the nation's most valuable asset, — manhood. From
an industrial point of view it would, if unrestricted,
exhaust the industrial resources of the working
people. Instead of being a way to develop a strong
and powerful working class, capable and efficient
in industry, it is the one most effective way of
weakening and rendering impotent the working
forces, of undermining their capacity, and of producing an inert, inefficient mass of laborers. To
the child it is ruinous. The conditions of labor
are neither healthful nor educative; the processes
are not suited to the development of the child;
on the contrary, they undermine his strength, stifle
his mental growth, and narrow his natural versatility
to routine mechanical actions. The present organization of industry is not calculated to produce
skilled workmen, but rapid, intense, and specialized
toilers. Furthermore, the intensity of modern
methods of work, made possible by the machine,
sets a pace so fast and uninterrupted as to tax the

strength of the strongest men, and naturally, there
fore, to rack the weaker bodies of the children.
Carlyle saw this half a century ago when he said
to the owners of the cotton-mills, "Deliver me
these rickety perishing souls of infants, and let
your Cotton-trade take its chance." [1]   And lastly,
child labor is now unnecessary; we are no longer
a nation on the verge of famine, calling all hands
to work; the industrial nations are too rich in
wealth and in various forms of mechanical power
to need the frail energies of the infants.

But the profit-seeking forces are never satisfied,
and a child, at a third of the wage, can take his
father's place in many of our present-day specialized
industries. The old cotton trade, which has murdered
unknown thousands of rickety infants in the North
and in England, has opened its mills in the South,
and the whole tragedy is now being enacted all over
again.   The cotton trade is growing, the South is
prosperous, and children of from five to fourteen
years, who formerly ran wild in the fields, can now
have ten, twelve, and fourteen hours of work and
earn ten, fifteen, and twenty cents a day — in a cotton-
mill! England was once proud of this same business
and talked much of how good it was for her children
to be at work and how much the children liked it;
but latterly she has become concerned about the
physical deterioration of her people and has about

decided to weigh and measure every workman in
England to see how far she has been ruined by her
cotton and other trades.

Not less than eighty thousand children, most of
whom are little girls, are at present employed in the
textile mills of this country.[1] In the South there are
now six times as many children at work as there were
twenty years ago. Child labor is increasing yearly
in that section of the country. Each year more
little ones are brought in from the fields and hills
to live in the degrading and demoralizing atmosphere
of the mill towns. Each year more great mills are
being built to reap the profits which these little hands
make possible. In one Southern town there are five
great mills and five settlements of workers — "pest-
ridden, epidemic-filled, filthy" settlements "to be
shunned like the plague"; each with its poverty-
stricken, hungry-looking wage-slaves; and each with
its group of box-houses, looking all alike and built
high above the malarial clay-mud. Tin cans, rubbish,
filth, are strewn everywhere inside and outside the
houses. The great mills shriek at 4.45. The men,
women, and children turn out of bed or rise from
mattresses on the floor, gulp down some handfuls of
food, and leave the home for the mills. Sleepy, half-
awake, frowsy girls, sleepy, yawning, half-dressed
children, drowsy, heavy men and women, hurry
along in crowds to be in time to begin their twelve or

more hours of continuous work. "The day in winter
is not born when they start their tasks; the night
has fallen long before they cease. In summer they
are worked far into the evenings." And after the
day of labor "they are too tired to eat, and all they
want to do is to turn their aching bones on to their
miserable mattresses and sleep."[1]

In the worst days of cotton-milling in England the
conditions were hardly worse than those now existing
in the South. Children — the tiniest and frailest —
of five and six years of age rise in the morning and,
like old men and women, go to the mills to do their
day's labor; and when they return home, they wearily fling themselves on their beds, too tired to take
off their clothes. Many children work all night —
"in the maddening racket of the machinery, in an
atmosphere insanitary and clouded with humidity and
lint."[2] It will be long before I forget the face of a
little boy of six years, with his hands stretched forward to rearrange a bit of machinery, his pallid face
and spare form showing already the physical effects
of labor. This child, six years of age, was working
twelve hours a day in a country which has established in many industries an eight hour day for men.
The twelve-hour day is almost universal in the South,
and about twenty-five thousand children are now
employed on twelve-hour shifts in the mills of the
various Southern states. The wages of one of these

children, however large, could not compensate the
child for the injury this monstrous and unnatural
labor does him; but the pay which the child receives
is not enough, in many instances, even to feed him
properly. If the children fall ill, they are docked for
loss of time. And if, "for indisposition or fatigue,
they knock a day off, there is a man hired (by the
mill) especially for this purpose, who rides from house
to house to find out what is the matter with them, to
urge them to rise, and, if they are not literally too sick
to move, they are hounded out of their beds and back to
their looms." [1] The mill-hands confess that they hate
the mills, and no one will wonder at it. A vagrant
who had worked in a textile mill for sixteen years once
said to a friend of mine: " I done that [and he made a
motion with his hand] for sixteen years. At last I
was sick in bed for two or three days with a fever,
and when I crawled out, I made up my mind that I
would rather go to hell than go back to that mill."

These are in part the conditions in the South
in 1903, — a half century after Lord Shaftesbury
awakened England to the bitter wrongs of the
children of the cotton-mills, and over one hundred
years after Thomas Jefferson defined the principle
of democracy as "equal rights to all and special
privileges to none." The South is keeping this
principle by sacrificing her children's rights and
guaranteeing to Northern capital the special privi-

leges of cheap labor. The history of child labor, when written, will be a tragedy of toil in which the bodies of children are maimed and their minds dwarfed solely that we may have cheap labor, increased profits on our capital, and a slightly reduced cost of commodities.

It is a curious fact that the people of any country can be easily aroused to protest against atrocities existing in another country. Injustice abroad causes great indignation among many of the very people who are insensible and apathetic to the injustice and cruelty in their own state and country. Many readers of Dickens will remember Muggleton, that "ancient and loyal borough, mingling a zealous advocacy of Christian principles with a devoted attachment to commercial rights; in demonstration whereof, the mayor, corporation, and other inhabitants have presented, at divers times, no fewer than one thousand four hundred and twenty petitions against the continuance of negro slavery abroad, and an equal number against any interference with the factory system at home."[1] We have had many like instances in this country. When the people of the North learned a few years ago of the conditions of child labor in the South, there was a great expression of public indignation. But while it is only fair to say that the conditions in the South are undoubtedly

worse than those in the North, there are nevertheless many conspicuous examples of child slavery
of the worst kind in almost every section of the
Union.* The South is not alone in its violation of
the Jeffersonian principle. It is violated in the
North, East, and West as well.

In the mining districts of Pennsylvania children
labor under conditions which are, if possible, even
more injurious to them than the child labor of the
cotton-mills is to the children of the South. In
the mines, mills, and factories, before the furnaces,
and in the sweatshops of Pennsylvania, that state
of colossal industrial crimes, one hundred and
twenty thousand little ones were, in the year 1900,
sacrificing a part of their right to life, most of
their right to liberty, and all of their right to happiness except perhaps of a bestial kind.[1] The
Commission appointed to settle the anthracite coal
strike of 1902 heard the cases of Theresa McDer-
mott and Rosa Zinka. These children represented,
though unknown to them, seventeen thousand little
girls under sixteen years of age, who were toiling
in the great silk-mills and lace factories of the
mining districts of Pennsylvania. The chairman
could not repress his indignation when these two
eleven-year-old children told the Commission how
they left their homes to report at the factory at

* See Appendix E.

half-past six in the evening and spent at work the long hours of the night until half-past six in the morning.[1]

The girls go to the mills, the boys to the breakers. A year or two ago Mr. Francis H. Nichols said regarding these working children: "I saw four hundred lads working in the breakers. One of the children told me, 'We go to work at seven in the morning and stay until six in the evening.'" "Are there many in the breakers younger than you?" he asked one of the children. "Why, sure, I'm one of the oldest; I'm making sixty cents. Most of them is eight and nine years old." Mr. Nichols then asked, "Did you ever go to school?" "To school?" the child echoed; "Say, mister, you must be a green hand. Why, lads in the anthracite doesn't go to school; they works in the breakers!"[1] They do not go to school, but instead they are put to work as soon as they may be trusted not to fall into the machinery and be killed. There is hardly an employment more demoralizing and physically injurious than this work in the breakers. For ten or eleven hours a day these children of ten and eleven years stoop over the chute and pick out the slate and other impurities from the coal as it moves past them. The air is black with coal dust, and the roar of the crushers, screens, and rushing mill-race of coal is deafening. Sometimes one of the children falls into the machinery and is terribly mangled, or slips into the chute and is smothered to death. Many children are killed in this way. Many others, after a time, contract coal-miner's asthma and consumption, which gradually undermine their health. Breathing continually, day after day, the clouds of coal dust, their lungs become black and choked with small particles of anthracite. There are in the United States about twenty-four thousand children employed in and about the mines and quarries.[1]

In New Jersey there is a great deal of child labor, for the reason that the law has been both inadequate and poorly enforced, if indeed not altogether ignored. The governor and others have been much aroused, in the last year or two, by numerous reports which have been made public concerning the extent of child labor. An appeal for state protection of the little ones, made public a short time ago, asserted that children of six years of age were employed in the glass factories. Great numbers of children worked all night. One factory alone, it was said, had two hundred and eighty workers, mostly children between ten and fourteen years of age. Over five thousand children are now employed as glass-workers in the United States, and most of these are at work in Pennsylvania and New Jersey. In the textile mills and in the tobacco and cigar factories, of the latter state, many thousand children are

employed. Working in tobacco is one of the employments most injurious to health. During the
recent agitation against child labor in New Jersey,
it was reported that many children working for the
American Cigar Trust fell down with weakness after
their day's labor.

New York has prided herself at various times
upon her laws restricting child labor. Two years
ago, when we began the agitation for new and better legislation, we were attacked by many as being
sentimentalists. Of all people, even the agent of
the Society for the Prevention of Cruelty to Children
felt called upon to denounce us and to say there
was no child labor in the state; but our investigations soon proved that many thousand children were
working because there was no law to protect them,
and many thousand others were working because
the law was so defective as to make it impossible of
enforcement. The new laws passed last year will
protect at least ninety-three thousand children in the
state of New York, and two hundred and thirty-one
thousand more will be benefited by the additions to
the compulsory school law. The little home-workers,
those making artificial flowers and those of the sweating trades, numbering many thousands in New York,
are as yet untouched by legislation and probably will
not be protected until the sweatshop system as a
whole is abolished. The Census for 1900 gives the

number of children under fifteen years of age at
work in New York State as nearly ninety-two thousand, but the result of our investigation three years
later showed that these figures certainly did not
include all of the working children.

The messenger and delivery boys were, previous
to 1903, unprotected by any law. Children of all
ages from eight to sixteen years were found working
almost unlimited hours at such occupations. Several
boys, striking for a shorter " day," had been working
from eighty to ninety hours a week. At the Christ-
mas season their hours were longest. At the time
of our inquiry a child was found frozen to death in a
delivery wagon. He had worked far into the night
and, being too tired to go home, lay down in his
wagon to sleep until morning. There were hundreds
of boys, under fourteen years of age, employed as
messengers. Their work often had no apparent
limit. Messengers were found who had been "on
duty continuously for twenty, thirty, thirty-two, forty,
and even seventy-two hours. The only rests during
these long periods were snatches of sleep taken
between messages on the wooden benches in the
office." Almost as this is being written the newspaper headlines announce : " Paralyzed from work.
Messenger boy lay unconscious in street for two
hours. Frank Depold . . . was found unconscious
. . . from overwork, his lower limbs temporarily

paralyzed. . . . Exhaustion, the physician said, was the cause of his condition. . . . The child thought he must have walked that day sixty miles." Our inquiries proved that the work of delivery and messenger boys was often as injurious physically as factory work, and morally it was much worse. The messengers of the "Tenderloin" district have small chance of becoming other than corrupt and vicious men.

Besides these children, upwards of seven thousand boys and girls, employed in street-trading, boot-blackening, peddling newspapers, etc., were working under conditions which made it often impossible for them to resist temptations of vice and crime. Several hundred children, pursuing street occupations, were without question descending as fast as possible into the most degraded and dangerous class in the community. Lord Shaftesbury, as a result of his investigation of the street lads of London fifty-five years ago, said, "Many of them retire for the night, if they retire at all, to all manner of places — under dry arches of bridges and viaducts, under porticoes, sheds, and carts; to outhouses; in sawpits; on staircases; in the open air; and some in lodging-houses." [1] Last year, in New York, Buffalo, and Chicago, children were found in precisely the same conditions that existed in London over half a century ago. These lads suffered few, if any, of the evils

which result to the factory worker ; but the temptations surrounding them in their work were fast
making of them petty thieves, loafers, and gamblers.
They broke all home ties, refused to continue in
school, and entered upon a street career which could
end only in making them diseased, drunken, and
shiftless vagrants and mendicants.

It is not my purpose in this chapter to mention
in detail the evil effects upon the child of exhausting toil amid conditions injurious to him mentally,
physically, or morally ; nor is it necessary or possible
to describe the conditions which surround him while
at work. Perhaps it would be well, however, to
mention the numbers of children, under fifteen years
of age, who are compelled to work in the various employments that are generally recognized as being in
themselves injurious.[1] Over 7000 children in this
country are working in laundries, some of which are
in basements, and nearly all of which are insanitary
and badly ventilated; nearly 2000 are working in
bakeshops, and the conditions here, as in the laundries,
are generally injurious to the health of adults as well
as of children ; 367 are employed in saloons as bar-
tenders and in other ways, and over 138,000 work as
waiters and servants in hotels and restaurants, in
both of which trades the hours are long and the
conditions often morally bad, especially for children ;
42,000 are employed as messengers, with work hours

R

often unlimited and the temptations to which they are exposed leading them often to immorality and vice; 20,000 are employed in stores.

While these trades injure the child in many ways, there are others which so endanger the child's health as often to render him incapable of future usefulness. The best examples are perhaps the following: On the railroads about 2500 children are employed; over 24,000 are working in mines and quarries; over 5000 are working in the glass factories; about 10,000 are employed in saw-mills and in the wood-working industries; over 7500 are employed in the iron and steel mills, and over 11,000 are working in cigar and tobacco factories. As has been mentioned before, over 80,000 children are engaged in the textile industry. Without exception all of these various employments are physically injurious to childhood. But the child is injured in still another way. He has been cut off by his work from all further opportunities for learning. His days of schooling are over, and he has once for all begun a life of labor which may not end until he is rendered incapable of industrial usefulness by age or some misfortune, such as injury or ill health.

Any one can realize what must be the effect upon the child's plastic body and pliable mind of hard work in the stunting or vicious surroundings of the above-mentioned trades. But in addition to such unavoidable evils connected with child labor, the above-mentioned dangerous trades cause yearly a great number of serious injuries and unnecessary deaths among the children. This country, as has been fully shown elsewhere, is far behind European countries in provisions to protect the life and health of factory employees. There are thousands of unnecessary deaths in this country and tens of thousands of needless accidents for no other reason whatever but that the owners of factories are not compelled by law to protect the workers in dangerous trades. To the child these dangers are ever menacing in all the industrial employments. We again and again hear of children's hands being taken off in stamping factories. Unguarded machinery of various kinds is maiming little ones for life. Several years ago it was estimated that from fifty to sixty were killed or injured daily through accidents occurring by operating buzz-saws. The materials used in frame gilding, a common occupation of children, stiffen the fingers of the little workers. The handling of poisonous paints and arsenical paper are employments which often result in injury or slow death. A woman factory inspector of Illinois recently said, " We find girls in the clothing trade contracting diseases from running machines by footpower — diseases that mean a life-long martyrdom and the loss of the crown of a woman's life, the

power to bear healthy children." [1] It has only been
as a result of the last Illinois Child Labor Law that
the younger children have been taken from the Stock
Yards of Chicago. Mrs. Florence Kelly said, a few
years ago, regarding the conditions there, "What
could be more revolting than the presence of three
hundred children in the Chicago Stock Yards, scores
of them standing ankle-deep in blood and refuse, as
they do the work of butchers?" *

These injuries which child labor inflicts upon the
children are terrible; but they are, perhaps, no more important than the injuries child labor inflicts on society.
As a matter of fact, child labor often retards industrial progress. Through cheap labor, manufacturers
are often able to retain and perpetuate methods of
manufacture which are unnecessary and antiquated.
The so-called belated industries, like the sweating system, are made possible only through the cheapness
of child and woman labor. Greed for profits alone
makes it necessary for children of six years to carry
the newly blown glass bottles from hot ovens to a
place for cooling. The same thing can be done by
mechanical means. Mechanical ingenuity and inventive skill are enabled to lie dormant because the
labor of children and women is cheap and plentiful.
Mrs. Sidney Webb of England gives this illustrative
fact, "When the employers in the woollen manufac-

* See Appendix E, p. 356.

ture found themselves debarred from the employment of children, they invented the piecing machine."[1] And Professor Franklin H. Giddings speaks even more broadly when he says : " Modern civilization does not require, it does not need, the drudgery of needle-women or the crushing toil of men in a score of life-destroying occupations. If these wretched beings should drop out of existence and no others stood ready to fill their places, the economic activities of the world would not greatly suffer. A thousand devices latent in inventive brains would quickly make good any momentary loss."[2]

Another evil of economic importance results from the well-known fact that the labor of children is constantly in competition with the labor of their elders. In most cases it means that the child displaces the adult. This year an employer, representing the dry-goods stores, came to me to ask that the Child Labor Committee repeal a certain section of the law which prohibits children under sixteen from working more than nine hours a day. He argued that, if we did not, the mercantile establishments would have to hire children over sixteen, and this he said would be a great injustice to those children, under that age, who were then at work. I asked him if the stores could procure the necessary number of children over sixteen years of age. " Oh, yes," he said ; " there are enough children over sixteen, but the smaller ones would be unemployed."

I then asked him if it did not seem fairer to all concerned, if there were enough children over sixteen who could do the work required, that those children should be at work and not idle, and that the other smaller children should be at school and not at work. This is a good illustration of the way in which children displace older workers. The children displace the men, and the younger children displace the older children. This widespread economic effect of the employment of children is perhaps more important than any other. Child labor, wherever it exists, must be counted as one of the important causes of unemployment among adults. Of course, the lower wages at which children may be hired is the greatest inducement for their employment. The competition of children with adults in the labor market can hardly fail to have the effect of reducing the wages paid to the latter, and it has been found by actual investigation that where child labor is most common the earnings of the children are at least partly offset by a corresponding loss in the earnings of the adults.

Opponents of child-labor legislation, seeking any possible excuse for their opposition, and wishing to appear humane rather than self-seeking, make much of the alleged fact that the earnings of the children are necessary to the support of the family. Widowed mothers, it is said, would suffer serious poverty if their children under fourteen were not permitted to work. Actual inquiry has shown, however, that these statements are rarely if ever justified. To begin with, there are very few widows who need to depend upon the earnings of children under fourteen years of age. Furthermore, the earnings of such children at best help but little, and in many cases their earnings are not sufficient to supply even themselves with a subsistence. But even if children could support themselves or even partially support their widowed mothers, it would be unwise to allow them to handicap their productive power by labor begun too early, especially as the earnings of these children are likely to be, at a later age, the sole support of the mother. It is hardly wise to force children to early labor, at the risk of their health, at the risk, indeed, in many cases, of their losing entirely all productive power, when we know that by further education and training their labor will become of much greater value to their parents, to themselves, and to the community.

Surely no one, except those selfishly interested, will maintain that the nation should any longer permit certain self-interested employers to benefit by the ruin of children. "Where there is only a cupidinous ravishment of the future, there, we think, is no true society," nor, it may be added, either a beneficial or a profitable industry.[1] Industry must be made to support its workers. This is its first duty, and anything short of the accomplishment of this duty proves the industry injurious to society and insolvent. An industry which does less is eating up more than its capital : it is destroying the source of capital. The industry which absorbs and burns up the energies of the little ones before their strength has had time to mature, and afterwards casts the wrecks of childhood upon public charity for support, very much as it would cast scrap-iron upon a rubbish heap, is a curse to any country. Those industries which coin into profits the vitality of childhood — and leave to the world, for its mercy to support, wrecks of manhood — rob the country of something which they can never return. They have contracted a debt to the child and to society which they can never repay. There is a debt to the child who must drag out a life of unproductive or half-productive manhood, and a debt to the nation which might have been enriched by his manhood's strength and by his matured mind. It is becoming general to call those industries parasitic that thrive only because of benefits accruing to them by reason of cheap labor.[1] They live by the destruction of human life, not by supporting and enriching human life. In many cases the employers of cheap labor do not pay wages sufficiently large to support, even while at work, the women or children. As a rule they are not compelled to support themselves, and can therefore work for wages which

are hardly sufficient to buy their clothes or food.
The husbands or fathers are ordinarily the ones who
are burdened with the family's support, and the wages
of women or children would be, in most cases, insufficient to support the latter in independence. For the
reason, therefore, that the employers do not as a rule
pay the children living wages, and for the reason also
that they are exhausting the immature energies of
childhood, they are in a real sense parasites, injurious
both to the child and to society. There is, to my
mind, nothing more astonishing in modern society
than the way in which the state seems ever willing to
support, as paupers and at public expense, the men,
women, and children who are brought into poverty
and misery by the parasitic industries. In this country the state has seldom demanded of such industries
more care and humanity in their treatment of employees. Instead of doing this, or of demanding that
the needless waste of life be stopped altogether, the
state has patiently built more almshouses and hospitals and free lodging-houses to care for the human
waste which parasitic industries produce in their
pursuit of profits. If any one is censured, it is the
broken-down workman — for his improvidence. The
national importance of the child-labor problem lies in
the fact that the working people can be exhausted by
parasitic employers in the same way that a coal mine
is exhausted.

Many persons in England and France are concerned to know whether or not this very thing has actually happened in their country. If it has, or if we are at some time afflicted with a degenerate working class, it will demonstrate that the captains of industry have, with insatiable greed, failed to pay their just debts; that they have been successful, not as a result of wisdom, ability, or inventive genius, but because they were parasitic and skilful in their methods of forestalling the labor of childhood, and of exploiting, greedily and without fair compensation, what should have been the untouched reservoirs of labor power.

All of this has a bearing on the present state of manufacturing art and its relation to the much-talked-of world's market. It is generally thought that the United States will dominate, in the near future, the commerce of the world. There will be few to question the important contribution which the working people of the United States have made to this marvellous industrial growth which enables us to take a prominent place in the world-wide commerce. This position of power is due to the superior ability and intelligence of American labor; in order to maintain it, we must as carefully guard the quality, ability, intelligence, and efficiency of labor as we now guard the security of capital. The whole country is alert to see that no laws are made which will impair the value and power of capital. Ought it not to be still more alert to prevent any injury to labor, and especially to prevent that most serious injury — the labor of children? One employer at least has taken this view of the matter. In a letter to the Wisconsin Bureau of Labor he says: "While our work is such that we can employ children to advantage, and for this reason it would be to our immediate interest to do so, we recognize the fact that early employment is not likely to result in the best class of men and women. This problem, therefore, involves the welfare not only of the children themselves, but of the state. It also seems to us that in the long run the interest of the employers lies in an efficient working class. Speaking from a purely business point of view, we should be glad enough to employ children, particularly at certain kinds of work. From the standpoint of society as a whole, we will say that a uniform law for all manufacturing states, under which no child under fifteen could be employed, and which compelled school attendance up to this age, would be preferable to the present laws. If we are ever to reach the industrial supremacy predicted for us, it can only be because of a superior industrial class. Such a class can nowhere be had without the most careful bringing up."[1]

This employer is, unfortunately, a very exceptional

one. Many of the employers of young children put
forth any argument, however specious, in order to
retain this or any other form of cheap labor. As
a class they have always protested, usually under
some humanitarian guise, against state protection of
the children. The same arguments which were used
against Joseph Hanway over one hundred years ago
were used sixty years later against Lord Shaftesbury.
The age of the children and the hours of their work
did not alter the arguments of the employers one
iota. The employers in Shaftesbury's day fought
legislation to protect children of five and six years
with even greater energy than employers now manifest against legislation to protect children of fourteen
years. The employers of the South are saying precisely the same things against those who are working
at the present time for the liberation of the children
of the South as the employers of England said years
ago against Lord Shaftesbury. Even Cobden spoke
scornfully of those who "talk sentiment over factory
children." [1] An English employer fifty years ago said,
"this kind of legislation would bring us back to the
barbarism of the Middle Ages." [2] In the South they
say "to the barbarism of the poor whites." And yet
in Cobden's time the children from the English almshouses were being sold into bondage as factory
slaves. Children of all ages, with aching backs,
inflamed ankles, and lacerated fingers, were beaten

and kicked to work by brutal overseers; the little
slaves toiled from morning till night, and often slept
by the machines until morning. Through "hunger,
neglect, over-fatigue, and poisonous air, they died in
terrible numbers, swept off by contagious fevers." [1]
Had the legislators heeded the arguments of the
employers of cheap labor, we should still have children of four and five years in the factories; we
should still sell pauper children to the highest bidder
among factory employers.

This destruction of the little ones, now so unnecessary and so obvious, is a kind of cannibalism. We
no longer eat each other, but there can be no question that some of us live, and even win our pleasures
and luxuries, by the ruin of others. A tailor who
had spent many years of his life in a sweatshop said
to me once, as we passed a poor, painted creature
of the street: "The man who won pleasure by the
degradation of that woman is a modern cannibal.
No," he continued fiercely, "he is worse than a
cannibal, for he not only destroyed her body, he ate
her very soul." There is a good deal more of such
cannibalism in our modern world than we realize.
The bodies and souls of many men and women are
destroyed by the selfishness of our present-day
society; but if we are to use the word "cannibal" in
this new sense, let us begin by applying it to those
employers, in the parasitic industries, who go to our

legislative halls in order to defeat child-labor laws, using the argument that only by the toil of infants are they enabled to make profits. Is it possible that this is saying too much? Perhaps it is — God knows. But I am not able to think as calmly as many of my friends, who discuss child labor as an academic question remote from human bodies and human souls, and who have never watched the children toiling in factories or mines or before the furnaces, nor wondered how many of these women of the street, or how many of the vagrants (crippled, deformed, and degenerate wastrels of the lodging-houses) were robbed of something in childhood which they vainly tried to find again in their vagrant and vicious womanhood or manhood. It cannot be said that all of these wasted lives are due to modern cannibalism, but it must be said that the child who is robbed of his childhood and forced to become a bearer of burdens while yet in his infancy is the victim of the brute either in man or in society. I am not sure what William Vaughn Moody had in mind when he wrote his terrible poem, " The Brute," but it means for me the mill or the mine or the factory which absorbs the life and energies of the children : —

" And they fling him, hour by hour,
  Limbs of men to give him power;
  Brains of men to give him cunning; and for dainties to devour

Children's souls, the little worth; hearts of women, cheaply
   bought;
He takes them and he breaks them, but he gives them scanty
   thought."

There could hardly be a more serious problem
than the one presented by the child of this machine-
made and tenement-dwelling age. Place in juxtapo-
sition the playing child of the street and the working
child of the factory, and it seems at first glance as
if there were, for the children of poverty at least, no
solution to the problem. Play, that is so precious to
the child of the country, and work, that was in the
home of the olden days so educative and valuable,
are now in our largest cities and factory towns either
dangerous or ruinous. To think of this problem in
part is to fall into error. When one has only in
mind the working child, one's first thought is — he
should be at play; when one has only the playing
child in mind, the first thought is — he should have
some occupation. It is a discouraging dilemma, facing
equally the man interested in street gangs and the
man interested in abolishing child labor. The brute
on the one side; the Reform School on the other. The
child is between the devil and the deep sea. The
choice offered is a choice of evils. But no one is
long in deciding which evil must be chosen. The
brute and the devil must be fought even though it
mean a swim for life in the deep sea.

But the dilemma is only a present one. We are in a transitional period in which the old individualistic ideas are still strong and the social ones as yet vague and groping. We are at present sufficiently developed socially to demand that the state protect the little ones; but we are not yet strong in our conviction that the community should provide institutions fitted so far as possible to replace what the child has lost as a result of industrial progress — nature, home, educative work, and noble recreation. If we go so far as to free the child from the brute, we are then inclined to cease our efforts for the child, feeling that the home must find ways of engaging his idle time profitably. We forget that the home is, for the working people, a few rooms in a crowded, yardless tenement, and that the individual parent cannot save the child from the deadening and aimless play of the city's streets. He may not give him work with tools, for there is no room in the tenement where the child can work ; the parent may not watch him at his play, for he is in a factory, and not in a home workshop or in the neighboring fields. In a word, the working-man cannot, as things now are, supervise the play of his child. We must therefore go farther than to liberate the child from slavery : we must see that his hours of freedom are utilized in those kinds of recreation and occupation which shall most develop him.

But it may be said that in the largest cities and

factory towns where the evils are greatest the thing
will adjust itself and that in other parts of the country there is no child problem. It is indeed a cause
for rejoicing that relatively so few children are suffering from the evils herein mentioned. Many hundred thousand children are still living in the country
and in villages, and about one million of the working
children are at work on farms away from the evils
of the factory, the mine, and the mill. These are
indeed hopeful things, which should not be forgotten
while considering the subject of poverty ; but neither
should we overlook the alarming fact that we are
only at the beginning of the industrial development
which is the cause of these problems. We can be
reasonably sure that under capitalism there will not
be any automatic readjustment of affairs which will
eradicate these evils. Indeed, it cannot be doubted
that cities are to grow larger and more numerous;
nor that city land is to become even more costly ; nor
that the homeless, yardless tenement and the factory
are to multiply; nor that the home, as a place for
social, educational, and recreational opportunities, is,
for a time at least, in certain large cities to be a
possession limited almost entirely to the wealthy.
It cannot, therefore, be doubted that the child problem is to grow year by year more and more serious.

However alarming, it is nevertheless reasonable to
think that we are only at the beginning of this prob-

s

lem of child life. In a general way two widely varying solutions are advocated. The Tolstoyan and
others, intense in their individualism and in their
love for the old order of things, urge upon us a
voluntary return to nature. They would have us
abandon the great city and the factory, with its
division of labor and its labor-saving mechanism.
They advocate reinstituting the primitive home and
the domestic workshop. In a word, we are to cure
the evils of modern society by voluntarily returning
to the extinct industrial order of previous centuries.
The other solution is a contrary one. It has faith in
the wisdom of our economic development, however
much it may deplore the misery at present incident
to it. It would build up the school and make known
to it the necessity of providing for the child, whether
working, playing, or learning. It would provide
social institutions for his development; it would give
him gardens, playgrounds, gymnasia, workshops, and
whatever other institutions are necessary to replace
the loss of the home workshop, and the fields of the
old industrial era. If, in great cities, there were no
other way of supplying these needs of the children
than by utilizing the roofs of tenements and of all
public buildings, it would be done. With proper
building regulations there is no reason why a new
Manhattan should not be created on the roofs of
tenements and public buildings which should be for

the exclusive use of the children, who are the larger
half of the population of the city. As was said
before, some cities abroad have already arranged to
feed the children who come from homes of poverty.
Berlin sends to the country daily several thousand
children who are physically weak or who are predis-
posed to tuberculosis. In the most healthful surroundings they are then given special instruction
and cared for by physicians and others until they are
entirely well and strong. The development of these
and similar social measures would soon solve many
of the more serious of the problems of the city child.

We are impatient and restless at the delay, but the
time will come when an awakened social conscience
will insist upon these necessary social measures.
Those of the new social faith are growing in numbers. To them the child is the world's supreme
treasure. For it the world moves and has its being.
Without the child the world were barren, riches but
dust, and life joyless. With the child (not mine
only nor yours, but every child born to man) the
world is forever new, forever hopeful, and forever
blessed. William Morris has said, in speaking of
the transitional time between serfdom and the wage
system of labor, " Ill would be the change were
it not for the change beyond the change." And
so may we think regarding the child evils incident
to the city and to the industrial organization of the

present era. The world must ever change, and for the benefit of the child must come the change beyond the change. But, in order that the little one may be nobler than his father, one change is just now imperatively necessary and presses upon us. The factory in displacing the home workshop has made no provision for the proper manual and industrial education of the child. The tenement in displacing the home and the common has made no provision for the child's play. The school must take upon itself these new responsibilities, both of which are educational problems, and both of which the school, more than any other public agency, is fitted to master. An awakening to the necessity of assuming the new duties should not be delayed, for the yardless tenement is multiplying, the children must be kept from the factory, and the little ones of the street may even now be counted by the million.

CHAPTER VI

THE IMMIGRANT

In the poorest quarters of many great American cities and industrial communities one is struck by a most peculiar fact — the poor are almost entirely foreign born. Great colonies, foreign in language, customs, habits, and institutions, are separated from each other and from the distinctly American groups on national or racial lines. By crossing the Bowery one leaves behind him the great Jewish colony made up of Russians, Poles, and Roumanians and passes into Italy; to the northeast lies a little Germany; to the southwest a colony of Syrians; to the west lies an Irish community, a settlement of negroes, and a remnant of the old native American stock; to the south lie a Chinese and a Greek colony. On Manhattan alone, either on the extreme west side or the extreme east side, there are other colonies of the Irish, the Jews, and the Italians, and, in addition, there is a large colony of Bohemians.[1] In Chicago there are the same foreign poor. To my own knowledge there are four Italian colonies, two Polish, a

Bohemian, an Irish, a Jewish, a German, a negro, a
Chinese, a Greek, a Scandinavian, and other colonies.[1]
So it is also in Boston and many other cities. In
New York alone there are more persons of German
descent than persons of native descent, and the
German element is larger than in any city of Germany except Berlin. There are nearly twice as
many Irish as in Dublin, about as many Jews as in
Warsaw, and more Italians than in Naples or Venice.[2]
No other great nation has a widespread poverty
which is foreign to its own native people except in
so far as it exists in distant colonies in foreign lands.
Our foreign colonies are to an important extent in
the cities of our own country. On a small scale we
have Russia's poverty, Poland's poverty, Italy's poverty, Hungary's poverty, Bohemia's poverty — and
what other nation's have we not? England, France,
Germany, or Italy may speak almost solely of her
native poor, her only poor, the poor of her own
blood. In those countries the rich and the poor
may meet together, talk together, worship together.
In addition to all the elemental bonds of union there
are many others growing out of national life. In
certain large cities of this country almost everything
separates "the classes and the masses" except the
feeling which inheres in the word "humanity." The
rich and well-to-do are mostly Americans; the poor
are mostly foreign, drawn from among the miserable

of every nation.   The citizen and the slave of Greece
were scarcely more effectually separated.

To live in one of these foreign communities is
actually to live on foreign soil.   The thoughts, feel-
ings, and traditions which belong to the mental life
of the colony are often entirely alien to an American.
The newspapers, the literature, the ideals, the pas-
sions, the things which agitate the community, are
unknown to us except in fragments.   During the
meat riots on the east side of New York City two
years ago, I could understand nothing, as I stood
among the mobs of rioters, except that heads were
being broken, windows smashed, and that the people
were in a frenzy.   A few years ago, when living in
Chicago in a colony of Bohemians and Hungarians
who had been thrown out of employment by the clos-
ing of a great industry, I went about among the
groups clustered in the streets or gathered in the
halls.   I felt the unrest, the denunciation, the growing brutality, but I was unable to discuss with them
their grievances, to sympathize with them, or to
oppose them.   I was an utter stranger in my own
city.   A fire was started by some one; a few buildings
were burned.   I watched the embittered and angered
faces light up with pleasure, but only by such expres-
sions of feeling could I understand what agitated the
people of this foreign land.   In London, there is an
English people; in Paris, a French people; in Mos-

cow, a Russian people. In all these countries there
are the masters and the workmen ; the rich and the
poor, separated by wealth, by position, and by place
of dwelling. But in the largest cities of America
there are many other things which separate the rich
and the poor. Language, institutions, customs, and
even religion separate the native and the foreigner.
It is this separation which makes the problem of
poverty in America more difficult of solution than
that of any other nation.

The movement of the poor from one nation to
another is one of the astonishing phenomena of modern society. The poor of any country find it possible
to move from one extreme of the world to another
extreme in quest of better economic or social conditions. The French Canadians move backward
and forward between this country and Canada. The
poor Italian peasantry of Sicily and southern Italy
are even able to come in great numbers from their
country to work here during the summer, returning
home again for the winter season. In 1898 sixty-six
thousand Italian emigrants returned to the port of
Genoa.[1] The poorest of the Jews of Russia, the most
oppressed peasantry of Asiatic countries, are able
to come to the United States to be freed from oppression, or in the hope that by so doing their
material condition will be bettered. Rapid and
cheap transportation has made possible these re-

markable migrations. Nothing shows more clearly than this the change which has taken place in the status of the worker; he is no longer slave or serf, fixed to master or soil; he is free to go where he will, but he has far less security of livelihood than formerly; he is propertyless and proletarian. As a result of these migrations of working men and women national barriers have been beaten down, prejudices overcome, and an intermingling of races and nationalities has ensued in the same country, city, or village, which would have been inconceivable fifty years ago.

While there is a great movement of population from all parts of the old world to all parts of the new, the migration to the United States is the largest and the most conspicuous. Literally speaking, millions of foreigners have established colonies in the very hearts of our urban and industrial communities. For reasons of poverty their colonies are usually established in the poorest, the most criminal, the most politically debauched, and the most vicious portions of our cities. These colonies often make up the main portion of our so-called "slums." In Baltimore 77 per cent of the total population of the slums was in the year 1894 of foreign birth or parentage. In Chicago the foreign element was 90 per cent; in New York, 95 per cent; and in Philadelphia, 91 per cent.[1] In recent years the flow of immigrants to the cities, where they are not needed, instead of to those parts of the country where they are needed, has been steadily increasing. Sixty-nine per cent of the present immigration avows itself as determined to settle either in the great cities or in certain communities of the four great industrial states, Massachusetts, New York, Pennsylvania, and Illinois. According to their own statements, nearly 60 per cent of the Russian and Polish Jews intend to settle in the largest cities. As a matter of fact, those who actually do settle in cities are even more numerous than this percentage indicates. As the class of immigrants, drawn from eastern and southern Europe, Russia, and Asia, come in increasing numbers to the United States, the tendency to settle in cities likewise increases. For many reasons the centripetal force of the foreign colonies seems irresistible. Already these great foreign cities in our slums have become wildernesses of neglect, almost unexplored and almost unknown to us. Even the settlements touch but few of their vast number. The padrone, enslaving industrially the Italians, the politician, seeking selfish ends, the Jew sweater, and the owner, or agent, of insanitary tenements are the ones who teach the immigrant what America is and what it stands for. Each new shipload increases the profits of these classes, adds to the population of the great cities and colonies, and incidentally adds to its misery.

It is amazing to consider the extent of the foreign element in this country.[1]   Ireland and Scotland combined had in the year 1889 less than ten million people, and yet there were considerably over that number of foreigners in the United States in the year 1900. There were almost twenty-one millions of our population with both parents foreign born; that is to say, more than the population of Portugal, Sweden, Holland, and Belgium combined in the year 1890. Considerably over six millions of our population, over ten years of age, were illiterate — a population about equal to that of Belgium.   Since the year 1821 over twenty million immigrants have arrived in this country.   Within the last twenty-three years considerably over half of this number, or upwards of ten million immigrants, have landed in the United States.[2]   The figures are really astounding.   In many towns nearly one-half of the population is foreign.   About 37 per cent of the people of New York City are foreign born, and over 80 per cent are either foreign born or of foreign parentage. In the latter sense about 80 per cent of the population of Chicago is foreign, in Milwaukee nearly 85 per cent, in Fall River about the same per cent.   In no less than thirty-three of our largest cities the foreign population is larger than the native.[3]   A man prominent in philanthropic work among the Jews claims, as a result of an independent census, that there are over half a million Jews foreign born and of foreign parentage in New York City. According to the United States Census, the immigrants from Germany and Ireland make up the largest numbers; but they are now being fast outstripped by those from eastern Europe. Assistant Commissioner of Immigration McSweeney said a couple of years ago, "A circle . . . including the sources of the present immigration to the United States would have its centre in Constantinople." [1] These facts and figures, even if there were nothing else to be said, would warrant the most serious consideration being given to the subject of immigration.

The problem of a foreign poverty, the growth of great colonies preyed upon by the worst classes, the immense number yearly of newcomers and the fact that the recent immigration brings us fewer Teutons and vastly more southern Europeans, Slavs, and Asiatics, are facts which the serious citizen should care to consider. Only the student of those ethnic changes wrought by great migratory movements, such as the one we witness in our day, can have any idea of the racial modifications which are likely to result from the coming of these strange peoples from all parts of the world. Far-reaching changes in our national characteristics will result. The American type must change in response to these new racial influences. Until 1860 the American was steadily

growing in stature. The recent immigration from
eastern and southern Europe, however, will, it seems
agreed, decrease the average stature of the American. It is said that the skull will become shorter
and broader.[1] There will also be psychological
changes resulting from the mixture of races. What
the final man will be no one can foretell, but the very
knowledge of the ethnic changes which must result
increases tremendously the responsibility of the
American people to this question of immigration.
By act of legislation there can be a selection practised which may result in infinite good to the people.
Foreign countries, by reason of oppression, wars, and
lack of education, have added greatly to their unfit
and abnormal classes. The strong and selected have
gone to war to be killed; the weak and mentally
deficient have been left at home to increase population. According to the Commissioner of Immigration these very classes of the unfit are at present
coming to our shores in vast numbers to exercise
their influence in these ethnic changes.[2] At the
same time the better classes of Italians are going to
South America; large numbers of skilled workers
from Germany and emigrants from other advanced
nations are now going to South America, Aus-
tralia and elsewhere in preference to America. The
Honorable James Bryce, one of the most careful
foreign observers of our social and political life,

said, about ten years ago : " Within the last decade new swarms of European immigrants have invaded America, drawn from their homes in the eastern parts of central Europe by the constant cheapening of ocean transit and by that more thorough drainage, so to speak, of the inland regions of Europe which is due to the extension of railways. These immigrants, largely of Slavonic race, come from a lower stratum of civilization than the German immigrants of the past, and, since they speak foreign tongues, are less quickly amenable to American influences, and probably altogether less improvable than are the Irish. There seems to be a danger that if they continue to come in large numbers they may retain their own low standard of decency and comfort, and menace the continuance among the working class generally of that far higher standard which has hitherto prevailed in all but a few spots in the country."[1] It is not sufficient to answer the manifold questions presented by these problems in the ordinary way of Americans by saying that some of the recent immigrants become rich. Many, it may be as truly said, remain poor. Unrestricted immigration involves more than wealth-getting or poverty. Many of the most subtle, social, and ethnological questions are involved. Here, however, we must speak of immigration in its relation to poverty and therefore mainly in its economic aspects.

A striking fact in connection with the movement of population is the influence of the profit-seeking forces upon its volume. It is stimulated by certain economic forces consciously exercised. Generally speaking, immigration is promoted by two classes: large employers of labor, seeking always and everywhere the cheapest form obtainable, and the owners of the transatlantic steamship companies. The former are responsible for large numbers of contract laborers. Mr. Jacob A. Riis said very recently: "Scarce a Greek comes here, man or boy, who is not under contract. A hundred dollars a year is the price, so it is said by those who know, though the padrone's cunning has put the legal proof beyond their reach. And the Armenian and Syrian hucksters are 'worked' by some peddling trust that traffics in human labor as do other merchants in foodstuffs and coal and oil." [1] These foreign people do not come as the early immigrants came, overcoming many obstacles and strong to overcome them for the sake of a new chance in the new world; they are seduced into coming, enticed by every available means and by every known scheme of advertising. Bolton King, writing on "Italy To-day," [2] says that in 1896 "there were over seven thousand emigration agents in the country (Italy), and too many of them have speculated on the peasant's ignorance, giving false information as to the labor market, sometimes cheating him (the Italian) of the little hoard he had taken with him, or deliberately sending him to a different locality from that agreed upon." * These agencies in Europe are spread "like a vast network," having representatives in every town, village, and hamlet for the purpose of making the ignorant peasantry believe fabulous stories of wealth to be had in America.[1] It is not difficult to deceive the illiterate and, consequently, they, in particular, are coming in larger and larger numbers. In fact, both the type and the nationality of the immigrants who come to America are very largely determined by the activity of these agents and by the ports from which the ships sail. If the steamship companies undertook to increase their business by opening a new port in the Baltic, we should have a great increase of immigrants from any Russian or Polish colony in which their agents worked. It is even said that a steamship company, in consideration of a certain number of yearly immigrants guaranteed by the government, has decided to open a new port in an eastern European country.[2] The people who come do not expect to fight a hard industrial battle after they have arrived; they have been deceived by the foreign agents, trafficked in for profits, and looted by the unscrupulous.

* The words in parentheses are interposed.

It should be realized that the forces promoting immigration are selfish forces caring neither for the welfare of the country nor for the welfare of the immigrant. Whenever a bill comes before Congress to restrict immigration, every effort is made by these private interests to prevent its passage. A few years ago the following letter was sent out by a general agent of the North German Lloyd Steamship Company to their many agencies in all parts of this country:[1]—

"Immigration bill comes up in the House Wednesday. Wire your congressman, our expense, protesting against proposed exclusion and requesting bill be defeated, informing him that vote in favor means defeat next election.

(Signed)

"H. CLAUSSENIUS & Co."

Similar intimidating telegrams were sent to every newspaper in which the steamship companies advertised. Official testimony also shows that bribery, in the form of passes, given to the editors and proprietors of newspapers, has helped to create newspaper opposition to restrictive legislation.

The class of large employers most active in preventing the restriction of immigration have usually been those paying the smallest wages. A repre-

T

sentative of the Southern Pacific Railroad, appearing before the Committee of the United States Senate on Immigration in 1902, for the purpose of opposing restriction, claimed that the railroad was unable to get sufficient workmen. The Commissioner General of Immigration, knowing well the wages and conditions of railway workmen, said, "Let it pay living wages and it will have laborers enough." The wages paid by the Southern Pacific, as shown before the same committee, were from $1.16 to $1.39 a day, or, in other terms, from $350 to $425 a year.[1] Those employers who use every means, fair or foul, to obtain an over-supply of laborers, and, in this way, to force wages down to the lowest possible limit, should be classed among the dangerous elements of any country. This policy, pursued for many years in the anthracite mining districts of Pennsylvania, caused violent disturbances until the men were organized in unions for the purpose of limiting the supply of laborers and of increasing wages. In order to keep wages down and to prevent the growth of trade unions, many employers advocate unlimited immigration. The reports to the Industrial Commission show that in those districts where there is an over-supply of laborers of many different nationalities, it is almost impossible to organize the workers until suffering makes the men realize the necessity of union, instead of competition, among themselves.[2]

In this way the selfish interests create serious social problems by promoting excessive immigration.

Curiously enough the only other class of Americans who are actively supporting a like policy of unlimited immigration are the revolutionary anarchists; the latter working consciously, and the former classes unconsciously, to bring about the same end. According to the anarchist theory, immigration is one of the active sources creating an intenser competition for bread, and, in consequence, a greater general poverty. In a miserable, half-lighted hall, I heard a few years ago a discussion of the subject by a group of revolutionary anarchists, mostly, I must say, foreigners. The speaker, a foreigner, using German and at times a broken English, said there was no hope of revolution in this country until conditions got worse. The immigrants were, however, breaking down the standards of living, and in a few years the workers, enraged by hunger and poverty, would rise up with arms and dynamite to destroy their masters and to establish the anarchist state. I have before me an anarchist leaflet called "A Letter to Tramps, the Unemployed, the Disinherited, and the Miserable." After appealing to these classes to realize their wretched condition and the cause of it, namely, the robbers who live in their "voluptuous homes" and "engage themselves at wanton sports," the letter urges a petition which the rich may read by the "red glare bursting from the cannon's mouth." It ends up with this significant phrase, in italics, "Learn the use of explosives." The anarchist knows there is no better school to prepare men for revolution than that of poverty. Anything which will make profits is favored by the steamship companies; anything which creates a greater supply of cheap labor is favored by certain employers; anything which makes poverty more general and more stinging is favored by revolutionary anarchists. This last body of men has no selfish interest in the present degradation of labor. Its position is based upon the principle that poverty, if severe enough, will bring a revolution. The other bodies of men have only in view their present selfish interests. Whatever difference there is in motive, the end they all seek is for the present precisely the same.

These are the ones who favor unrestricted immigration. The actual conditions of the workers show, I think, that there is in many places in this country a large supply of labor which our industries are not using — and, in fact, cannot use. The figures of unemployment mentioned in other places show this conclusively; but for further proof any one may visit these colonies at any time and see for himself the great numbers of idle men walking the streets. This enforced idleness, due to

inability to find employment, is also shown by the
figures gathered by the Department of Labor at
Washington, in the investigation of the Italians
in Chicago.[1] During the year of the investigation
the Italian workman was actually employed on an
average but little more than four months out of the
twelve. The other eight months were spent in
idleness. The average wage of the Italian workman
was less than $6 a week, and, in the most unskilled
trades, it fell in one class to $5, and in another as
low as $4.37.[2] These wages, these long months of
unemployment, mean wretched poverty. They mean
starvation, insanity, and tuberculosis. Let any one
look about in the colonies. The evidences of poverty are everywhere. The local doctor will tell you
that there is a great prevalence of rickets among
the Italian children, a disease due to malnutrition;
the settlement worker will tell you that the child is
taken from school at the earliest hour and sent
to work; the woman is taken from her children
and put to work; the neglected children are left to
the vice and crime taught by the street gang; the
policeman will tell you, if you ask, that the Italians
of the poorest class obtain their food to a large extent from the garbage boxes. He will also tell you
that the fighting and the drunkenness result naturally from unwilling idleness. Mr. Jacob A. Riis,
speaking of the Italians who swarm about the city

dumps, says, "Whenever the back of the sanitary
police is turned, he will make his home in the filthy
burrows where he works by day, sleeping and eating
his meals under the dump, on the edge of slimy depths
and amid surroundings full of unutterable horror."
He adds, the city is content to board the Italian "so
long as he can make the ash-barrels yield the food
to keep him alive." [1] It would seem that our industries fail to absorb some few at least of the newcomers.

Since these facts and figures concerning the conditions of poverty in these Italian colonies were
made public, several hundred thousand more Italians
have immigrated. In the last five years over six
hundred thousand Italians have arrived in this country.[2] Last year, 1903, almost three hundred thousand new immigrants were admitted to the Italian
colonies of this country, to share with those already
here whatever may be rescued from the city's garbage, or to fight with them, or against them, for a
chance to work and for means of livelihood. The
wages given above do not, however, represent the
extent of their poverty. The padrone must get his
commissions and profits out of these poverty-stricken
people.[3] By organization under a padrone, for the
padrone's benefit, the men work for wages, the
amount of which they often do not know; but when
there is work, they get it, because the sort of slavery

which they are willing to suffer and the standard
of life which they are willing to accept is most
satisfactory to those contractors who desire to get
labor at the cheapest possible rates. The padrone
is a parasite. He lives and grows rich by fleecing
ignorant immigrants from his own country. He
helps the steamship companies to stimulate immigration. He gets his commission for bringing
tenants to a vile tenement. He farms out laborers
to railroad companies and other employers. When
they are working, he supplies them with food at
excessive prices. It is even said that he is sometimes
the owner of the Italians, and that they are actually
his slaves.[1]

These conditions of poverty are not peculiar to the
Italians. They are only worse with them. Among
the Jews, who have been admitted in great numbers
to this country, and who have settled almost entirely
in the largest cities, distress and poverty are widespread. Not to speak from observation, but to quote
only from published reports, there is more than
enough to be said. The annual report of the United
Hebrew Charities for 1901 says: "A condition of
chronic poverty is developing in the Jewish community of New York that is appalling in its immensity.
Forty-five per cent of our applicants, representing
between twenty thousand and twenty-five thousand
human beings, have been in the United States over

five years; have been given the opportunities for economic and industrial improvement which this country affords; yet, notwithstanding all this, have not managed to reach a position of economic independence." The same report says, "The statement can safely be made that during the year from seventy-five thousand to one hundred thousand members of the New York Jewish community are unable to supply themselves with the immediate necessaries of life." [1] In the report of the same society for 1898 the following passage occurs, "Those who are familiar with the crowded section on the lower east side know that vices are beginning to spring up which heretofore have been strangers to the Jewish people." [2] In the report for 1901 this observation is confirmed and made more explicit, "The horrible congestion in which so many of our co-religionists live, the squalor and filth, the lack of air and sunlight, the absence, frequently, of even the most common decencies, are too well known to require repetition at this writing."

I do not know whether or not, all considered, the Italians have improved their lot by coming to America. Many of them have, doubtless, bettered themselves financially, but I do know that nothing in Polish Russia can compare with the conditions stated above concerning the Jewish community of New York City. From careful observation in both places, I should say, offhand, that, except for advantages of education, the Jews of the Polish part of the Russian Pale are better off morally, physically, religiously, and perhaps even financially, than those of the east side of New York. It is never safe to make such a statement without searching inquiry, but, so far as my observation goes, it is true.

Distressing as these conditions seem, many people will, doubtless, feel inclined to say that immigrants arriving in poverty would, very naturally, have to suffer some of these conditions for a few years at least. The fact is, however, that the competition of recent immigrants increases the poverty among the native as well as among the more or less Americanized working classes. The poverty of the Irish, and the degeneration which has resulted from it, is an excellent example.

I think any one who has lived in the poorer quarters of any large city or industrial community will agree that the Irish-American has degenerated in recent years in the most astonishing way. Certain districts, formerly flourishing, in which the people were prosperous, thrifty, and energetic, are at present the very worst pauperized and most criminal districts of our cities. For instance, the "Archy Road" section of Chicago, the home of Peter Dunne's "Mr. Dooley," was a few years ago a prosperous district of sober, self-respecting, working people. The Irish were at

that time doing almost all the common laboring work
of the city, the unloading of barges on the river, the
unskilled work in the railroad yards, the street-clean-
ing work, and other common laboring jobs about the
mills and factories.   Little by little the padrones
began to bargain on political lines with corrupt alder-
men, and the Italians were put to work on city jobs.
Johnnie Powers, whose district is largely an Italian
one, could, at one time, it is said, "make the proud
boast that he had two thousand six hundred people in
his ward upon the public pay roll." [1]   The Poles
and Hungarians have taken away much of the unskilled work at the mills and at the stock yards; the
Bohemians have. monopolized the wood-working
trades.   As a result, the Irish have had either to rise
to higher positions or to compete successfully with this
poorer paid labor.   They were unable to do the one
and refused to do the other.   In consequence, the
homes are being mortgaged and lost; the young lads
are becoming gamblers and drunkards and vagrants.
I have recently seen a statement that crime is decreasing in Ireland; but in the larger cities of this country
the Irish make up an undue proportion of vagrants,
criminals, paupers, and defectives.   Over 76 per cent
of the paupers of foreign birth in Massachusetts a few
years ago were Irish, although they constituted only
46 per cent of the foreign born in that state.[2]   I do
not believe that there are any qualities inherent in the

Irish to which may be attributed the cause for this degeneration. It seems difficult to explain it except on the ground of excessive competition among the workers. In the rural communities, where the competition of recent immigrants has not been felt, the Irish, on the whole, have developed into very excellent Americans. Nothing would be of greater value to one interested in the effects of immigration than a study showing the degeneration which results from this battle between the wage-earners of different nationalities, in the cities and in the industrial communities, for the means of livelihood.

This general poverty which exists among the immigrants brings us very naturally to the consideration of the actual burden which immigration places upon the state. This burden is principally borne by the benevolent, charitable, and penal institutions. The thing which most strikes one in a visit to the public institutions of the state is the great number of foreigners of all nationalities which one finds there. The only figures which exist of pauperism, in the United States as a whole, are those gathered by the Census Bureau. They are by no means complete; the number of the poor supported in their homes is unknown. Nevertheless, the burden of the dependent foreign born is shown to be a very heavy one. It is well known that various societies in foreign countries have pursued the policy of send-

ing to us large numbers of paupers, imbeciles, and
aged persons, as well as criminals and other dangerous persons. They have employed such means
to evade the responsibility and expense of continuous
support for these classes. This has been partially
stopped by recent laws prohibiting the entrance of
such persons. But it has not altogether ceased.
During the month of September, 1903, three hundred
and sixty-two persons were debarred on the ground
that thay were likely to become public charges.
During the year over three thousand immigrants
were rejected because they were insane, idiots,
afflicted with dangerous, contagious diseases, or
likely to become paupers.[1] Vigilance alone prevents
the entry of those obviously unfit. There is, however, no possibility of sifting out of the immense
immigration of about one million persons annually
all of the unfit persons. The inspection at best must
be too cursory, and it is inconceivable that any agent
of the Immigration Bureau should be skilled enough
to determine unfitness by merely looking a person
over. The Commissioner General has recently said
that even those who have been rejected at the port
of New York as unfit come over the borders elsewhere in large numbers.[2] If this is true even those
whom our laws recognize as unfit often succeed in
making an entrance, and the immigrants who are
generally undesirable because unintelligent, of low

vitality and of poor physique, are not even prohibited from coming. It is difficult to keep out the latter class. For instance, it is not an easy matter to discover, except as a result of most careful, painstaking examinations of all immigrants, incipient tuberculosis or insanity of a recurring character. In fact, it is estimated that twenty-three thousand consumptive immigrants arrived in New York in 1902. It is well known that certain kinds of insanity are only temporarily cured. Furthermore, how is it possible to know at sight dangerous persons and criminals or the morally insane, who have been helped, by friends and relatives, to leave a foreign country? A case I came across recently in Switzerland is doubtless typical of the kind of dependents who come of their own will when they are not actually sent to us. An itinerant tailor, apparently strong, but afflicted with an incurable disease, was making his way through the mountains to Davos, where, he said, there was a hospital which he hoped would take him in. When he learned that we came from America, he exclaimed : " How I wish I could get there! The hospitals are free in your country."

According to the Census of 1890 there were, in proportion to population, over twice as many foreign-born inmates of charitable and penal institutions as there were native-born.[1] Of paupers alone the foreign classes supply an even larger

proportion. As long ago as 1887 there were
in the city poorhouses of New York State over
thirty-four thousand foreign born, while there were
only eighteen thousand of the native born. Over
44 per cent of the paupers of Massachusetts are
of foreign birth.[1] Taking an equal number of persons from the foreign element and the native
element, the foreign element furnishes four times
as many paupers. These figures represent most
important facts and should be given careful consideration. In view of them it can hardly be questioned that the recent immigrants were not all
needed, for, granting that they came to the country
in condition to be independent, self-supporting citizens, the wages they received were evidently not
sufficient to prevent them from depending upon
public relief for support. An interesting commen-
tary upon what has been previously said concerning
the Irish may be given here. By far the largest
proportion of paupers in the almshouses are Irish.
From observation, I should say that this is even
more true of the paupers receiving outdoor relief,
although there are no figures to be obtained on this
matter. It must, however, be said that a large
number of children of foreign parentage in charitable institutions are not there solely because of
poverty. A great many of the poorest and most
ignorant foreigners desire to have their children sup-

ported in public institutions. They often refer to
such places as the "college" to which they are sending their children.

There has been no effort to determine the amount
of money spent by the various states for the support
of foreign-born paupers. It is reasonable, however, to
suppose that it amounts to an immense sum yearly.
The insane hospitals, to which the foreign element
supply an unduly large proportion, are among the
most expensive public institutions. Mr. Goodwin
Brown, of the State Commission of Lunacy of New
York, estimates that, in the course of ten years,
about $50,000,000 are expended by the United States
to care for the excess of foreign-born insane.[1] The
Italians show a very large proportion of insane in
the asylums, hospitals, etc. Out of about twenty-
four thousand insane persons in New York State,
almost exactly one-half are foreign born, although
only about one-fourth of the people of the state are
foreign born. Mr. Brown says, in another place:
"We know of instance after instance, in fact there
are thousands of them, where they (the insane) have
been only a few months out of a hospital on the
other side. They are sane when they are admitted
here — that is, they will pass the ordinary inspection; they find difficulty in procuring employment;
they get out of money; they are away from their
friends, and, naturally, they soon go to pieces, and

then they are re-committed. . . . There are instances of persons who have been re-committed
as many as fifteen or twenty times." [1]

The number of crimes committed by the foreign
born is only slightly, if at all, above the due proportion. In the matter of intoxication and disorderly
conduct, the foreign born furnish about three times
as many offenders as the native born. For assault,
burglary, larceny, and grand larceny, there is a
slight predominance of foreign born.[2] It is, however,
among the children of foreign parentage that criminals are found in greatest number.[3] The most
vicious, confirmed, incorrigible child criminal is the
child of foreign parents.   As a tough and outlaw
he has few, if any, equals.   In the chapter on
" The Child " some of the reasons for this have
been given.   The tremendous struggle with poverty which the foreigner makes in order to survive
in the competitive labor strife means, in a great
many cases, the sacrifice of the child; in other
words, the ruin of the Americanized foreigner.
The parents, when they are illiterate or belong to
Slavic, Balkan, or Mediterranean races, are rarely
Americanized.   Vice and crime, inconceivable to
the adult immigrant, become habitual to the most
neglected of the children of foreign parentage.
It is really appalling to observe the extent of this
ruin of childhood.   Among all the foreign peoples,

and especially among the Jews and the Italians of
New York and Chicago, many of the children are
developing habits of vice which are revolting in
the extreme. A Jewish society has recently published in one of its reports, " The vice and crime, the
irreligiousness, lack of self-restraint, indifference to
social conventions, indulgence of the most degraded
and perverted appetites, . . . are daily growing more
pronounced and more offensive." [1] Out of every
million of the voting population in Massachusetts,
there were about *nineteen thousand* male criminals
of foreign parents, while among the children of
native parents there were only *three thousand and
ninety*.[2] In the five states where the recent immigrant most often finds his home, his children supply from two to six times as many criminals as the
children of native parents. This is perhaps as
strong an argument as any against excessive immigration. It not only illustrates clearly the fact that
the recent immigrants must neglect their children
in order to gain a livelihood, but also that the recent
immigrants settle in the most degraded portions of
our cities, and, while not themselves becoming in
excessive numbers addicted to vice, bring up their
children in surroundings which make them in large
numbers vicious and criminally dangerous.

It is unnecessary to speak here especially of the
amount of illiteracy which exists by reason of re-

U

cent immigration. Despite the fact that it has
been our national custom to spare no expense to
educate our citizens, about half the foreigners in
the slums are illiterate. And we are presented
yearly with an enormous number of adults — this
year there will be approximately one million immigrants — a large proportion of whom are illiterate.
When they arrive after their fourteenth year, it is
very unlikely that they will ever become literate.
In a political democracy, where it is of the utmost
importance that every citizen should understand
the institutions of his country, and should be prepared by reading for intelligent voting, the illiteracy, which extends to over six millions of our
population, should be a matter of concern. The
relation of illiteracy to crime is not fully known,
but some figures gathered in Massachusetts show
that, with the increase of illiteracy, there is an
increase in the number of commitments to penal
institutions for every crime except that of drunkenness.[1] The immigrants from Austria, Poland, and
Italy, being the most illiterate, were the most often
committed to penal institutions. It is, however,
only fair to repeat that the poor of the four
great industrial states are largely foreign born or
children of foreign parents. We should expect,
therefore, that the foreign element would supply
an excess of dependents. It is true of every coun-

try — it is true of purely American communities — that the poor supply an excess of criminals and dependents. It is one of the natural results of poverty. How far in excess the dependent foreign born and the criminals of foreign parentage are, it is not possible to determine from our present inadequate data. The facts, however, if they were known, would doubtless make a much less unfavorable showing for the foreign element than the proportions heretofore given indicate. It is not possible to give actual figures showing the cost to the state of almost unrestricted and indiscriminate immigration. That it is a great expense to the state and that it becomes increasingly large, because of the neglected children of immigrants, there is no question.

The heaviest burden of the immense immigration is, however, not borne by the state, which, after all, can, when necessary, afford to bear even larger burdens of this character. The real weight is borne by the poorest classes of our community (except those in the almshouses); namely, the unskilled workers. Unskilled labor is already too plentiful; nothing shows it more than the conditions which exist in many parts of the country; in those places where unskilled laborers might profitably employ themselves, the recent immigrants refuse to go, and instead herd in factory and mining towns and in large cities, pulling like a heavy weight upon that class of laborers which is already too plentiful there. In times of industrial depression, such as we are facing now, the amount of unskilled labor vastly over-supplies the demand for it, and the distress, by reason of unemployment at such periods, becomes a calamity of national importance. We have seen elsewhere how serious the problem of unemployment is at all times. It is nowhere so great as among the classes which are increased by recent immigration. A surplus of laborers enables the meanest employer to oppress his workmen to the very limit of endurance. If it is to his advantage to have short seasons, an over-supply of labor enables him to push through large contracts of work in short periods of time, leaving the workmen at other times unemployed and in poverty. In the same way that surplus labor enables the individual manufacturer to supply his market in a short period of time, leaving his plant and workmen idle at other times, all manufacturers are enabled by surplus labor to supply sufficient products for the market, in a few years of great business activity, thereby necessitating, periodically, a long season, sometimes extending over years, when both plant and men must be idle. Both the Honorable Carroll D. Wright and Professor Richmond Mayo-Smith have shown how important a factor this over-supply of labor is in creating industrial depressions. The relation of immigration to the over-supply of labor, which, in part, causes industrial depressions, can be clearly seen. Even in times of increasing prosperity and of unusual industrial activity, the unskilled workers are not permitted to profit by the better times. Immigration instantly increases, the labor market is progressively overcrowded, and the wages in unskilled trades are thereby reduced to the lowest limit.

The unskilled workers are most largely drafted from the Chinese, Croatians, Greeks, Italians, Lithuanians, Magyars, Poles, Portuguese, Ruthenians, and Slovaks. When the women come, they also commonly work at such employments as they find open to them. I have seen hundreds of women employed in the stock yards, working in great tubs of blood and entrails, employed in this manner week in and week out, leaving their children at home uncared for in order to assist the men in their fight for livelihood. The assistance of the women has made the Italian a formidable competitor in any trade which he has undertaken. It happens, however, that women often become the competitors of their own husbands and sons, and, by their willingness to accept a lower wage, decrease the wage scale of all laborers. The fear of poverty intensifies the competition between the different nationalities, between the native and the foreigner, between the women and the men, between the adults and the children, so that it is absolutely impossible for the unskilled classes to successfully resist oppression. They will work any hours, at any speed, and for almost any wages; they will suffer the direst poverty; they will under-feed their children and themselves; they will sleep in the most insanitary hovels of factory towns or in the darkest rooms of the worst tenements in the cities. The Italians are perhaps as successful as any, and succeed because they are willing to accept the low-est standard of living, the greatest poverty, and the highest mortality. It can almost be said that many who win in this competitive struggle win at death.

It is a competition of standards, and the lowest standard prevails. Among the common laborers in coal mining and in the clothing and textile trades, this competition is always too intense. It amounts, at times, almost to a race war, so that the bitterest hatred often exists between the different nationalities. The recent pitched battle between fifty Italian laborers and seventy Irish rock-drillers in one of the Subway pits is an example of what often occurs between the conflicting races. In 1892 a visitor to the anthracite district of Pennsylvania was amazed at the heartless and cruel way in which the foreigners were treated by the Americans; but after remaining in the dis-trict some time, he began to excuse, if not to justify, the Americans, for he saw "a thousand idle Ameri-cans, and a like number of foreigners slaving for eighty or ninety cents per day." [1] Professor John R. Commons says, concerning the coal miners displaced by foreigners: "Many coal miners sought the western and northern metal fields; others turned to farming. In case migration is not available, the displaced workman may be able to rise on top of the immigrant and become his foreman, his boss, or the proprietor of his working place. On the other hand, the inferior individuals of the displaced classes, refusing to compete alongside the immigrant, and incapable or unwilling to rise and better their condition, fall into the class of hoodlums, tramps, and paupers." [2]

The tragedy which results from this surplus of labor was strikingly shown in the work of a sculptor, exhibited at the World's Fair in Chicago. It is the custom in some places, in England for instance, for the foremen of the great factories to go out in the morning to the gate where the workmen, seeking employment, are gathered, and to throw out tickets to the number of employees needed. The group represents an intense struggle to obtain one of these tickets. The man fortunate enough to get it is the central figure. He holds it high above his head, resistant, but looks with compassion upon the struggling ones about him. A withered old man clings to him, begging for the ticket; a youth behind is plotting to seize it; a woman with babe in arms, trampled under the feet of the others, strives to protect the child; a tiny lad, with a wolfish hunger in his face, endeavors to clamber up on others in the hope of seizing the ticket. Let him, who will, go about the factory districts of the country and see this thing enacted in real life, not so obviously dramatical but with agony that is actual. It will then be easy for him to question a national policy of unrestricted immigration.

The political consequences are perhaps out of our province, although they are becoming more and more serious as the foreign colonies become an increasing source of power to corrupt politicians. The greater the poverty, the greater is the dependence of the foreigner upon either padrone or politician. It has been recently shown that naturalization papers can be had for $5; and a vote means a job.[1] The present methods of naturalization outrage the principles and ideals which formerly underlay this legal process of initiating the foreigner into the full rights of American citizenship. At present it involves no qualifications on the part of the immigrant and becomes simply another method of encouraging venal voting. It is not easy to say to what extent the foreign elements are responsible for the political corruption in those sections in which they predominate. Our own history is an unclean one. The native element is guilty of the most dangerous political corruption. The Americans are the ones principally who buy up the state legislatures and city councils, who bribe the representatives of the people, and steal every privilege which yields a profit. The Irish-Americans are mainly responsible for bribe-taking because they are the successful politicians. The recently arrived immigrants are an unknown quality, but they are learning the game. Their igno-rance and poverty make them easy tools. It is undoubtedly true that they play, though perhaps innocently, into the hands of the politicians, and temporarily, at any rate, enhance their power. The conditions in certain sections of New York City and Chicago — and especially in certain sections of Penn-sylvania — prove this beyond question. Whether or not the dangers to democratic government, which reside in the present political corruption, can be as clearly demonstrated to these foreign elements as to the native element, and whether or not they will respond to the higher appeal, are momentous ques-tions. The personal power of ward politicians and saloon keepers and its appeal to the immediate selfishness of poor immigrants is a mighty political force, perhaps too mighty for the higher appeal to overcome until the mass of immigrants have been sufficiently educated and informed to be reached by the minority from which reform and revolt always emanate. The minority cannot build up a machine; they cannot gain their ends through personal power;

they are necessarily dependent to a large extent upon public appeals and literature to make evils known and to demonstrate clearly their proposed reforms. The love and devotion which many of the immigrants manifest for democracy is beautiful and pathetic; but their ignorance prevents them from knowing that their votes commonly support the very men who are selling themselves and their country to the most sinister *Enemies of the Republic*.

There are certain results of migratory movements which are even more important than those hitherto considered. It is generally thought that emigration has been of great value to Europe in that it has relieved a condition of over-population and congestion, thereby benefiting the poorer classes especially. It would seem, in support of this theory, that the twenty million persons who have emigrated to this country since 1820 must have left behind them less crowding and better industrial opportunities for the workers who remained at home. In other words, it is the popular belief that the migrations of the last century have worked a redistribution of population which has been of inestimable value both to foreign countries and to our own for the reason that additional workers have come here, where they have been needed for the development of the new country, and a less congested population left abroad, where there is at all times a large surplus of unemployed and suffering workers. Upon the face of the matter this view seems a right one, but it fails to take any account whatever of the influence of migratory movements upon the birth-rate. It is obvious that if when large numbers of persons emigrate from a country, their places are soon filled by an increase in the number of births, the result will not be as imagined, but instead that emigrating races will greatly increase in numbers. There seems to be little question but that this does result from emigration. It has been observed again and again that emigration from a country causes an increase in the number of children born in that country. William Farr noted that in Norfolk, England, emigration was followed by large families. Commenting upon this fact, he says that when the young people emigrate, the parents remaining at home "have on an average five children instead of two or three, or none." [1]   In almost every country of Europe the same tendency has been observed. Ireland is perhaps the only exception, and certain very definite economic causes are responsible for its extremely low birth-rate.*   Professor Richmond Mayo-Smith says: "Emigration does not threaten to depopulate the countries of Europe. Had there been no emigration during this century, it is not probable that the popu-

* See Appendix F, p. 360.

lation of Europe would have been any greater than it is. The probabilities are all the other way. Europe has never grown so fast as during the present century." [1] These statements by two of the ablest students of vital statistics could be supported by facts from other writers if it were necessary. There is a strange and rather startling probability that the twenty million persons who have emigrated to this country have been replaced by twenty or so million persons *who would not have been born* had these emigrants remained at home. Their leaving Europe has simply meant more births. As paradoxical as it seems, the population of Europe has in all likelihood not been decreased at all by the leaving of the twenty million emigrants who have come to the United States. Economic conditions abroad have not been bettered for the reason that an increased number of children have been born to fill the places left vacant by the emigrating millions. Neither has the poverty nor the congestion abroad been diminished by emigration.

It is also generally thought that immigration to the United States has increased the population of this country by some twenty million persons, and therefore has vastly aided in the growth of our industrial life. But this popular impression has also been called into question. Professor John R. Commons, who is now perhaps our foremost student

of the subject, says, in his study of Immigration for
the Industrial Commission, "It is a hasty assumption which holds that immigration during the nineteenth century has increased the total population
in the United States."[1] Professor Commons' statement is based upon the same principle of the growth
of population which was considered in the previous
paragraph. Immigration to this country has a striking influence upon our birth-rate. As emigration
tends to increase the number of births among those
remaining at home, so immigration, it is thought,
causes a decrease in the birth-rate of the persons
already in the country to which immigrants come.
The late President Francis A. Walker, who was the
superintendent of the censuses of 1870 and 1880, and
therefore at the fountainhead of information on the
subject, vigorously maintained that had there been
no immigration to this country during the last seventy years, the native element would have filled, by
an increased number of births, "the places which
the foreign element has usurped."[2] According to
his belief, had there been no immigration since 1830
we should nevertheless have had as large a population (of native American stock) as we now have with
the twenty million foreign immigrants. He claimed
that the coming of the foreign element caused a great
decrease in the birth-rate of the native Americans,
and that in consequence the foreign peoples are

here in place of the native children who would have
been born had there been no immigration during
these years.   This is one of the most important
explanations of the much-discussed question of race-
suicide, or, as one may choose to call it, the annihilation of the native American stock.

To certain people this reasoning will seem absurd,
and especially will it appear so to those who are
not familiar with the economic forces which act and
react upon the birth-rate.   There are certain facts,
however, concerning the annihilation of the native
American stock which cannot be questioned.   During the last seventy years the birth-rate of the
American element in certain sections of the United
States has declined from one of the highest in the
world to one of the lowest.   Throughout the so-
called civilized world the greatest decline in birth-
rate, shown in the last century, is in Massachusetts.[1]
The native population in this and in one or two other
New England states is not increasing.   A writer in
The Quarterly Journal of Economics concludes an
instructive paper on the subject by saying that the
native stock actually "seems to be diminishing."[2]
In the northeastern division the native birth-rate
has fallen so enormously that the annual increase of
children of foreign white parents is ten times as
great as the increase of the children of native parentage.[3]   In the several states of Connecticut, Maine,

Massachusetts, New Hampshire, Rhode Island, and Vermont the annual *death-rate* in 1900 of the whites of native parentage *exceeded the birth-rate by* 1.5 *per thousand*, while among those of foreign white parents the *birth-rate exceeded the death-rate by* 44.5 *per thousand.*[1] In passing it is well to note that this birth-rate among the foreign whites is considerably greater than that of Hungary, which has the highest birth-rate in Europe, and this would go to prove that the birth-rate among immigrants is increased as a result of their migration, although it might be explained on the ground of the age distribution among the foreign element. The main conclusion, however, which is to be drawn from these facts, is that, if this decrease in the birth-rate of the native stock continues, the annihilation of the native element is only a matter of time.

However, the question which many persons will ask is not answered by these facts. Granting that the native element is disappearing, can it be proved that immigration is responsible for the annihilation? To account for the connection between immigration and the decreasing birth-rate, certain economic changes which have been found to affect the birth-rate must be considered. There is a great mass of collected data showing that the birth-rate is in all countries affected by economic changes. For instance, Farr in his "Vital Statistics" concludes that "war, abundance, dearth, high wages, periods of speculation," etc., have a direct effect upon the birth-rate.[1] Von Mayr and others have shown that the number of births fluctuates with a change in the market price of wheat or rye.[2] Professor Richmond Mayo-Smith, in summing up a chapter on "Births" in his "Statistics and Sociology," says that where the number "decreases suddenly, it shows the effect of war or of commercial distress or of *economic disaster*. Where it increases, it is generally a sign of economic prosperity." [3] Hadley, Marshall, Newsholme, and others (not to go back as far as Malthus) have all reviewed more or less the influence of economic conditions upon the birth-rate.[4] It is not a matter of theory, it is an observed fact that economic disaster and similar influences operate to decrease the birth-rate, and that prosperity or any improvement in economic conditions operates to increase the birth-rate. On the basis of these well-established facts we should expect a decrease in the birth-rate of Americans as soon as the foreigners began to come in sufficiently large numbers to cause distress among the native working-men; we should also expect an increase in the birth-rate abroad because of a large emigration, for the reason that industrial opportunities are temporarily improved; and lastly, we should expect an increase in the birth-rate of foreigners in this country for the reason that the better wages and conditions here represent to them prosperity.

It has been repeatedly mentioned in this chapter that the coming of foreign immigrants presents itself to the workers already in this country as the coming of an economic disaster.[1] The conflicts which occurred between the foreigners who came to this country in the forties and fifties and the native element are too well known to require mentioning. Their coming was a terrible economic disaster to the native workers. The Irish and Germans came to compete, they had a lower standard of living, and they drove the American element out of certain classes of work. It was a bitter conflict, and on that level the foreigner won. The native rose above the foreigner, or fell below him and became vagrant or hoodlum. An effect upon the native birth-rate was noticed immediately. A lower rate of increase was to be observed wherever the foreigner came. It is not a theory but a fact that the decline in the rate of increase among the native element began in those very districts to which the foreigner came in considerable numbers. There was to be observed a remarkable correspondence between the number of immigrants arriving and the decrease in the growth of the native population. In other words immigration to this country means not an increase in population, but, as President Walker says, "the substitution of one kind of man for another."

This position is very well stated by President

x

Walker in Volume II of his "Discussions in Economics and Statistics." "The population," he says,
"of 1790 was almost wholly a native and wholly an
acclimated population, and for forty years afterwards
immigration remained at so low a rate as to be
practically of no account; yet the people of the
United States increased in numbers more rapidly
than has ever elsewhere been known, in regard to
any considerable population, over any considerable
area, through any considerable period of time. Between 1790 and 1830 the nation grew from less
than four millions to nearly thirteen millions — an increase, in fact, of 227 per cent, a rate unparalleled in
history. That increase was wholly out of the loins
of our own people. Each decade had seen a growth
of between 33 and 38 per cent, a doubling once in
twenty-two or twenty-three years. During the thirty
years which followed 1830, the conditions of life
and reproduction in the United States were not
less, but more, favorable than in the preceding
period. Important changes relating to the practice
of medicine, the food and clothing of people, the
general habits of living, took place, which were of
a nature to increase the vitality and reproductive
capability of the American people. Throughout
this period the standard of height, of weight, and
of chest measurement was steadily rising, with the
result that, of the men of all nationalities in the

giant army formed to suppress the slaveholders' rebellion, the native American bore off the palm in respect to physical stature. The decline of this rate of increase among Americans began at the very time when foreign immigration first assumed considerable proportions; it showed itself first and in the highest degree in those regions, in those states, and in the very counties into which the foreigners most largely entered. It proceeded for a long time in such a way as absolutely to offset the foreign arrivals, so that in 1850, in spite of the incoming of two and a half millions of foreigners during thirty years, our population differed by less than ten thousand from the population which would have existed, according to the previous rate of increase, without reënforcement from abroad. These three facts, which might be shown by tables and diagrams, constitute a statistical demonstration such as is rarely attained in regard to the operation of any social or economic force.

"But it may be asked, Is the proposition that the arrival of foreigners brought a check to the native increase a reasonable one? Is the cause thus suggested one which has elsewhere appeared as competent to produce such an effect? I answer, yes. All human history shows that the principle of population is intensely sensitive to social and economic changes. Let social and economic conditions remain as they were, and population will go on increasing from year to year, and from decade to decade, with a regularity little short of the marvellous. Let social and economic conditions change, and population instantly responds. The arrival in the United States, between 1830 and 1840, and thereafter increasingly, of large numbers of degraded peasantry, created for the first time in this country distinct social classes, and produced an alteration of economic relations which could not fail powerfully to affect population. The appearance of vast numbers of men, foreign in birth and often in language, with a poorer standard of living, with habits repellent to our native people, of an industrial grade suited only to the lowest kind of manual labor, was exactly such a cause as by any student of population would be expected to affect profoundly the growth of the native population. Americans shrank alike from the social contact and the economic competition thus created.* They became increasingly unwilling to bring forth sons and daughters who should be obliged to compete in the market for labor and in the walks of life with those whom they did not recognize as of their own grade and condition." [1]

There is another closely associated economic cause of the annihilation of the native stock. There are certain classes of the population who may be said to

* See Appendix F.

be the main population-producing classes. It is a well-established fact that the wealthiest class in most countries is continually dying out — that is, the birth-rate is so low that were it not for accessions to the class from other classes in the community, it would disappear. Benjamin Kidd says: "The attempts which have been made in the past by the nobles and power-holding classes in almost every country to perpetuate the stock of the privileged classes to which they have belonged have invariably failed."[1] Galton, Lageneau, and others have shown that in both England and France the aristocratic families would entirely disappear were it not for recruits from below. This is well illustrated by the following table, prepared by Dr. J. Bertillon, and placed before the meeting of the International Statistical Institute held in St. Petersburg in 1897:[2] —

BIRTHS PER 1000 WOMEN PER ANNUM

CLASSIFICATION	PARIS	BERLIN	VIENNA	LONDON
Very poor quarters	108	157	200	147
Poor quarters	95	129	164	140
Comfortable quarters . . .	72	114	155	107
Very comfortable quarters .	65	96	153	107
Rich quarters	53	63	107	87
Very rich quarters	34	47	71	63
Average	80	102	153	109

Certain things in this table have been criticised,
perhaps quite properly, but it will serve as an illustration of the well-known fact that births are most
numerous among the poorer classes. The deaths
are also most numerous. The death-rate among
the wealthier classes is low and varies little, while
among the poorest it is often high but it varies
much, — sometimes 100 per cent in two different
blocks or wards.[1] But it is true, notwithstanding the
higher death-rate, that the poorer, if not the poorest,
classes are the great population-producing classes.
There are many reasons for this, some physiologi-
cal, such as decreased fecundity due to excessive
nervous or mental strain among the higher classes,
some ethical, and others social. But the economic
causes which affect a whole social or industrial class
are the most powerful and far reaching. For instance, one is the desire which the propertied classes
have of leaving their children a large income.
"The fear of losing social standing," as President
Hadley puts it,[2] or, as Benjamin Kidd says, "the unwillingness of men . . . to marry and bring up families
in a state of life lower than that into which they themselves were born" is one of the most powerful of the
known influences working to restrict the birth-rate.[3]
This cause alone is probably mainly responsible for
the extremely low birth-rate in France. Professor
Alfred Marshall says, "The birth-rate in France is

known to vary inversely with the predominance of small properties, being lowest in those departments in which the largest proportion of the agricultural population own land, and highest in those in which there are fewest peasant proprietors."[1] There are other causes for a low birth-rate among the propertied classes, such as the later age at which they marry, but the most important seems unquestionably to be this desire to retain or better the social standing attained.[2] A similar desire among the working classes operates toward producing a high birth-rate. Their highest wages are earned between the years of eighteen and thirty-five. They consequently marry early, and for this reason alone they would be likely to have larger families than other classes. But the main incentive which operates to increase the number of children is, it seems to me, the fear of becoming in old age dependent upon the public. To the poor, children are a form of old-age insurance. They are taught that they must care for their parents when they are old, and it is one of the commonest of sayings among these classes that "a large 'family' of boys is a good thing, for they will care for us when we are old." For several reasons, therefore, the great population-producing class is the wage-working class.

It is a generally observed fact that the mass of laborers in certain parts of the United States are either foreign born or of foreign parentage. To a remarkable extent the native born have risen out of this class, although a certain portion have evaded competition by emigrating to states having fewer immigrants, and not a few have been crushed beneath the foreigners. In the manufacturing, mechanical, and common laboring classes of several Eastern states the foreigners are three or four times as numerous as the natives.[1] In other words, the natives of these states have been forced out of that class, which is known to be the great population-producing class. Those who have fallen below the foreign workers have been largely forced into the vicious classes, who fortunately never have a large birth-rate, and those natives who have been successful have, to a considerable extent, entered into the propertied and the professional classes, which always have relatively a small birth-rate. They were able to rise out of the lower class by marrying later and by having fewer children or none, and the desire to maintain the higher social position has been a continued incentive to limit the number of children.

The process which is at work in this struggle of the races has, therefore, not only in the past lowered the birth-rate among the natives, but will continue to lower it as the natives leave the classes which have the higher birth-rate. It can hardly be expected that any incentive toward the increase of population will become powerful enough to counteract the forces which are increasingly diminishing the birth-rate of the native stock. In the South and West, where there are fewer immigrants, the native stock will probably remain dominant in the population groups, but in the northeastern division of the states the foreign element is fast becoming dominant.[1]

The evils, therefore, of immigration, if they are to be called evils, are not temporary. The direct descendants of the people who fought for and founded the Republic, and who gave us a rich heritage of democratic institutions, are being displaced by the Slavic, Balkan, and Mediterranean peoples. This is the fact in the problem of immigration which is of greatest importance. Discussion of the problem should be elevated to a different plane from that which has been taken in the past. It involves too much socially and politically in the world's progress to be ignored or lightly considered. It is a question of babies and birth-rates, and whatever decision is made regarding immigration, it is perforce a decision concerning the kind of children that shall be born. The decision for Congress to make consciously and deliberately is simply whether or not it is better for the world that the children of native parents should be born instead of the children of foreign parents. The making of the decision cannot be avoided. It is made now, although unconsciously, and it is a decision against the children of native parents. Immigration, therefore, means that, by permitting free and unlimited entry, we are stimulating the birth-rate both in this country and abroad of Italians, Hungarians, Lithuanians, Ruthenians, Croatians, and Polish, Roumanian, and Russian Jews. This increase means that the places of those who emigrate to this country are filled in a generation, and the misery and oppression, which emigration is supposed to relieve, continue unimproved, while in the United States the peasantry from other countries, degraded by foreign oppression, are supplanting the descendants of the original stock of this country. This is the race-suicide, the annihilation of our native stock, which unlimited immigration forces upon us, none the less powerfully because it is gradually and stealthily done. The native stock of America, possessed of rare advantages, freed by its own efforts from oppression and the miseries of oppression, might have peopled the United States with the seventy millions which now inhabit it. It has not done so for the reason that "we cannot welcome an indefinite number of immigrants to our shores without forbidding the existence of an indefinite number of children of native parents who might have been born."

Immigration presents for our serious consideration a formidable array of dangers. It is unnecessary to summarize the facts and the arguments which have been given. These are the two things which, of all that have been stated, seem the most important: the likelihood of race annihilation and the possible degeneration of even the succeeding American type. It seems unquestionable that the unfittest class of immigrants that have ever come to our shores is increasing yearly in numbers. We may and should be willing to permit our native stock to be annihilated by a superior people; but it is inconceivable that we should knowingly promote, by conscious act, an intermarrying and intermingling of peoples, which will indefinitely lower the standard of American or any other manhood. If this is to result from an unrestricted and practically unselected immigration, that conscious act is taken at Ellis Island and at other ports of entry, after the legal decision compelling it has been made by Act of Congress. Our philanthropic institutions are yearly making larger provision for segregating the feeble-minded in order to prevent propagation. This is observing the necessity for exercising some selection, when it is possible, as to the kind of children that shall be born. There is extreme necessity in such cases, which does not exist in the case of immigration. In the latter case, however, selection may be powerfully exercised in deciding the class of immigrants that may land in America. The fathers and mothers of American children can be chosen, and it is in the power of Congress to decide upon what merits. By wise regulation of immigration selection can be exercised so as to increase the number of strong-minded children, as it is used, in the former instance, to decrease the number of feeble-minded children.

There are few questions which it would seem easier to decide upon purely moral grounds than this one of immigration. Whether or not we should restrict immigration is perhaps after all not so fundamentally important as the fact that in deciding the question, as it is now decided, our governing bodies have not considered the welfare of the people, either immigrants or Americans. The decision has been made as a result of pressure brought to bear upon public officials by private and selfish interests. Our national characteristics may be changed; our love of freedom; our religion; our inventive faculties; our standard of life. All of the things, in fact, for which America has been more or less distinctive among the nations may be entirely altered. Our race may be supplanted by another, — by an Asiatic one, for instance, — and not because it is better so nor because it is for the world's good. On the contrary, it is in order that the individuals interested in steamships may be benefited and in order that the employers may have cheaper labor. These selfish forces may be disguised, but they are there and they are active.

One appalling social problem, which caused a terrible civil war and which still awaits solution, was forced upon us by the selfishness of the slave-traders, the ship-owners, and the southern land-owners. One entire race, the Negro, came for their profit. It almost ruined the South, and it is still problematical whether, in the face of race hatred, we shall be able to maintain in the South a political democracy. Like selfish forces are to-day at work creating new social problems which may be even more baffling to the future generations.

CONCLUSION

In the previous chapters I have only touched here and there upon the struggle with poverty which the poor themselves make. We are perhaps too prone to think of those in poverty as effortless beings, who make no fight for themselves and wait in misery until some one comes to assist them. Such an opinion is without any foundation. It is based upon knowledge gained by acquaintance with the pauper and vagrant, and is in no wise applicable to the workers in poverty. It is small wonder that workers who are underfed, underclothed, and poorly housed, are sometimes won from their hard and almost hopeless toil by sensual pleasures. Nor is it surprising that they are driven to despair by the brutal power of the economic forces which dominate their lives. Without the security which comes only with the ownership of property, without a home from which they may not be evicted, without any assurance of regular employment, without tools with which they may employ themselves, they are pathetically dependent upon their physical efficiency, — their health and strength, and upon the activity of machinery, owned by others,

and worked or left idle as the owners consider it wise
or profitable.   In their weak and unorganized condition, they are unlike the skilled workers, made powerful by their unions and by their methods of collective
bargaining; they are fighting alone, each one against
another.   In watching during the last few years
the struggle with poverty of this poorest class of
workers I have again and again read the allegory
with which Dante begins his great poem, each
time feeling more and more how wonderfully it
pictures this struggle.   The bewildered traveller,
weary and terrified, is toiling up a steep and uncertain path of a mountain.   His eyes are lifted to
the "rose of dawn," which sends to him a glow of
hope and leads him on.   As he laboriously toils
upward, a leopard (significant of sensuality), bright
and beautiful, almost irresistibly attracts him; and
from time to time, as he wearily pauses for rest,
"that fair creature with the spotted hide" fills him
with sensations of pleasure.   Suddenly his heart
is filled with terror by a lion, fierce and terrible,
which threatens to devour him; and from another
quarter appears a lean and hungry she-wolf with
"all ill-greed defiled."   Losing all hope, he turns
and flees from the dangers which beset his "life's
course."

It would be absurd to think that Dante meant to
picture the problem of poverty.   The statesman, the

theologian, the psychologist, has each made the allegory serve a purpose, according to the bias of his thought. And, in the same way, reading our own thought into the lines, there could hardly be a more powerful picture than this one of the dangers and difficulties which beset those of our people who are in poverty, or of the almost hopeless struggle which presents itself as life to those of our people who are underpaid, underfed, underclothed, badly housed, and overworked.

To make the matter clear, a few words — and these, unfortunately, too much of a personal nature — are perhaps necessary. Having been drawn, about twelve years ago, to some interest in the problems of poverty, there happened to me the common experience of all those of like interests. The poor in the broader sense of that word were busily at work and trying rather to conceal than to make evidence of their poverty; while the beggars, vagrants, idlers, and dependents of all sorts were more or less always pressing forward their necessities. It was natural, therefore, for me to confuse the problem of poverty with that of pauperism and to take up with some enthusiasm the ideas which are a part of the propaganda of many useful charitable organizations. To the charitable workers these problems of vagrancy and pauperism seem possible of solution. Many reforms —

among which wise giving, friendly visiting, workrooms, work-tests, model lodging-houses, rent-col-
lecting, etc., are a few — were, in the early
nineties, making rapid headway. They were, at
that time, ranked first in importance in the cate-
gory of organized movements for diminishing the
evils of pauperism. Many committees were at work
promoting these reforms, and in different cities I
was able to help in their efforts. The result of
their work was not discouraging, but in every
instance they came hard up against one almost
insurmountable obstacle. The pauper and the
vagrant were not dissatisfied; they clamored for
alms, but they did not wish to alter their way of
living. Even those who possessed the capacity
for industrial usefulness and who might have
become self-supporting did not wish to go back
again into the factories, mills, or mines. In fact,
so far as one could see, they were as unwilling as
the others to alter their ways of living. However
miserable their lot seemed to those of us on the
Committees, to them it seemed to be, on the
whole, acceptable enough to bring a certain sort
of content. However malarious and poisonous and
undrained, they loved their valley of idleness and
quiet; they hated the hill upon which they were
constrained to toil; they shrank from its disappointments, its bruises, its weariness and bitterness,

Y

while its meanness and ugliness of life were but slightly less mean and ugly than their own. The children, bred into the ways of pauperism, nearly always took up the vices of their parents. They were pleasure-loving, and whatever was toilsome seemed abhorrent to them. The girls took the easier path; it appeared unquestionably more desirable to their childish standards, and for a time at least it gave them more of everything, for which most human beings seem to hunger, — finery, leisure, and a kind of pleasure. The men and boys liked vagrancy, and those who were not attracted to these ways settled down into a satisfied, imperturbable pauperism. They lived in God only knows what misery. They ate when there were things to eat; they starved when there was lack of food. But, on the whole, although they swore and beat each other and got drunk, they were more contented than any other class I have happened to know. It took a long time to understand them. Our Committees were busy from morning until night in giving them opportunities to take up the fight again, and to become independent of relief. They always took what we gave them; they always promised to try; but as soon as we expected them to fulfil any promises, they gave up in despair, and either wept or looked ashamed, and took to misery and drink again, — almost, so it seemed to me at times, with a sense of relief. I am reminded now of a vagrant whom I knew well and for many years believed to be sincerely trying to become "a man," as we used to say. He has turned up wherever I have happened to be — in Chicago or New York. He has always looked me up, and together we have conspired to overcome his vagrant instincts. We have always failed, and after a few weeks' work Jerry disappears, and I know what has become of him. At last, in his case as in many others, I have become convinced that he is more satisfied and content with the life of a vagrant than with the miserable lot of an unskilled, underpaid workman.

But as long as one works with, or observes only, the dependent classes, the true, or at least what seems to me the true, explanation of this apparent satisfaction of vagrants and paupers remains in the dark. It was not until I had lived for several years among the toilers in a great industrial community that the reason for the content of the dependent classes became clear to me. In this community of workers several thousand human beings were struggling fiercely against want. Day after day, year after year, they toiled with marvellous persistency and perseverance. Obnoxious as the simile is, they worked from dawn until nightfall, or from sunset until dawn, like galley slaves under the sting of want and under the whip of hunger. On cold, rainy mornings, at the dusk of dawn, I have been awakened, two hours before my rising time, by the monotonous clatter of hobnailed boots on the plank sidewalks, as the procession to the factory passed under my window. Heavy, brooding men, tired, anxious women, thinly dressed, unkempt little girls, and frail, joyless little lads passed along, half awake, not one uttering a word as they hurried to the great factory. From all directions thousands were entering the various gates,— children of every nation of Europe. Hundreds of others — obviously a hungrier, poorer lot than those entering the gates; some were most ragged and almost shoeless, but all with eager faces — waited in front of a closed gate until finally a great red-bearded man came out and selected twenty-three of the strongest, best-looking of the men. For these the gates were opened, and the others, with downcast eyes, marched off to seek employment elsewhere or to sit at home, or in a saloon, or in a lodging-house, until the following morning, when they came wistfully again to some factory gate. In this community, the saddest in which I have ever lived, fully fifty thousand men, women, and children were all the time either in poverty or on the verge of poverty. It would not be possible to describe how they worked and starved and ached to rise out of it. They broke their health down; the men acquired in

this particular trade a painful and disabling rheumatism, and consumption was very common. The girls
and boys followed in the paths of their parents.
The wages were so low that the men alone often
could not support their families, and mothers with
babies toiled in order to add to the income. They
gave up all thought of joyful living, probably in the
hope that by tremendous exertion they could overcome their poverty; but they gained while at work
only enough to keep their bodies alive. Theirs was
a sort of treadmill existence with no prospect of anything else in life but more treadmill. When they
were not given work in the mill, they starved; and
when they grew desperate, they came to my office
and asked for charity. Here was a mass of men
whose ways of living were violently opposed to those
of the vagrant or the pauper. They were distorting
themselves in the struggle to be independent of
charity and to overcome poverty. That they hated
charity must be taken without question. The testimony of scores of men is proof of it, even if, indeed,
their very lives were not. But despite all their efforts
they lived in houses but little, if any, better than those
of the paupers ; they were almost as poorly dressed;
they were hardly better fed.

In other words, these men, women, and children
were, to my mind, struggling up the face of a barren
precipice, — not unlike that up which Dante toiled,

— sometimes in hope, sometimes in despair, yet bitterly determined; the abyss of vice, crime, pauperism, and vagrancy was beneath them, a tiny ray of hope above them. Flitting before them was the leopard, persistently trying to win them from their almost hopeless task by charms of sensuality, debauch, and idleness. The lion, predatory and brutal, threatened to devour them; the she-wolf (Greed), hungry for them, enriched herself by their labors. Some were won from their toil by sensual pleasures, some were torn from their footholds by economic disorders, others were too weak and hungry to keep up the fight, and still others were rendered incapable of further struggle by diseases resulting from the unnecessary evils of work or of living.

This may seem to many persons an overdrawn simile; so, at any rate, it would have seemed to me several years ago. But it is a true picture, and I am convinced a just simile of the conditions in which the mass of those workers live who are already defined as being in poverty. At any rate, two or three things seem clearer to me now, after arriving at the conclusion so well represented by Dante's picture. It is easier to understand the reason for the abhorrence which the pauper and the vagrant and the prostitute have for that terrible struggle with poverty, and only less easy is it to understand their apparent willingness to live on rubbish or alms. Furthermore, it is clear that the poverty which undermines the workers is the great and constantly active cause of the fixed states of degeneracy represented by the pauper, the vagrant, the inebriate, etc. In other words, when the working people, by reason of whatever misery poverty brings, once fall into the abyss, they so hate the life of their former struggles and disappointments and sorrows that almost no one, however well-intentioned or kindly, can induce them to take it up again. In the abyss they become merely breeders of children, who persist in the degeneration into which their fathers have fallen; and, like the tribe of Ishmael or the family of the Jukes, they have neither the willingness nor the capacity to respond to the efforts of those who would help, or force, them back again into the struggle.

However merciful and kind and valuable the works of the charitable and the efforts of those who would raise up again the pauper and the vagrant, they are not remedial. In so far as the work of the charitable is devoted to reclamation and not to prevention, it is a failure. Not that any one could wish that less were done in the direction of reclamation. The fact only is important that effort is less powerful there than in overcoming the forces which undermine the workers and those who are struggling against insurmountable difficulties. It is an almost hopeless task to regenerate the degenerate, especially when, if the

latter are to succeed, they must be made to take up
again the battle with those very destructive forces
which are all the time undermining stronger, more
capable, and more self-reliant men than they. The
all-necessary work to be done is not so much to
reclaim a class which social forces are ever active in
producing, as it is to battle with the social or economic forces which are continuously producing recruits
to that class. The forces producing the miseries of
pauperism and vagrancy are many, but none are so
important as those conditions of work and of living
which are so unjust and degrading that men are
driven by them into degeneracy. When the uncer-
tainties, hardships, trials, sorrows, and miseries of a
self-supporting existence become so painful that good,
strong, self-reliant men and women are forced into
pauperism, then there is but little use in trying to
force the paupers and the vagrants back into the
struggle.

It is not necessary to debate the relative importance of individual or social forces, or of heredity or
environment, upon the extent of poverty, in order to
prove that social forces are constantly and everywhere active in bringing poverty to a great mass of
people. Leaving all such questions out of the discussion, we can nevertheless be certain that obstacles
can be too great for even the strongest of men to overcome. And this is almost precisely what happens to

the masses in poverty. As a class they have the
longest hours of work, they have the lowest pay —
often not even living wages; they have competition
of the severest kind to face — unskilled workers from
every land come to seek their employment; they are
oppressed by sweating methods, their employment is
irregular; their tenements are the most insanitary,
and their rents relatively the highest that any class
pay; the prices for food and fuel are exorbitant,
because they must buy in small quantities; when
they find it necessary to go into debt they are fleeced
by loan sharks; they are most often ill; they bear
the burden of more deaths than any other class;
and being without savings, they are in actual distress as soon as they are unable to work, or as soon
as they are unemployed as a result of economic or
other causes.   Furthermore, the children are prevented from having fair opportunities to master the
difficulties which ruined their fathers. Their health
is imperilled and not seldom destroyed by insanitary
homes; they are injured morally and otherwise by a
necessary street life; their food is in many cases so
poor that it will not feed the brain, and they are consequently unable to learn; they are early pressed to
do a man's labor and are often ruined physically and
blighted in other ways by this early and unnatural
toil.   With all of these and many other obstacles and
disadvantages working their ruin, only the strongest

and most fortunate are able to put forth the struggle necessary to master their fate. For the others, their life's course lies up an almost baffling precipice.

About a half-century ago there were so many persons in London becoming paupers, vagrants, mendicants, etc., that a group of people organized together to make the way of the pauper, vagrant, and mendicant so thorny and difficult that the workers, toiling up the precipice, would hold the abyss beneath them in even greater aversion than it was thought they were in the habit of doing, and that the able-bodied dependents in the abyss would be forced to turn from their way and seek again the path of self-support. This may, in certain places and at certain times, be necessary; but would it not seem a more wholesome, not to say kindlier, policy to see that the obstacles — the unnecessary obstacles, now preventing the rise of those workers in poverty — be removed?

This, however, is not by any means easy of accomplishment. The first difficulty lies in the complex nature of the problem itself. It is inextricably woven in with all other social and economic problems. If what Charles Booth says is true (and many economists agree with him), that our "modern system of industry will not work without some unemployed margin, some reserve of labor"[1]; if it is necessary, as another economist has said, that "for long periods of time large stagnant pools of adult effective labor power must lie rotting in the bodies of their owners, unable to become productive of any form of wealth, because they cannot get access to the material of production "; and if at the same time "facing them in equal idleness are unemployed or under-employed masses of land and capital, mills, mines, etc., which, taken in conjunction with this labor power, are theoretically competent to produce wealth for the satisfaction of human wants,"[1]—if these things are essential to our modern system of production, then the poverty of this large mass of workers must continue unrelieved until the system itself is reorganized. As a matter of fact, it would be useless to deny or ignore the fact that much of our poverty is directly due to a whole series of economic disorders which seem actually to make waste of human life necessary. And, in so far as poverty is a result of such deeply seated and fundamental economic disorders, due either to the method by which industry is organized or to the present ownership of the means and materials of production, it will, in all probability, find a solution only through struggles between the workers and the capitalists. No one who watches the trend of the times can doubt that these struggles, both in the industrial and in the political field, are growing more and more serious. Furthermore, in so far as poverty is a result of individual weaknesses, not them-

selves due to social causes, it can be dealt with only
by moral and personal forces. But complex as the
problem is, and varied as the remedies must be,
we may be sure that poverty is, to a considerable
extent, due to social causes which are clearly to be
seen and which are possible of remedy.

Besides the complexity of the problem, there is
still another, perhaps an even greater, obstacle firmly
set in the path of constructive reform. And this is
a political difficulty; namely, the anarchic principle
of state rights which divides this country into two
score and more small legislative areas. National
problems of the character herein dealt with cannot
therefore be treated in a national way, as they are
in most countries abroad. Legislation concerning
child labor, tuberculosis, tenements, factories, dangerous trades, sanitation, etc., must be of a variety of kinds, often warring with each other, throwing industrial advantages now to this state and now
to that. The child-labor laws which have been won
in the Northern states by years of vigorous agitation give an advantage to the parasitic industries
of the South. It is even likely that the textile industry may move to the South partly at least in order
to have the privilege of employing little children.
Manufacturers threaten the state legislatures (more
often, to be sure, than they carry out the threat) that
they will move into another state if any laws protect-

ing the workmen are passed. There is perhaps a certain business justification for such protests, for, unquestionably, by reason of our legislative anarchy, a parasitic industry in one state may thrive while an industry in another state, shorn of its parasitic privileges by legislation, may remain at a standstill, if it does not actually lose its trade. For this reason social and industrial legislation is usually more difficult to obtain in America than in any other great industrial country. Our political machinery itself, therefore, seriously retards and perhaps renders impossible any national standard of education, of sanitation, of working or of living conditions, etc. It is probable that there can be no national solution of some of these more remedial of the problems of poverty.

Another obstacle stands in the way of justice. The selfish interests of capitalists and land-owners too often either prevent good legislation or vitiate, by their influence, its enforcement. One can understand the determined opposition of men to socialistic measures seriously changing or violating the so-called rights of property; but it is not so easy to understand opposition to measures which, while affecting property interests, do not destroy any rights which may be exercised without injury to another. When property rights become property wrongs by injuring others, especially when they cause the physical degeneration and the human misery represented in poverty, they

may for a time, but will surely not always, stand in
the way of remedial action. The sense of justice
may for a time be so warped and distorted as to
value property more than human life, but only for
a time. The real cause of our present errors of
judgment in this matter lies in the corruption of
our political institutions. The business and propertied interests have bought the bosses of our political
machinery, and at present our laws are made and
enforced in the interest of the owners. When the
shame of our cities is notorious; when state and
national governments are in the hands of corrupt
politicians, owned by corporate interests; when "the
laws which should preserve and enforce all rights
are made and enforced by dollars;" when "it is
possible . . . with dollars to 'steer' the selection
of the candidates of both the great parties for the
highest office *in our Republic,* . . . so that the
people, as a matter of fact, must elect one of the
'steered' candidates;" when "it is possible to repeat the operation in the selection of candidates for
the executive and legislative conduct and control of
every state and municipality in the United States, and
with a sufficient number of dollars to 'steer' the doings
of the law-makers and law-enforcers of the national,
state, and municipal governments of the people, and
a sufficient proportion of the court decisions to make
absolute any power created by such direction;" when

the country is being daily betrayed by the "enemies of the republic,"— it seems utopian to appeal to these powers to do justice to their workers.[1] This may seem a dark view to take of our political institutions, but, considering the great mass of evidence accumulated in the last few years, it is surely warranted. So far as the problem of poverty is concerned, we can perhaps hope for little in the way of justice or reform during the next few years. For, by the help of this corruption, reform is fought at three stages: in the legislature, in the courts, and at the time of its enforcement.

In consequence of this temporary perversion of our democratic institutions pessimism runs high. Professor Franklin H. Giddings, our most distinguished sociologist, says: " We are witnessing to-day, beyond question, the decay — perhaps not permanent, but at any rate the decay — of republican institutions. No man in his right mind can deny it."[2] A president of one of our greatest universities prophesies that we shall have an emperor in the United States in twenty-five years. Charles Fourier may have been right when he prophesied one hundred years ago that "vast joint-stock companies, destined to monopolize and control all branches of industry, commerce, and finance, would establish an industrial or commercial feudalism that would control society by the power of capital, as did the old baronial or

military feudalism by the power of the sword" and
"by the monopoly of the land." [1]   Or again we may
have Mr. Ghent's "benevolent feudalism." [2]   If this
be the tendency of the times, the poverty of the ten
million people of this country will receive scant attention.   Indeed, poverty will become wider spread
and grow more distressing.   Even the moderate proposals for reform made in this book will, if viewed
solely from the standpoint of their effect upon property, seem radical, and, in so far as they affect property interests, unjust.   This is not mere speculation.
I could mention a score of incidents connected with
efforts to get child-labor or tenement-house legislation in Illinois and New York to prove that this
is even now true.   Progress on these reform lines
has been so slow in the last decade as to seem almost
no progress.   Much of the best legislation has been
won only after a bitter fight with the propertied
interests; and legislation, once secured, simply cannot, in most cases, be enforced because the political
machine is owned by the propertied classes.   Furthermore, when any so-called reform administration
does enforce the laws, the corporate interests lump
their campaign donations and punish the reformers
with ignominious defeat.

However, the difficulties which lie in the way of
any progress along social reform lines are beside the
purpose of this book.   That purpose is largely satis-

fied when the problem is stated, and, in so far as possible, I have summarized it in the following sentences. There are probably in fairly prosperous years no less than 10,000,000 persons in poverty; that is to say, underfed, underclothed, and poorly housed. Of these about 4,000,000 persons are public paupers. Over 2,000,000 working-men are unemployed from four to six months in the year. About 500,000 male immigrants arrive yearly and seek work in the very districts where unemployment is greatest. Nearly half of the families in the country are propertyless. Over 1,700,000 little children are forced to become wage-earners when they should still be in school. About 5,000,000 women find it necessary to work and about 2,000,000 are employed in factories, mills, etc. Probably no less than 1,000,000 workers are injured or killed each year while doing their work,* and about 10,000,000 of the persons now living will, if the present ratio is kept up, die of the preventable disease, tuberculosis. We know that many workmen are overworked and underpaid. We know in a general way that unnecessary disease is far too prevalent. We know some of the insanitary evils of tenements and factories; we know of the neglect of the street child, the aged, the infirm, the crippled. Furthermore, we are beginning to realize the monstrous injustice of compelling those who are unem-

* See Appendix A, p. 344.

z

ployed, who are injured in industry, who have acquired diseases due to their occupation, or who have been made widows or orphans by industrial accidents, to become paupers in order that they may be housed, fed, and clothed. Something is known concerning these problems of poverty, and some of them at least are possible of remedy.

To deal with these specific problems, I have elsewhere mentioned some reforms which seem to me preventive in their nature. They contemplate mainly such legislative action as may enforce upon the entire country certain minimum standards of working and of living conditions. They would make all tenements and factories sanitary; they would regulate the hours of work, especially for women and children; they would regulate and thoroughly supervise dangerous trades; they would institute all necessary measures to stamp out unnecessary disease and to prevent unnecessary death; they would prohibit entirely child labor; they would institute all necessary educational and recreational institutions to replace the social and educational losses of the home and the domestic workshop; they would perfect, as far as possible, legislation and institutions to make industry pay the necessary and legitimate cost of producing and maintaining efficient laborers; they would institute, on the lines of foreign experience, measures to compensate labor for enforced seasons of idleness, due to sickness, old age, lack of work, or other causes beyond the control of the workman; they would prevent parasitism on the part of either the consumer or the producer and charge up the full costs of labor in production to the beneficiary, instead of compelling the worker at certain times to enforce his demand for maintenance through the tax rate and by becoming a pauper; they would restrict the power of employer and of ship-owner to stimulate for purely selfish ends an excessive immigration, and in this way to beat down wages and to increase unemployment.

Reforms such as these are not ones which will destroy incentive, but rather they will increase incentive by more nearly equalizing opportunity. They will make propertied interests less predatory, and sensuality, by contrast with misery, less attractive to the poor. Or, in the terms of our simile, the greyhound — which Dante promised would one day come — will come to drive away the lion, the leopard, and the she-wolf. This does not mean that there is to be no struggle, — the mountain must still remain, — but rather that the life of the poorest toiler shall not be a hopeless thing from which many must turn in despair. In other words, the process of Justice is to lift stony barriers, against which the noblest beat their brains out, and from which the ignoble (but who shall. say not more sensible?) turn away in despair. Let it be this, rather than a barren relief system, administered by those who must stand by, watching the struggle, lifting no hand to aid the toilers, but ever succoring those who flee and those who are bruised and beaten.

APPENDICES

APPENDIX A

HOUSING AND TUBERCULOSIS

If there were no other evidence of poverty than that supplied by the insanitary housing conditions in which the mass of unskilled workers live, we should be warranted in believing that poverty is widespread in this country. The housing problem in the United States has attracted very little attention outside of the largest cities, and such facts as we have are almost solely those gathered in these largest cities. But the housing problem is by no means limited to the larger centres of population. Generally considered, housing conditions may be classified under three heads: first, the tenement-house evils of the largest cities, and especially those insanitary evils which result from the most vicious of all tenements, the double-decker dumb-bell; second, the evils of those tenements which have been made by remodelling old abandoned private houses, stores, warehouses, and even factories; and, third, the evils of those small houses, shanties, and cabins which are overcrowded and devoid of all sanitary conveniences and necessities. While New York has the worst conditions which result from the large block form of dwelling, this form of housing is increasing in all large cities. Nearly all of the cities and many of the small towns suffer from the last two evils. And many of the industrial towns of the manufacturing states are so insanitary from the last evil, and from lack of drainage, and of all housing and health regulation, as to rival the worst conditions of New York.

The housing problem of New York City arises largely from the scarcity of land and from the wholly mischievous construction of the tenements. In addition to miserable living conditions, resulting from insanitary surroundings and overcrowded rooms, the tenants have been, in certain portions of the city, so deprived of light and air as to seriously endanger health. No other city in the world has so many dark and windowless rooms, or so many persons crowded on the acre, or so many families deprived of light and air. There are about 360,000 dark rooms in Greater New York. Although these evils are most serious, they are by no means all of the problem. In New York and in all other large cities there are houses so badly constructed, so saturated with filth, and so infested with vermin — in a word, so thoroughly insanitary — as to make demolition the only process worthy to be called a remedy. In the smaller towns, in every industrial community which I have happened to know, about the mines, mills, and about iron, steel, and glass works, along the inland rivers, and, in fact, wherever large masses of the poorest workers live, insanitary conditions and miserable and dilapidated homes are to be seen. In a few of the largest cities, the housing problem stands out distinctly from other sanitary problems because the latter have received considerable attention; but in these more neglected places the housing problem is all messed up with inadequate drainage or none, with an impure water supply, and with an utter lack of enforcement of health laws concerning privies or disposal of rubbish and decaying matter. One industrial town is, I venture to think, fairly typical of some of those which have most neglected all sanitary measures. The wood shanties of this settlement are built along the railroad, up a hillside and down into a swamp. The houses are built of rough planks, roofed mainly with rusty scraps of tin. Some are unpainted, while others are worn of whatever paint once covered them. Those in the undrained swamp are built on piles or stilts above the foul, stagnant water and accumulated waste. There is no sewerage, and the wells are contaminated by natural drainage from the privies. I nearly always think of Dickens's description of a London street when seeing this or other of the wretched mill and mining towns : —

" It is a street of perishing blind houses, with their eyes stoned out; without a pane of glass, without so much as a window frame, with the bare, blank shutters tumbling from their hinges, and falling asunder; the iron rails peeling away in flakes of rust; the chimneys sinking in ; the stone steps to every door (and every door might be Death's Door) turning stagnant green; the very crutches on which the ruins are propped decaying."

I am convinced that when a careful inquiry is made into the housing conditions in which those who are in poverty in this country live, they will be shown to be as bad as, if not, indeed, worse than, the conditions abroad which have created great concern and been the subject of many official inquiries.

Two other indications of poverty are important. Both are closely associated with evils of wretched living, long hours, and low pay. It has been observed in the cities of this country and abroad that the density of population and the death rate from tuberculosis increase with the increase of poverty. A careful investigation, made by a resident of the College Settlement of New York for the Tenement House Commission of 1894, showed that the density of population increased with the decrease in wages, and that overcrowding was greatest where wages were lowest. The overcrowding of the population on the acre in certain sections of Chicago exceeds that of the densest portions of

London. In New York the conditions are three times as bad as they are in London. Unfortunately, we cannot compare the overcrowding in the rooms, for there are no figures for our cities. This, of course, is the better test.

The other indication of widespread poverty is the death rate from tuberculosis. An eminent German specialist, in speaking to me about tuberculosis, gave it as axiomatic almost that this disease is a sort of social yardstick by which one can measure social misery. It is not an absolute test, of course, because improved prophylactic measures will reduce the death rate very greatly; but in the present state of preventive measures New York's rate can, I think, be fairly compared to that of London. An excessive death rate is invariably associated with poverty and the evils incident to poverty. The death rate from this disease in New York greatly exceeds that in London. And this is true in spite of the more favorable climate here. The Jewish population, among whom there is always a very low death rate from this disease, is much larger in New York than in London. This factor, therefore, is also in our favor, and yet the death rate here is in excess of that of London.

THE NUMBER OF ACCIDENTS IN THE UNITED STATES

The number of accidents occurring in the United States can only be estimated. I have asked Mr. Frederick L. Hoffman of The Prudential Insurance Company to prepare me an estimate upon the basis of such facts as he may have of the number of accidents occurring in this country. His assistant has very kindly sent me the following statement. " As nearly as we can judge from such facts as we have before us, the fatal accident rate in the United States as a whole is between 80 and 85 to every 100,000 of popu-

lation. . . . The percentage of fatal accidents to total
accidents varies from 2.1 in factory labor to 40.2 % in
accidents from boiler explosions. Probably it would be
safe to say that from twenty to thirty persons are more or
less seriously injured to every one killed. If we say that
twenty-five are injured to every one killed and consider the
population of the United States to be 80,000,000 and the
fatal accident rate to be 80 in every 100,000, we have it
that 1,664,000 persons are annually killed or more or less
seriously injured in the United States. If all minor accidents were taken into consideration, it is probable that the
ratio of non-fatal accidents to fatal accidents would be
nearly 100 to one. In McNeill's book he treats of
1000 consecutive accidents, and of this number only six
were fatal. At the Convention of the National Association of Accident Underwriters in 1896, reporting on the
statistical information of accidents among physicians in-
sured for one year, there were five death claims and 965
indemnity claims. It seems to be the experience of accident insurance companies that the ratio of fatal to non-fatal
claims is at least 100 non-fatal to one fatal."

APPENDIX B

A LIVING WAGE

John Mitchell says, in his book on "Organized Labor":
"For the great mass of unskilled workingmen, . . .
residing in towns and cities with a population of from five
thousand to one hundred thousand, the fair wage, a wage
consistent with American standards of living, should not
be less than $600 a year. Less than this would, in my
judgment, be insufficient to give to the workingman those
necessaries and comforts and those small luxuries which
are now considered essential."

The General Advisory Committee of the Chicago Bureau of Charities, on March 17, 1904, " agreed that no American family, or family of any other nationality whose standards of living are similar, could comfortably live on any less than $1 a week per capita at the present time, owing to high prices of foods." — *Coöperation*, March 26, 1904.

Mr. Ernest Poole says, in an article on the meat strike, in *The Independent*, July 28, 1904: "Of the 60,000 men on strike, 40,000 are engaged in different kinds of unskilled labor. Under the union's last annual agreement, these unskilled men received 18½ cents per hour. A few received 19 cents, many others 17½ cents, but the largest number, like the 15,000 in Chicago, received 18¼ cents an hour. This wage is much lower than at first appears, for as the men average but 40 hours' work a week throughout the year, 18¼ cents per hour means only $7.40 a week."

Mary E. McDowell says in an article called "At the Heart of the Packingtown Strike" (*The Commons*, September, 1900): "A Polish doctor in that district says: ' Any man who has a family of little children here simply cannot keep it alive on the un-American wage of $6 or $7 a week, especially since the cost of living is rising so high. . . . With no money for wholesome recreation, and with the home so overcrowded with boarders, it is natural enough that drinking is so heavy, and that in many cases immigrant wives and daughters grow inured to sexual immorality — or rather unmorality. . . . I have never had a child come to me for treatment who has not had enlarged glands of the neck. These glands are meant to absorb poisonous matter. These little children live in homes so foul and overcrowded, they take in so much poison that their glands are overworked. They suffer too from underfeeding, and hence anaemia. In the blood of a healthy person the 'count' should be between 85 and 95. Among my patients I rejoice at finding a count of 50. I have found it as low as 28.'

" The whole community says with a weary mother, 'We can't even live decently on eighteen cents an hour working but three days a week, and then, there's the sickness, and the deaths.'

" Eighteen cents an hour, ten hours a day, four days a week, seven in a family — this is the economic problem that Packingtown is trying to solve, and the question that is stirring them at present is, What can bring a peace that will leave the community with a standard of living higher, not lower; with a self-respect strengthened, not weakened? "

Mr. Franklin H. Wentworth says in *The Worker*, August 28, 1904, under the head of " Stricken Fall River ": " Fall River cannot compete with the child labor of the South without using skilled operatives and grinding out their very lives. Fall River is going steadily to ruin. That is the cause of the strike. The profit system in Fall River has worn itself out, and the future is dark and cold. The wages here for the past year average $7.24 a week. This isn't a living wage. Who would not strike at the proposal to reduce this wretched wage $12\frac{1}{2}$ per cent further? "

Dr. Peter Roberts says concerning the physical condition of the poorer paid classes of workers in the anthracite district: " During the recent strike in these coal fields, Lieutenant J. P. Ryan, of the United States Navy, was sent here to recruit sailors for the navy, and then ordered to leave the regions for the following reason: One curious outcome of the recruiting was that very few of the strikers who applied for enlistment could pass the physical requirements. Lieutenant Ryan found that nearly all of those who were willing to go into the navy are under size, weak-chested and round-shouldered, and physically undesirable in nearly every way. This is attributed to going to work at an early age, lack of nourishment, and hard labor in unsanitary surroundings."

APPENDIX C

RATES OF WAGES FOR MALE WORKERS OVER SIXTEEN YEARS OF AGE

PER CENT OF EMPLOYEES RECEIVING, IN 1900, UNDER $6.00 A WEEK

TRADE	NEW ENGLAND STATES	MIDDLE STATES.	SOUTHERN STATES	CENTRAL STATES	TOTAL
Cotton Mills: All occupations	10.9	31.5	59.1	—	30.4
Cotton Mills: Spinners	13.4	44.5	—	—	32.8
Woollen Mills: Bobbin hands, doffers, etc. .	68.9	90.5	--	—	70.1
Woollen Mills: Card tenders	36.6	—	60.	—	48.9
Bakeries: General hands, helpers, etc. .	21.7	43.8	—	55.	46.7
Shoes: General hands and helpers . .	22.6	87.2	—	80.3	51.

This table is adapted from the Census volume on Employees and Wages, and includes in the main only data concerning unskilled laborers, although the first item is for all occupations. These workers can only hope to receive $312 a year if they are employed every day in the year.

The New York Bureau of Labor Statistics shows the following wages paid to the classes of workers designated ("Industrial Commission," Vol. XV, pp. 338–340): —

KIND OF WORK DONE	WAGES	
	1897	1898
Coat operators	$277.49	$
Basters	414.24	
Coat makers	349.23	344.80
Pressers	375.56	317.36
Vest makers	375.85	260.45

Professor Commons, in his study of the Sweating Trades for the Industrial Commission, gives the following figures (Vol. XV, pp. 352–369): —

NUMBER OF ESTABLISHMENT	WAGES FOR BASTERS	WAGES FOR OPERATORS
3	$208.00	$388.92
4	274.56	274.56
5	242.32	402.00
6	189.28	156.00
8	291.20	201.76
11	210.08	390.00

These two tables give the wages for certain classes of the poorest paid laborers. The first table is drawn from returns of the organized workers numbering altogether about 20,000; while the second table is made from a study of the unorganized workers numbering about 80,000.

APPENDIX D

ESTIMATES ON EXTENT OF POVERTY

I have endeavored to be as conservative as possible in my estimate of the extent of poverty, so as to have it remain absolutely unquestioned. It would probably be fairer to use the population of the following sixteen foremost industrial states as a basis for an estimate. (See Census, 1900, Vol. on Occupations, p. 98.)

Rhode Island	428,556
Massachusetts	2,805,346
Connecticut	908,420
New Hampshire	411,588
New Jersey	1,883,669
New York	7,268,894
Pennsylvania	6,302,115
Delaware	184,735
Maine	694,466
Ohio	4,157,545
Maryland	1,188,044
Vermont	343,641
Illinois	4,821,550
Wisconsin	2,069,042
Michigan	2,420,982
Indiana	2,516,462
	38,405,055

75,994,575   Total population of United States.
38,405,055   Population of sixteen foremost industrial states.
37,589,520   Population of other states.

Ten per cent of the last number is 3,758,952, and twenty per cent of the population of the foremost industrial states is 7,681,011, making altogether a population of 11,439,963 in poverty.

Still another method of working an estimate is as follows (see Abstract of Census, 1900, p. 85) : —

29,074,117 Total number of persons engaged in gainful occupations.
11,640,504 Total number of persons engaged in agricultural and in
          professional pursuits.
17,433,613 Total number of persons engaged in mechanical work, in
          trade, transportation, etc.

The total population, 75,994,575, divided by persons engaged in gainful occupations, gives the number of dependent persons in proportion to each worker. The result is 2.6 persons. Assuming that each worker in trade, transportation, mechanical work, etc., has 2.6 persons dependent upon him, we may then estimate the "industrial" population at 45,427,391, and 20 per cent of this number gives the number in poverty — 9,085,478. This leaves out any estimate of the number of persons in the agricultural districts who are in poverty. This, I feel sure, could, as I have said, be shown to be in many communities close on to 10 per cent of the population.

APPENDIX E

General Gobin, in his testimony before the Anthracite Coal Strike Commission, stated that the greatest wrong of the strike of 1902 was the lawlessness taught the youths of these regions. . . . It was the custom for the family to teach the children the lessons of right and wrong, but it is so no more. This is not done by the public school, and the church cannot effectively do it by a few hours' teaching once a week, while there are many who never come within its influence. Is it astonishing that under such circumstances youths grow up without an intelligent sense of right and wrong? The results are ingratitude to parents, disregard to the rights of men and of property, insubordination to superiors, lack of respect for women, indulgence in sensuous enjoyments, lack of truthfulness and honor, a contempt for civil authority that presages anarchy, and loss of faith in all save material realities. Society must suffer because of this, and it can only be remedied by establishing an efficient machinery for the instruction of the young in righteousness.

. . . As far as our public schools are concerned, no systematic instruction is given in right and wrong, and the mass of our youths is suffering moral atrophy. Their moral faculties are undeveloped, and our system of instruction assumes that moral conduct will take care of itself if only the common branches are taught. Need we wonder that harmless people are assaulted, women insulted, peaceful citizens maligned on the street, and our politics are corrupt ? — " Anthracite Coal Communities," by PETER ROBERTS, Ph.D.

CHILD LABOR IN THE UNITED STATES

(Census, 1900. Volume on Occupations)

OCCUPATIONS	TOTAL
All occupations	1,752,187
Agricultural pursuits	1,062,251
Agricultural laborers	1,054,700
Dairymen and dairywomen	301
Lumbermen and raftsmen	571
Stockraisers, herders, and drovers	4,247
Turpentine farmers and laborers	1,201
Woodchoppers	1,133
Other agricultural pursuits	98
Professional service	2,956
Actors, professional showmen, etc.	617
Architects, designers, draftsmen, etc. . . .	147
Artists and teachers of art	225
Electricians	550

Occupations	Total
Engineers (civil) and surveyors	60
Musicians and teachers of music	712
Teachers in colleges, etc.	453
Other professional service	192
Domestic and personal service	280,143
Barbers and hairdressers	1,656
Bartenders	367
Janitors and sextons	218
Laborers (not specified)	128,890
Launderers and laundresses	7,017
Saloon keepers	
Servants and waiters	138,284
Watchmen, policemen, firemen, etc.	151
Other domestic and personal service	3,560
Trade and transportation	122,507
Agents	945
Boatmen and sailors	497
Bookkeepers and accountants	2,169
Clerks and copyists	22,034
Draymen, hackmen, teamsters, etc.	11,582
Foremen and overseers	
Hostlers	1,811
Hucksters and pedlers	2,277
Merchants (except wholesale)	2,568
Messenger and errand and office boys . . .	42,045
Packers and shippers	4,611
Porters and helpers (in stores, etc.) . . .	2,633
Salesmen and saleswomen	20,342
Steam railroad employees	2,480
Stenographers and typewriters	1,486
Street railway employees	98
Telegraph and telephone linemen	51
Telegraph and telephone operators	1,315
Others in trade and transportation	3,563
Manufacturing and mechanical	284,330
Carpenters and joiners	1,924

2 A

Occupations	Total
Masons (brick and stone)	582
Painters, glaziers, and varnishers	3,253
Paper hangers	304
Plasterers	131
Plumbers and gas and steam fitters	1,691
Roofers and slaters	62
Mechanics (not otherwise specified)	85
Oil well and oil works employees	208
Other chemical workers	583
Brick and tile makers, etc.	2,413
Glassworkers	5,365
Marble and stone cutters	338
Potters	1,039
Fishermen and oystermen	2,275
Miners and quarrymen	24,217
Bakers	1,948
Butchers	1,382
Butter and cheese makers	399
Confectioners	2,056
Millers	249
Other food preparers	1,972
Blacksmiths	1,525
Iron and steel workers	7,592
Machinists	4,170
Steam boiler makers	321
Stove, furnace, and grate makers	301
Tool and cutlery makers	830
Wheelwrights	111
Wireworkers	842
Boot and shoe makers and repairers	8,235
Harness and saddle makers	536
Leather curriers and tanners	1,377
Trunk and leather-case makers, etc.	866
Bottlers and sodawater makers, etc.	751
Brewers and maltsters	532
Distillers and rectifiers	24
Cabinet makers	297
Coopers	990

Occupations	Total
Saw and planing mill employees	4,925
Other woodworkers	5,721
Brassworkers . . . . :	915
Clock and watch makers	617
Gold and silver workers	1,408
Tin plate and tinware makers	2,874
Other metal workers	1,890
Bookbinders	1,965
Boxmakers (paper)	3,333
Engravers.	268
Paper and pulp mill operatives	1,557
Printers, lithographers, and pressmen	6,289
Bleachery and dye works operatives	803
Carpet factory operatives	1,319
Cotton mill operatives	44,427
Hosiery and knitting mill operatives	8,267
Silk mill operatives	8,938
Woollen mill operatives	6,625
Other textile mill operatives	12,428
Dressmakers	6,709
Hat and cap makers	980
Milliners	3,227
Seamstresses	7,673
Shirt, collar, and cuff makers	3,635
Tailors and tailoresses	10,927
Other textile workers	1,961
Broom and brush makers	639
Charcoal, coke, and lime burners	505
Engineers and firemen (not locomotive) . , . .	848
Glovemakers	826
Manufacturers and officials, etc.	
Model and pattern makers	115
Photographers	238
Rubber factory operatives	1,039
Tobacco and cigar factory operatives	11,462
Upholsterers	724
Other miscellaneous industries	36,477

Mr. A. M. Simons, writing of conditions in the Chicago stockyards, says, regarding the " benefits " of child labor :

" As the machinery grew more perfect and the newly-invented processes of canning and preserving taught the packers how to rob the rendering vat to feed the tables of the world, a new competitor was brought to the auction block. The woman and the child took the place of the husband and father, because they could live for less than the man. Some attempt has been made to restrict the employment of children, and this is one of the things complained of in the official statement of the packers. This precious document declares : —

" ' The child-labor law has done more harm than good in the stockyards' industry. Before the enactment of the statute forbidding the employment of children under 16 years of age, many of them obtained profitable work in the packing plants. Now they run at large in the neighborhood, for their parents will not keep them in school. As a matter of fact, a boy who has not learned to work by the time he reaches 16 years of age, never will learn. He has, on the other hand, acquired habits that make him unfit for work. Many people hold that the best industrial condition is that in which all the members of a family who wish can find employment at the same place. This was the condition in the packing industry before the passage of recent laws.'

" When it is remembered that these children were employed in catching the blood that flowed from the slaughtered animals, cleansing intestines for sausage casings, etc., some idea of the elevating influences from which the child-labor law took them is gained." — " The Packingtown Strike," by A. M. SIMONS.

" FALL RIVER, MASS., March 11. — Situated in the very centre of Fall River's wharf line and flush with the waters of Mount Hope Bay is the mammoth plant of the American Printing Company, the largest establishment of the kind in America, and the individual property of Matthew Chandler Durfee Borden, the millionnaire resident of New York.

"Hundreds of small boys work for Mr. Borden, and many of them toil ten hours a day without a thread of clothing on their bodies. No one except employees is allowed to enter the works, and therefore when it was stated before a woman's club in New York, last week, that naked babies were at work in the Fall River mills, much interest was aroused. . . .

"They work in the big tanks called ' lime keer,' in the bleach house, packing the cloth into the vats.

"This lime keer holds 750 pieces of cloth, and it requires one hour and twenty minutes to fill it. During that time the lad must work inside, while his body is being soaked with whatever there is of chemicals which enter into the process of bleaching, of which lime is a prominent factor.

"The naked bodies of the children who do this work day after day are never dry, and the same chemicals which effect the bleaching process of the gray cloth naturally bleach the skin of the operator, and after coming out of the vats the boys show the effects in the whiteness of their skins, which rivals the cotton cloth." — " The Child Labor Evil," by Hon. JAMES F. CAREY.

WOMAN AND CHILD LABOR IN JAPAN

"The immensely rapid development of Japan from a feudal state, with its natural production, to a capitalistic modern state is well known. Hardly any other country in the world has passed through a similar evolution in such a short period of time; no other country has shown such extraordinary adaptability to this process of development as Japan has. . . .

"A black spot in Japan's industrial life is child labor. . . . The children live sometimes several thousands together, with board and lodging in the factories. From the earliest age up, having been used to open air and play outdoors, they see themselves pressed into the low, dark rooms of the factories and mills, cut off from everything that was dear to them before. Some try to escape; many of them die before the contract is fulfilled, for also the children have to work at nights, at times fifteen to eighteen hours continuously." — *The Worker*, July 10, 1904.

APPENDIX F

Professor John R. Commons, writing on the effect of immigration on population, says: "It is, of course, impossible to measure the effect of immigration upon the population of the country, but at any rate it is a hasty assumption which holds that immigration during the nineteenth century has increased the total population. The late Francis A. Walker, superintendent of the censuses of 1870 and 1880, maintained that had there been no immigration whatever into this country during the past ninety years, 'the native element would long have filled the place the foreigners have usurped.' President Walker's argument gains statistical plausibility from the estimates, which he quotes, made by Elkanah Watson, in 1815, of the future population of the United States, on the basis of the first three censuses.

"Taking Watson's predictions and comparing them with the actual census returns (see table below), Walker found that in the censuses of 1820 and 1830, when immigration was so slight as to be negligible, the predictions were within four one-thousandths of the actual population; and

Year	Population	Watson's Estimate	Watson's Error	Foreign Immigration for Decade
1790	3,929,214	—	—	—
1800	5,308,483	—	—	50,000
1810	7,239,881	—	—	70,000
1820	9,633,822	9,625,734	−8,088	114,000
1830	12,866,020	12,833,645	−32,375	143,439
1840	17,069,453	17,116,526	+47,073	599,125
1850	23,191,876	23,185,368	−6,508	1,713,251
1860	31,443,321	31,753,824	+310,503	2,598,214
1870	38,558,371	42,328,432	+3,770,061	2,314,824
1880	50,155,783	56,450,241	+6,294,458	2,812,191
1890	62,622,250	77,266,989	+14,644,739	5,246,613
1900	75,559,258	100,235,985	+24,676,727	3,687,564

again, in 1840 and 1850, with immigration amounting to 599,125 in one decade, and 1,713,251 in the second decade, Watson's predictions were again as close as before. Speaking of these predictions, Walker says : ' Here we see that, in spite of the arrival of 599,000 foreigners during the period 1830–1840, four times as many as had arrived during any preceding decade, the figures of the census coincided closely with the estimate of Watson, based on the growth of population in the pre-immigration era, falling short of it only by 47,073 in 17,000,000 ; while in 1850 the actual population, in spite of the arrival of 1,713,000 more immigrants, exceeded Watson's estimate by only 6508 in a total of 23,000,000. Surely, if this correspondence between the increase of the foreign element and the relative decline of the native element is a mere coincidence, it is one of the most astonishing in human history.' " — " Report of the Industrial Commission," Vol. XV, 1901.

EMIGRATION FROM IRELAND

The effect of emigration upon the population of Ireland does not appear to be the same as its effects upon the population of other countries. There are probably many reasons for this, but the two following quotations from Thomas Lough's book partly explain it: —

"In the ten years ending in 1881, the total number of emigrants was 630,000, but in the succeeding ten years this number increased to 770,000. This great company was made up of the bone and sinew of the island. No less than 85 per cent of the whole number were between the ages of ten and forty-five, only 5 per cent being above the latter age. Thus *the old are left to die* in Ireland, while those who should be the support and comfort of their declining years are forced to seek a shelter in other lands."

"Dealing with the figures of deaths from famine or starvation, Mulhall shows that in the year 1879 there were 312 deaths in England, 260 in France, 101 in London, and in Ireland no less than 3789, or 37.6 per thousand of the entire number of deaths." — "England's Wealth, Ireland's Poverty," by THOMAS LOUGH, M.P., pp. 138 and 170.

AUTHORITIES

CHAPTER I. POVERTY

2–1 Past and Present, by Thomas Carlyle, p. 203.

5–1 Principles of Economics, by Professor Alfred Marshall, Vol. I, Book II, pp. 119–122 and Poverty — A Study of Town Life, by B. S. Rountree, pp. 86, 132 *et. seq.*

7–1 John Ruskin — Social Reformer, by John A. Hobson, p. 88.

8–1 Marshall, *op. cit.*, p. 121.

9–1 Carlyle, *op. cit.*, p. 23.

2 Life and Labor in London, by Charles Booth, Vol. I, p. 33. Marshall, *op. cit.*, p. 122, note. Rountree, *op. cit.*, p. 110.

10–1 Rountree, *op. cit.*, p. 133.

12–1 Unto This Last, by John Ruskin, p. 177.

14–1 Practical Sociology, by Carroll D. Wright, Chap. XVIII, and American Charities, by Dr. Amos G. Warner, Chap. II.

2 Wright, *op. cit.*, p. 344.

15–1 The Social Unrest, by John Graham Brooks, p. 209.

16–1 America's Working People, by Charles B. Spahr. The Workers, by Walter A. Wyckoff. The Woman Who Toils, by Mrs. John Van Vorst and Marie Van Vorst. By Bread Alone, by I. K. Friedman. Packingtown, by A. M. Simons.

2 How the Other Half Lives, The Battle with the Slum,

PAGE AND NUMBER

etc., by Jacob A. Riis.   The Plague in Its Stronghold, by Ernest Poole.   The Leaven of a Great
City, by Lillian W. Betts.

3 Tramping with Tramps, etc., by Josiah Flynt.

17–1 Booth, *op. cit.*   Final volume, p. 9.

19–1 Rountree, *op. cit.*, pp. 299, 300, 301.

20–1 The Dictionary of Statistics, by M. G. Mulhall, pp.
439 and 444.

2 Report of Special Committee on Outdoor Alms
(Hartford), p. ix.

21–1 North American Review, April, 1891.

2 Census of 1890, Special Report.

3 Hartford Report, *op. cit.*, p. 6, Table V.

22–1 How the Other Half Lives, by Jacob A. Riis, pp. 243
et. seq.

2 Report of United Hebrew Charities, 1901, p. 30.

3 Annual Reports of New York State Board of
Charities.   Consult appendices.

24–1 Bulletin of the Statistics Department, City of Boston,
Vol. VI.   Nos. 4 and 5, appendix, p. 95.

2 Municipal Court Review, February, 1904, p. 20.

25–1 Report of the Department of Corrections, New York,
1902, p. 71.

28–1 Report of the Mosely Industrial Commission, 1903.

2 Atlantic Monthly, February, 1904.

29–1 Census of 1900, Vol. on Occupations, pp. ccxxviii*et seq.*

2 *Idem*, p. ccxxvi.

3 *Idem*, p. ccxxxv.

4 Census of Massachusetts, 1895, p. 105.

30–1 *Idem.*

3 Statistics and Economics, by Professor Richmond
Mayo-Smith, p. 97.

3 Anthracite Coal Communities, by Dr. Peter Roberts.

4 Bulletin of the New York Department of Labor, September, 1903, p. 260.

31-1 *Idem*, p. 261.

32-1 Problems of Poverty, by John A. Hobson, p. 17.

33-1 Ninth Special Report of the Federal Bureau of Labor, p. 29.

   2 *Idem*, p. 28.

34-1 Census of 1900, Vol. on Occupations, p. ccxxxii.

35-1 Workingmen's Insurance, by W. F. Willoughby, p. 7.

36-1 Brooks, *op. cit.*, p. 209.

   2 Annual Reports of the Interstate Commerce Commission.

37-1 Bulletins of the Interstate Commerce Commission.

38-1 Bulletin No. 37 of the Department of Labor, p. 1036.

40-1 Roberts, *op. cit.*, p. 273.

   2 Report of Bureau of Labor of New Jersey for 1884.

   3 Roberts, *op. cit.*, p. 82.

41-1 Fifth and Final Report of the Royal Commission on Labor, p. 128.

42-1 Political Science Quarterly, Vol. VIII, 1893, p. 591.

   2 Abstract of the Twelfth Census, p. 28.

   3 *Idem*, pp. 133-135.

43-1 Political Science Quarterly, *op. cit.*

44-1 Distribution of Wealth in the United States, by Charles B. Spahr, p. 56.

   2 Brooks, *op. cit.*, p. 163.

45-1 For criticisms, Statistics and Economics, by Richmond Mayo-Smith, pp. 431-437, and Evolution of Industrial Society, by Professor Richard T. Ely, pp. 264 *et seq.*

49-1 Report of the Industrial Commission, Vol. XV, pp. 309-311. Principles of Biology, by Herbert Spencer, Vol. II, § 368.

51-1 Report of Massachusetts Bureau of Statistics of Labor, Part III, 1901.

   2 Organized Labor, by John Mitchell, p. 118.

PAGE AND NUMBER

3 Report of New York Bureau of Labor Statistics, 1902, p. 72.

53–1 Report of the Industrial Commission, Vol. IV, p. 46.

54–1 *Idem*, p. 47.

   2 *Idem*, Vol. VII, pp. 406, 414, 415.

   3 *Idem*, p. 574.

   4 Roberts, *op. cit.*, p. 346.

   5 Census of 1900, Vol. on Employees and Wages, p. 616.

55–1 Census of Massachusetts, 1885.

   2 Census of 1900, Vol. on Employees and Wages, pp. 324–325.

56–1 Rountree, *op. cit.*, p. 136.

60–1 Abstract of Twelfth Census, p. 32.

61–1 American Economic Association Studies, 1897, p. 56.

CHAPTER II. THE PAUPER

68–1 General references : Proceedings C. O. S. Section of the National Conference of Charities and Corrections, 1880–1904. C. O. S. Occasional Papers (London). Charity Organization, by C. S. Loch. How to Help Cases in Distress (London). Handbook of Charity Organization, by H. S. Gurteen. Tracts of the Boston Associated Charities and of the New York, Baltimore, and London Charity Organization Societies.

69–1 The Jukes, by R. L. Dugdale, p. 47.

   2 The Tribe of Ishmael, by Oscar C. McCulloch.

70–1 Parasitism, Organic and Social, by Massart and Vandervelde, p. 26.

72–1 Dugdale, *op. cit.*, pp. 48–49.

74–1 How the Other Half Lives, by J. A. Riis, p. 243.

   2 Annual Report Charity Organization Society, New York, 1894.

PAGE AND NUMBER

3 Report of United Hebrew Charities, 1901, p. 30.

4 Tenement House Problem, by DeForest and Veiller, pp. 113–114.

75–1 Report of United Hebrew Charities, 1901, p. 39.

2 American Charities, by Amos G. Warner, p. 30.

77–1 Report from His Majesty's Commissioners on the Poor Laws, 1834 (London). The Poor Law, by T. W. Fowle. History of the English Poor Law, by Sir G. Nicholls, 1898. State of the Poor, by Sir F. M. Eden, 3 vols., 1798.

78–1 Report of New York State Board of Charities, 1877, pp. 18–19.

79–1 Charities, weekly, of Charity Organization Society, XI, p. 441 (New York).

80–1 Report of Standing Committee on Outdoor Relief, New York State Board of Charities, 1884. Outdoor Relief, by Alexander Johnson. Ohio State Conference of Charities, 1893. Warner, *op. cit.*, p. 162.

2 McCulloch, *op. cit.*

81–1 The Old Poor Law, by F. C. Montague, p. 9.

85–1 Mutual Aid, by P. Kropotkin, pp. 103–104.

86–1 Unto This Last, by John Ruskin, p. 226.

89–1 See authorities, Chap. IV.

92–1 Inebriety, by Norman Kerr.

2 Abnormal Man, by Dr. Arthur McDonald.

93–1 Warner, *op. cit.*, p. 44.

101–1 Economic Crises, by Edward D. Jones, pp. 100–101.

2 Workingmen's Insurance, by W. F. Willoughby. Insurance of Workmen, Massachusetts Bureau of Labor, 1901. Compulsory Insurance in Germany, Washington, 1893.

103–1 Workmen's Insurance Abroad, by Dr. Zacher, 1898, Berlin, p. 2.

PAGE AND NUMBER

104–1 *Idem*, p. 6.
   2 *Idem*, p. 29.
   3 *Idem*, p. 7.

CHAPTER III.   THE VAGRANT

128–1 Degeneration, by E. Ray Lancaster.
129–1 Principles of Sociology, by Herbert Spencer, Vol. I,
       pp. 75, 76.
132–1 The Tramp Problem, by J. J. McCook, p. 289 of
       Twenty-second Annual Conference of Charities
       and Corrections.
133–1 The Unemployed, by Geoffrey Drage, p. 160.
134–1 Life and Labour in London, by Charles Booth,
       Vol. I, p. 152.
135–1 The Unemployed, by John Burns, M.P., Fabian
       Tract, No. 47, p. 8.
138–1 Paper before Twenty-sixth Conference of Charities
       and Corrections, by Washington Gladden, p. 144.
   2 McCook, *op. cit.*, p. 288.
139–1 Census, Vol. on Occupations, p. ccxxxv.

CHAPTER IV.   THE SICK

141–1 Report of Ohio Board of State Charities, 1902, p. 6.
   2 Vital Statistics, by William Farr, pp. 512–513.
143–1 American Charities, by Amos G. Warner, p. 40.
144–1 Tenement Conditions in Chicago, by Robert
       Hunter, p. 157.   Report of New York Tenement
       House Committee of 1894, p. 33.
147–1 Hunter, *op. cit.*, p. 63.
150–1 Hunter, *op. cit.*, pp. 156–157.   Roberts, *op. cit.*, p. 80.
   2 Farr, *op. cit.*, p. 121.
151–1 Britain's Homes, by George Haw, p. 30.   London,
       1902.

PAGE AND NUMBER

152–1 *Idem*, p. 28.

153–1 See Advance Sheets of Report of New York Tenement House Commission, 1900, p. 72.

154–1 Report of Royal Commission on The Housing of the Working Classes, Vol. I, pp. 13–14.

2 New York Commission, *op. cit.*, 1894, p. 12.

156–1 Royal Commission, *op. cit.*, Vol. II, p. 4.

158–1 Industrial Democracy, by Sidney and Beatrice Webb, Vol. II, p. 354.

159–1 The Diseases of Occupations, by Dr. J. T. Arlidge, p. 553.

161–1 *Idem*, p. 423. Dangerous Trades (Indianapolis), by W. English Walling.

162–1 The Diseases of Occupations, by Dr. J. T. Arlidge, p. 5.

165–1 Twenty-sixth Conference of Charities and Corrections, p. 120.

166–1 Municipal Care of the Consumptive Poor, by S. A. Knopf, M.D., pp. 3–4. Boston.

167–1 The Plague in Its Stronghold, by Ernest Poole, in A Handbook on the Prevention of Tuberculosis, p. 305.

168–1 Social Aspects of Tuberculosis, by Lillian Brandt, in A Handbook, etc., pp. 88–92.

2 *Idem*.

3 *Idem*, pp. 66–68.

169–1 A Handbook, etc., p. 167.

171–1 Koch in Tuberculosis, monthly of the International Bureau, May, 1903, pp. 107–109.

172–1 A Handbook, etc., pp. 166–167.

175–1 Philadelphia Medical Journal, Dec. 1, 1900.

2 Koch in *op. cit.*, p. 107.

178–1 Poole, *op. cit.*

188–1 Sesame and Lilies, by John Ruskin, p. 55.

CHAPTER V. THE CHILD

PAGE AND NUMBER

194–1 The Outlook, Aug. 22, 1903.

196–1 Portions of this and following paragraphs have been taken from Tenement Conditions in Chicago, pp. 150–152.

199–1 Report of Industrial Commission on Immigration, Vol. XV, p. 288.

201–1 Social Progress, by Josiah Strong, p. 151.

204–1 On the Old Road, by John Ruskin, Vol. I, § 277.

207–1 Municipal Government in Continental Europe, by Albert Shaw, pp. 119–122.

214–1 Charities, May, 1903.

217–1 Underfed Children Attending School, Report of Committee of School Board of London, 1898–1899.

219–1 The School and Society, by John Dewey.

221–1 Report of Commissioner of Education, July, 1903.

223–1 Wieland, see p. 11 of The Child, A Study in the Evolution of Man, by A. F. Chamberlain.

224–1 The First Years of Childhood, by Margaret Mac-Millan, Manchester.

227–1 Fors Clavigera, by John Ruskin, Vol. I, p. 196.

230–1 Past and Present, by Thomas Carlyle, p. 255.

231–1 Census, 1900.

232–1 The Woman Who Toils, by Van Vorst, pp. 217, 240, 252, 263.

232–2 Child Life vs. Dividends, by Irene Ashby-Mac-Fadyen, American Federationalist, May, 1902.

233–1 Van Vorst, op. cit., p. 240.

234–1 Pickwick Papers, by Charles Dickens, p. 105.

235–1 Census, 1900.

236–1 Kellogg Durland's Report for the New York Evening Post.

2 The Children of the Coal Shadow, McClure's, 1902.

PAGE AND NUMBER

237–1 Census, 1900.

240–1 Life and Work of the Seventh Earl of Shaftesbury, Edwin Hodder, p. 400, London, 1893.

241–1 Census, 1900. See, also, Social Progress, by Josiah Strong, p. 81.

244–1 Mrs. Alzina P. Stevens, National Convention of Factory, Inspectors, 1893, pp. 46–47.

245–1 The Economics of Factory Legislation in The Case for the Factory Acts, ed. by Mrs. Sidney Webb. See several instances in Capital, by Karl Marx, Chapter XV, sec. 2, Vol. II, pp. 240, etc.

    2 Ethics of Social Progress, by Professor Franklin H. Giddings, in Philanthropy and Social Progress, p. 226, 1893.

247–1 Letters of a Chinese Official, p. 8.

248–1 Mrs. Sidney Webb, *op. cit.*, pp. 18–35.

251–1 Report of Factory Inspectors, Illinois, 1900, pp. 12–13.

252–1 Shaftesbury, *op. cit.*, pp. 226–227, note.

    2 *Idem*, p. 235.

253–1 *Idem*, p. 77.

CHAPTER VI. THE IMMIGRANT

261–1 Tenement House Problem, by DeForest and Veiller, Vol. II, pp. 67–89.

262–1 Tenement House Conditions in Chicago, by Robert Hunter, p. 72.

    2 City Life, Crime, and Poverty, by Professor John R. Commons. Chautauquan, April, 1904.

264–1 Italy To-day, by Bolton King and Thomas Okey, p. 312.

265–1 Seventh Special Report of Commissioner of Labor, p. 44.

267–1 Abstract of the Twelfth Census, 1900, p. 8.

PAGE AND NUMBER

267–2 Immigration to the United States, 1820–1903, Washington, p. 4336.

3 Commons, *op. cit.*, p. 117.

268–1 Century, March, 1903, p. 675.

269–1 *Idem*, p. 688.

2 Report of the Commissioner of New York, p. 70.

270–1 The American Commonwealth, Vol. II, pp. 862–963.

271–1 Century, *op. cit.*, p. 681.

2 King and Okey, *op. cit.*, p. 320.

272–1 Report of the Commissioner-General, 1903, p. 85. Speech of Hon. Charles W. Fairbanks, United States Senate, Jan. 11, 1898; Senate Document, No. 2119, p. 21.

2 Daily Papers, April, 1904.

273–1 Publications of the Immigration Restriction League, No. 22.

274–1 Regulation of Immigration, Senate Report, No. 2119, p. 473.

2 Industrial Commission, Vol. XV, p. 311.

277–1 Ninth Special Report of the Federal Bureau of Labor, p. 29.

2 *Idem*, p. 28.

278–1 How the Other Half Lives, by Jacob A. Riis, p. 52.

2 Immigration into the United States, 1820–1903, Washington, p. 4348.

3 Federal Bureau of Labor, *op. cit.*, p. 49.

279–1 Charities, Vol. VIII, p. 247.

280–1 Report of United Hebrew Charities, 1901, p. 29.

2 *Idem*, 1898, p. 21.

282–1 Democracy and Social Progress, by Jane Addams, p. 234.

2 Emigration and Immigration, by Professor Richmond Mayo-Smith, p. 159.

284–1 Private Statement of the Commissioner-General.

2 Senate Report, No. 2119, p. 243.

PAGE AND NUMBER

285–1 Census of 1890, Crime, Pauperism, and Benevolence, p. 10.

286–1 Emigration and Immigration, by Richmond Mayo-Smith, p. 159.

287–1 Senate Report, No. 2119, p. 238.

288–1 *Idem*, p. 236.

2 Industrial Commission, Vol. XV, p. 288.

3 *Idem*, p. 288.

289–1 Report of United Hebrew Charities, 1901, p. 30.

2 Industrial Commission, Vol. XV, p. 288.

290–1 Publication of the Immigration Restriction League, No. 30, p. 9.

295–1 Forum, Vol. XIV, September, 1892, p. 114.

2 Industrial Commission, Vol. XV, p. 311.

296–1 Burdens of Recent Immigration, by Frank H. Ainsworth.

299–1 Vital Statistics, by William Farr, p. 62.

300–1 Emigration and Immigration, by Richmond Mayo-Smith, p. 23.

301–1 Industrial Commission, Vol. XV, p. 277.

2 Discussions in Economics and Statistics, by Francis A. Walker, Vol. II, pp. 417–426.

302–1 Vital Statistics, by A. Newsholme, p. 77.

2 Quarterly Journal of Economics, November, 1901 ; February, 1902.

3 Census of 1900, Vol. III, pp. li and lii.

303–1 *Idem.*

304–1 Farr, *op. cit.*, p. 69.

2 Statistics and Sociology, by Richmond Mayo-Smith, p. 74.

3 *Idem*, p. 89.

4 Newsholme, *op. cit.*, Chap. IX. Principles of Economics, by Professor Alfred Marshall, Book IV, Chap. IV. Economics, by Arthur T. Hadley,

pp. 42–49.   Principles of Sociology, by Franklin
H. Giddings, pp. 367–369.

305–1 The Slav Invasion, by F. G. Warne, pp. 80–83.
Industrial Commission, Vol. XV, pp. 310–311.

308–1 Walker, *op. cit.*

309–1 Social Evolution, by Benjamin Kidd, p. 257.

2 Newsholme, *op. cit.*, p. 75.

310–1 Britain's Homes, by George Haw, p. 28.

2 Hadley, *op. cit.*, p. 48.

3 Kidd, *op. cit.*, p. 260.

311–1 Marshall, *op. cit.*, p. 238.

2 Journal of Royal Statistical Society, 1890.

312–1 Census of 1900, Vol. on Occupations.   Table 41,
pp. 220–423.

313–1 Census of 1900, Vol. III, p. lii.

CHAPTER VII.   CONCLUSION

330–1 Life and Labour in London, by Charles Booth,
Vol. I, p. 152.

331–1 The Social Problem, by John A. Hobson, pp. 8–9.

335–1 The Shame of the Cities, by Lincoln Steffens.
Frenzied Finance, by Thomas Lawson, Everybody's
Magazine, 1904.
The Enemies of the Republic, by Lincoln Steffens,
McClure's Magazine, 1904.

2 Address before the Nineteenth Century Club, by
Professor Franklin H. Giddings.

336–1 Theory of Social Organization, by Charles Fourier,
p. 6.

2 Benevolent Feudalism, by W. J. Ghent.

NOTE. — In a few instances I have been unable to find the original
sources of certain quotations and therefore have found it necessary to
omit references.

INDEX

373

The Principles of Sociology

An Analysis of Phenomena of Association and of Social Organization

By FRANKLIN HENRY GIDDINGS, M.A.
Professor of Sociology in Columbia University

Cloth   8vo   **$3.00 net**

"It is a treatise which will confirm the highest expectations of those who have expected much from this alert observer and virile thinker. Beyond a reasonable doubt, the volume is the ablest and most thoroughly satisfactory treatise on the subject in the English language." — *Literary World*.

"The distinctive merit of the work is that it is neither economics nor history. . . . He has found a new field and devoted his energies to its exploration. . . . The chapters on Social Population and on Social Constitution are among the best in the book. It is here that the method of Professor Giddings shows itself to the best advantage. The problems of anthropology and ethnology are also fully and ably handled. Of the other parts I like best of all the discussion of tradition and of social choices; on these topics he shows the greatest originality. I have not the space to take up these or other doctrines in detail, nor would such work be of much value. A useful book must be read to be understood."
— Professor SIMON N. PATTEN, in *Science*.

The Elements of Sociology

A Text-book for Colleges and Schools

By FRANKLIN HENRY GIDDINGS, M.A.
Professor of Sociology in Columbia University

Cloth   8vo   **$1.10 net**

"It is thoroughly intelligent, independent, suggestive, and manifests an unaffected enthusiasm for social progress, and on the whole a just and sober apprehension of the conditions and essential features of such progress."
— Professor H. SIDGWICK in *The Economic Journal*.

"Of its extreme interest, its suggestiveness, its helpfulness to readers to whom social questions are important, but who have not time or inclination for special study, we can bear sincere and grateful testimony." — *New York Times*.

"Professor Giddings impresses the reader equally by his independence of judgment and by his thorough mastery of every subject that comes into his view." — *The Churchman*.

THE MACMILLAN COMPANY

66 FIFTH AVENUE, NEW YORK